William Henry Holcombe

Letters on Spiritual Subjects in Answer to Inquiring Souls

William Henry Holcombe

**Letters on Spiritual Subjects in Answer to Inquiring Souls**

ISBN/EAN: 9783337334536

Printed in Europe, USA, Canada, Australia, Japan

Cover: Foto ©Lupo / pixelio.de

More available books at **www.hansebooks.com**

# LETTERS

ON

# SPIRITUAL SUBJECTS

IN ANSWER TO

## Inquiring Souls.

BY

WILLIAM H. HOLCOMBE, M.D.

AUTHOR OF "OUR CHILDREN IN HEAVEN," "THE OTHER LIFE,"
"THE END OF THE WORLD," ETC., ETC.

---

PHILADELPHIA:
PORTER & COATES.
1885.

# PREFACE.

IN the early part of 1882 there appeared in the *New Church Independent*, four essays upon the Opening of the Interior Degrees of the Human Spirit, and the Descent of the Lord into Ultimates. They attracted considerable attention, and I have received many letters from earnest and anxious souls, desirous of learning more of the Second Coming of the Lord by interior processes, and of that New Life which his coming will establish in the world.

Some of my responses to those letters are here collected, and so arranged as to give an appearance of order and continuity to the subjects discussed. If the reader discovers occasional reiterations of the same ideas, he will understand that it was scarcely avoidable in writing to different persons about the same things. Fortunately the reiterations relate to important truths which cannot be too often repeated or too deeply impressed on the mind.

The four Essays which elicited the correspondence, are here published in the form of Appendix. Those who are acquainted with the philosophical and theological teachings of Swedenborg, will do well to read the Essays first and the Letters afterwards. Those who know little or nothing of the doctrines of the New Church, will find the reading of the Letters a suitable preparation for a more thorough understanding of the Essays.

It is useless to say anything to prejudice the reader's mind in favor of the contents of this volume. It is already "made up" by the necessities of its own organic conditions. Those who see truth by a certain interior light, will hail these things with faith and joy, without caring for the name of the author, or the sources of his enlightenment. Those who believe in the authority of Authority, will doubt and cavil and very generally reject. The great majority of the reading and thinking public, if it gives the subject any attention at all, will dismiss it as an idle tale or a poetic dream.

To the receivers of the heavenly doctrines revealed through Swedenborg I would say, that the book makes no claim to any special revelation, nor its author to any spiritual state not accessible to and attainable by all others under similar conditions.

The Lord is perpetually striving to manifest Himself, and the New Life continually presses for utterance; but the effort can be successful only so far as suitable environments have been prepared for its reception. Hence the injunction: "Prepare ye the way of the Lord: make straight in the desert a highway for our God."

During the century preceding Swedenborg's active career, there was a remarkable development of religious fervor, limited in extent but of great intensity, and many abortive attempts were made to manifest the genuine life of heaven upon earth. The cause of the failure of Molinos, Guyon, Fenelon, Bourignon, and others, is very instructive. It was from ignorance of the true relations between internal and external things, which led to a total separation—theoretical and sometimes practical—of the spiritual from the natural or social and business life. Their beautiful and mysterious castles in the air, had no solid foundation on the earth.

Swedenborg was sent, like John the Baptist, to prepare the way of the Lord and make his paths straight. This was done by teaching a vast system of spiritual truth which not only leads to repentance, but delivers us from falsities and brings us into judgment. This system shows the organic connection and correspondence between spiritual and natural things, and demonstrates scientifically, that internal religion without its external basis, and external religion without its internal spirit, are equally sentimental, unreal, and fantastic.

It is very certain that old things are passing away, and a new basis of faith is being gradually constructed in the world. Will it be a "highway in the desert for our God"? Will it be the solid ground-work and foundation of a higher, and purer, and holier life than has ever before been realized in the church? Are the environments ready? If the New Man of the New Era were now ushered into the world, would he survive or would he perish?

W. H. H.

NEW ORLEANS, LA.,
    Dec. 4, 1884.

# Contents.

## Letter I.
The Second Coming of the Lord, a Descent from Within, both General and Special . . . . . . . . 15

## Letter II.
Three Degrees of Human Life: Celestial, Spiritual, and Natural. . . . . . . . . . . . 30

## Letter III.
The Three-fold Appearance of the Lord . . . . 41

## Letter IV.
The Lord as Physician: "Who Healeth all Thy Diseases" 45

## Letter V.
Remains: "The Remnant:" The Old and New Proprium . 56

## Letter VI.
Ecclesiastical and Vital Religion . . . . . . 67

## Letter VII.
The New Life.—Madam Guyon.—The Religious Proprium . 77

## Letter VIII.
Shall We Know Ourselves, or Not? . . . . . 82

## LETTER IX.
SWEDENBORG AND PAUL ON THE NEW BIRTH, AND THE GRAND MAN . . . . . . . . . . . 87

## LETTER X.
ANSWER TO INQUIRIES ABOUT THE NEW LIFE . . . . 100

## LETTER XI.
THE INNER WAY.—JONES VERY . . . . . . . . 107

## LETTER XII.
THE INTERNAL AND THE EXTERNAL WAY . . . . . 122

## LETTER XIII.
THE SEED GROWING: THE PROPRIUM AND THE NEW LIFE. . 126

## LETTER XIV.
THE TERRORS OF THE NEW LIFE: SPIRITUAL TEMPTATIONS . 130

## LETTER XV.
THE CELESTIAL MAN AGAIN . . . . . . . . 139

## LETTER XVI.
THE DESCENT OF THE LORD THROUGH THE CONJUGIAL SPHERE . 143

## LETTER XVII.
DIVORCE, FROM THE STAND-POINT OF THE CELESTIAL CHURCH . 153

## LETTER XVIII.
OBJECTIONS ANSWERED . . . . . . . . . 164

## LETTER XIX.
THE CELESTIAL FORGIVE ALL THINGS, EVEN ADULTERY . . 177

## LETTER XX.
SWEDENBORG'S VIEW OF EXTERNAL AND INTERNAL . . 181

## LETTER XXI.
THE PHILOSOPHY OF CREATION: NATURE ABSOLUTELY DEAD . 189

## LETTER XXII.
ADVICE TO A WOUNDED SPIRIT . . . . . . . 194

## LETTER XXIII.
COERCION IN RELIGIOUS MATTERS . . . . . . . 199

## LETTER XXIV.
CONVICTION OF SIN: INFIDEL DOUBTS: THE TWO PROPRIUMS . 205

## LETTER XXV.
CONFIRMED IN FALSE DOCTRINES: BROUGHT INTO JUDGMENT . 211

## LETTER XXVI.
UNFOLDING OF INTERIOR STATES . . . . . . . 217

## LETTER XXVII.
FREEDOM OF THOUGHT, ETC.—HOW IS THE LORD NEARER TO US?
—REMNANTS OF THE MOST ANCIENT CHURCH . . . 223

## LETTER XXVIII.
WHY SHOULD WE NOT COMMUNICATE WITH THE DEPARTED?—
SWEDENBORGIANS AND SPIRITUALISTS . . . . . 231

## LETTER XXIX.
MEDIUMS IN THE NEW CHURCH: THE PHENOMENA AND THE LAW
OF THE PHENOMENA . . . . . . . . . 239

## LETTER XXX.

THE BIBLE OF THE SPIRITUALISTS.—THE TRUE TESTS OF REVELATION.—RELIGIOUS CRANKS . . . . . . . 249

## LETTER XXXI.

THE DIVINE MOTHERHOOD CRITICISED. . . . . 254

## LETTER XXXII.

TO A NEWCHURCHMAN INFESTED BY SPIRITS . . 256

## LETTER XXXIII.

IF THE HELLS WERE SUBJUGATED BY THE LORD, WHAT NEED OF A SECOND COMING?—WHY IS SPIRITISM SO GENERALLY EVIL AND FALSE? . . . . . . . . . . 259

## LETTER XXXIV.

THE OPENING OF DEGREES.—THE NEW ERA.—RETICENCE OR REVELATION? . . . . . . . . . . 263

## LETTER XXXV.

ON SOME OBSCURE PASSAGES OF SCRIPTURE . . . . 275

## LETTER XXXVI.

SHALL WE STAY IN THE OLD CHURCH?—MARRYING OUTSIDE OF THE NEW CHURCH.—HOW SHALL WE BE SAVED? . . 284

## LETTER XXXVII.

THE NEW MOVEMENT, OLD AS WELL AS NEW—THAT SKELETON IN THE NEW-CHURCH CLOSET . . . . . . 294

## LETTER XXXVIII.

SHALL WE JOIN AN EXTERNAL NEW CHURCH? . . . 301

## LETTER XXXIX.

THE DESCENT OF THE CELESTIAL THROUGH THE SPIRITUAL INTO THE NATURAL . . . . . . . . . . 308

## LETTER XL.

RESTATEMENT OF FUNDAMENTAL PRINCIPLES . . . . 314

# APPENDIX.

### THE LORD'S DESCENT INTO ULTIMATES.

## ESSAY I.

OPENING OF THE INTERIORS . . . . . . . 325

## ESSAY II.

THE LORD'S DESCENT THROUGH THE HEAVENS . . . . 341

## ESSAY III.

THE LORD'S DESCENT INTO THE NATURAL PLANE OF THE HUMAN MIND . . . . . . . . . . 358

## ESSAY IV.

THE LORD'S KINGDOM ON EARTH.—THE NEW LIFE . . 382

# ABBREVIATIONS

OF THE WORKS OF SWEDENBORG QUOTED OR REFERRED TO IN THE FOLLOWING PAGES.

| | | |
|---|---|---|
| A. C. | stand for | Arcana Cœlestia. |
| T. C. R. | " | True Christian Religion. |
| H. H. | " | Heaven and Hell. |
| D. P. | " | Divine Providence. |
| A. R. | " | Apocalypse Revealed. |
| A. E. | " | Apocalypse Explained. |
| S. D., or Spl. D. | " | Spiritual Diary. |
| C. L. | " | Conjugial Love. |
| L. J. | " | Last Judgment. |
| Contin. L. J. | " | Continuation of the Last Judgment. |
| N. J. D. | " | Doctrine of the New Jerusalem. |

# LETTERS
## ON
# SPIRITUAL SUBJECTS.

## LETTER I.

*THE SECOND COMING OF THE LORD, A DESCENT FROM WITHIN, BOTH GENERAL AND SPECIAL.*

MY DEAR FRIEND:—You are astonished at my declaration that the Lord Jesus Christ has come again, with his own personal divine-human sphere, and that He now stands upon the earth, ready, under the proper conditions, to reveal his presence and power to men, just as truly as He stood upon the earth when He appeared to Mary in the garden, to the disciples by the way, to the incredulous Thomas in the room closed from fear of the Jews, and to Peter and John by the seaside, when the disciples durst not ask Him, Who art Thou? "knowing that it was the Lord."

This, you say, is a statement so remarkable, so remote from the perceptions and cognitions of men, that it requires to be very fully and clearly explained, or to be immensely qualified. I will offer a few suggestions which may give you a little more light on the subject.

In the first place, let us seriously consider what is meant by the coming and going away of the Lord. He said to the Pharisees, "Ye cannot tell whence I come, and whither I go," and immediately gives the reason of their ignorance: "Ye judge after the flesh," that is, ye judge from your sensuous, scientific, and rational standpoints, from which you never can discover any spiritual truth. But He said to his disciples, "Whither I go ye know, and the way ye know;" and to the ever-doubting Thomas, who still does not comprehend Him, He says, "I am the way, the truth, and the life." The coming and going of the Lord are therefore spiritual phenomena, dependent upon personal states and experiences, and explicable by spiritual and not by natural laws.

God is one and indivisible. In Himself there are no differentiations or divisions into Father, Son, and Holy Ghost. These differentiations or different conceptions of Him are made in the triune, organic, finite structures of the human mind, just as the white ray of light is broken up in the prism into several rays differing in appearance and properties. We know nothing whatever of God except as He has revealed Himself in the Lord Jesus Christ (Jno. i. 18), in whose person "the fulness of the Godhead" or the Divine Trinity resides. Now the Lord is omnipresent; neither here nor there, but everywhere simultaneously. When He is said to come and go, it is clearly an appearance due to changes occurring, not in Him, for He is unchangeable, but in the states of the human mind itself, which at one time, or under certain circumstances, recognizes his presence, and at another time, or under other conditions, does not recognize it.

In the next place let us look at some peculiar features of his first coming, or incarnation. How could that event possibly have occurred without there being the slightest change in the

Divine whereabouts? While the historical man, Jesus Christ, was living out his divine life in Judea, his spirit was everywhere and simultaneously present throughout the universe. The Jesus Christ perceptible and cognizable by men, was only the Divine Being as received, limited, and projected through the mind of the Jewish church. His career was therefore representative and significative of the organic spiritual states of that church and determined by them. Therefore, also, all his words and deeds were parables, representative and significative of spiritual truths. He could force no external belief in Him. Unbelief even suspends the working of his power. Every man saw Him and judged of Him from his own standpoint. To some, He was only the carpenter's son, and how could they comprehend the sources of his knowledge? To others, He was a gluttonous man and a wine-bibber, "a friend of publicans and sinners," and how could they appreciate his mission? To some, He "had a devil and was mad;" and why should they listen to his words? To others, He was a deceiver and a blasphemer, and why should they not crucify Him? To some, He was Elias, or John the Baptist, or one of the old prophets risen from the dead. But to his disciples He was "the Christ, the Son of the living God," or the divine truth emanating from the divine good. Nor did they perceive Him in his true light from the "flesh and blood," or the external standpoints of the Jewish church, which altogether rejected Him, but from the interior illuminating power of the Divine Love, "the Father which is in heaven." And this interior perception of truth from the standpoint of good, is the rock upon which the church is built.

But why was the Divine Being, at his first coming, projected through the mind of the church as an external man like ourselves? But first mark in this place, that Jesus Christ was a genuine objective human being, and not a mere appearance, as Tulk and some others have supposed. Our sun, with its heat and light, is a projection of the Divine mind through the sun of the spiritual world, but what can be more real and substantial? And so of the body and the external life of Christ. The reason why He became a man in the lowest or sensuo-corporeal degree, was this: The Divine Life found no plane or resting-place in the affections of the church, for they were confirmed in evils; and so their celestial degree was closed to the influx of the divine love. It could find no plane or resting-place in their thoughts, for they were confirmed in false doctrines, and the spiritual degree was closed to the influx of the divine wisdom. It could find no plane or resting-place in their natural degree of life and conduct, for that was the ultimate effect of their interior evils and falsities. There was, therefore, no abiding place for Him. The foxes and birds of the old selfhood had ample provision, "but the Son of man had not where to lay his head." "He came unto his own, and his own received Him not."

The Divine Life therefore, impregnating the virgin affection for truth, the last feeble remains of genuine good and truth in the world, produced that extraordinary human being, the historical Christ, born without natural father, both God and man, living a divine life but tempted as we are, putting off everything derived from the mother, and passing away, even as to his physical remains, entirely out of the sphere of human perception; disappearing or ascending from without inwards, exactly as He had descended from within outwards. This was "the eternal life" about whom his favorite disciple uses these solemn and wonderful words:

"*That which was from the beginning, which we have heard, which we have seen with our eyes, which we have looked upon, and our hands have handled, of the Word of life:*

"(*For the life was manifested and we have seen it, and bear witness and show unto you that eternal life which was with the Father and was manifested unto us :*)

"*That which we have seen and heard declare we unto you, that ye also may have fellowship with us : and truly our fellowship is with the Father and with his Son Jesus Christ.*"

The divine love produces the divine wisdom just as heat produces light. It was the divine love, in its outflowing endeavor to save the human race from hell, that, passing through the organic spiritual forms of the Jewish church, produced the manifestation of the divine wisdom embodied in the person and life of Christ. This divine love was called the Father, who was prior, superior, and greater than He; from whom He came forth, who sent Him, who gave Him every word that He spoke, and who did through Him everything that was done. "I am in the Father, and the Father in me : the words that I speak unto you I speak not of myself, but the Father that dwelleth in me, He doeth the works."

Such was the first coming of the Lord. He was compelled to manifest Himself in the lowest or sensuo-corporeal sphere of human life, because He had been interiorly rejected and could not be manifested through its higher and interior spheres of affection and thought. He looked, "and behold! there was no man," no genuine image and likeness of God in the world. So He apparently descended because man had descended, and could only see Him on his own plane. He became man in order to restore the broken and desecrated order of heaven to humanity, and to make it divine.

If He could have found a receptive plane for his influx in the affections of that age, it would have produced such people as Fenelon, Wesley, and William Law. If He could have found a receptive plane for his influx into the thoughts of that age, it would have produced a Swedenborg, and the spiritual sense of the Word would have been opened, and not merely guessed at, as by Paul, Origen, and others. If He could have been received at that time in the natural plane of human life, all our modern discoveries in science, our political revolutions and social advances would have then been possible. But the interior degrees of the human race were closed, and it was sinking into animalism, and would have perished morally and physically, had not the Lord taken on or entered into its lowest environments, prepared for Himself a human nature, with its infirm human conditions and propensities to evil derived from the mother, and perfected and glorified his humanity by the conquest of the influent hells, and by the reopening of all the closed degrees of life, becoming successively a divine natural, divine rational, divine spiritual, and divine celestial man, until He and the Father were one, and He had "all power in heaven and upon earth."

But I find myself, my dear sir, carried away by that most sublime and sacred of all themes, the philosophy of the incarnation, and must return to the simpler purpose of this letter, which was to show that the three apparent movements of the Lord—his coming from the Father, his going back to the Father, and his return or second coming to us, were dependent, not upon any changes in Himself, but upon his accommodation of the divine love and wisdom to the varying spiritual states and organic receptivities of his creatures.

His going away, his returning to the Father, was the elevation of his human states into such a degree of unition with the divine love, that our human perceptions and cognitions could no longer retain Him. So He passed away from us, becoming invisible simply because He was no longer comprehensible, even by the highest finite intelligences. This was the lifting up which draws all men unto Him, a state not attained by the death of the cross, as is commonly supposed, but by the far more important death of the selfhood or old proprium derived from the mother. We follow Him in the regeneration by a similar death of the selfhood and a similar elevation of our natural states of life into spiritual states, which are "the heavenly places in Christ Jesus" mentioned by Paul: "If we have been planted together in the likeness of his death, we shall be also in the likeness of his resurrection."

We ourselves "come to the Father," or attain to states of heavenly peace and love, only by Jesus Christ, who is "the way, the truth, and the life." The way is the external rule or conduct, the truth is the spiritual light or guide, the life is the celestial essence or power. It is only by the divine presence of the threefold spirit of Christ within ourselves, that we enter into union with the Father as He did, and become one with Him even as He was one with the Father. These heavenly states of life are the many mansions in our Father's house—the spiritual places or conditions prepared for us by his going away, or by the unition of the human nature with the divine.

Observe, my dear friend, the stress which our Lord lays upon the expediency and necessity of his going away:

"*It is expedient for you that I go away; for if I go not away, the Comforter will not come unto you; but if I depart, I will send Him unto you.*"

*"If ye loved me, ye would rejoice because I said, I go unto the Father; for my Father is greater than I."*

*"I go to prepare a place for you;*

*"And if I go and prepare a place for you, I will come again, and receive you unto myself, that where I am, there ye may be also."*

It is clear from these considerations that the race cannot be saved so long as the divine life flows through distorted mediums into the external sphere of our being, as it did through the Jewish church. Nor can even a perfect medium, like the Christ, do us any good, so long as He seems to remain in our own external sphere, or to operate upon us only in an external manner. He must be lifted up into higher and more and more interior standpoints, even to his own divine centres, or into union with the Father, so that He may come back or return from above downwards, from within outwards, and, by the spiritual laws of creation, reconstruct and re-create us after the model of his own divine image.

The Divine Being contains within Himself all possible states of humanity as to goodness and truth, for He is the infinite good, the infinite truth. In the process of his incarnation He never laid aside or lost any of those states; in the process of glorification he never obtained any state which He did not have before in infinite fulness. He underwent no change at all. But He projected Himself outwardly into visible human form, not directly from Himself, but mediately through the human race. In that form He bore the sins and iniquities of the world; through it He combated against all the powers of hell; and into it He infused the fulness of the divine life, until it passed away from the perceptions and cognitions of men. It was a manifestation of Himself, a means of bringing us into rapport with Him. The places prepared for us are states of goodness and truth which his divine love and power have thus opened to us and made possible to us, for He now draws all men unto Him. We are where He is, when we can appropriate his divine love and wisdom, and conform our wills to his will, until we are clothed upon with the spirit of Christ. Similarity of thought and feeling makes presence in the spiritual world.

Our Lord's first coming was only preparatory to the second. It was exceedingly limited on the earthly or external side, made so by the influx of the divine life through interior spheres which repudiated and rejected Him, crucifying his divine truth in their own spirits before they condemned his external manifestation to the cross. But by the glorification or divinization of his assumed humanity, He has elevated our states, or so spiritualized our being that states of affection and thought, "heavenly places" in our religious life, are ready to receive Him at his second coming. It will, therefore, not be a coming from without, as the Christian world expects, but a genuine coming or descent from within; not special to one race or religion, but universal; an influx of a divine-human life into the Body of Humanity, which will finally purify the affections, illumine the understandings, and regulate the conduct of men.

Every coming of the Lord is, therefore, not a voluntary movement on his part, such as we imagine that He made, but a revelation to us of his presence, made always according to spiritual laws; for God is the supreme law of laws. It is a change within ourselves, which enables us in some manner to realize the fact that He is here and is always here—that "open secret" which is so hard for us to comprehend. This revelation of the Lord occurs with infinitely varying phenomena to human souls in the course of their religious experiences and regeneration. But all human souls are bound together by spiritual laws into a great, invisible solidarity; and in the course of the evolution of the race there are mighty epochs or crises, caused really by the reaction of the heavens against a perverted church and an evil world ("the kingdom of heaven suffereth violence"), and accompanied by new influxes, internal and external revolutions, the destruction of old and the establishment of new orders, revelations of some sorts, or rather of many sorts, from within, and the unfolding of a better and wiser life in the world. Such epoch or crisis constitutes a general coming of the Lord. Such phenomena occurred in the time of Christ; and similar phenomena are now occurring, and are still to occur, for the Lord has come again.

The historian and the scientist cannot discover the real causes of these extraordinary movements of humanity, for those causes do not lie upon the same plane or level with their researches. The dog that hunts with his nose along the ground, can never reach the bird that flies in the air over his head. The causes are spiritual, and can only be made known by revelation; and they have been revealed through Swedenborg for the benefit of the new age which is dawning upon us. And if Swedenborg is a star of very small magnitude to some people, and entirely out of sight to others, it is only because they are too remote from him to recognize his solar immensity.

From Swedenborg we learn that there is a perfect continuity and solidarity of law and life throughout the universe. The human race, as a spiritual totality, does not stand alone deriving its life from natural sources, but is organically connected by internal bonds with the world of spirits, with heaven and with hell. Its life is a composite problem, the result of a vast series of actions and reactions between the spiritual world and the natural world. Every coming of the Lord is therefore attended by rearrangements of societies in the heavens and the hells; by judgments executed in the world of spirits and repeating themselves in different forms in the world of men; by removal of obstacles from the interior, and a consequently greater influx of spiritual heat and light, which are love and wisdom, into the hearts and minds of those who are in conditions to receive them.

Those disciples of Swedenborg who are teaching that the second coming of the Lord consists wholly and solely in the revelation of the spiritual sense of the Word, do great injustice to Swedenborg and to the Christian world. That is one statement of Swedenborg, and a reiterated and a most important and truthful statement; but it is not the whole truth. Swedenborg also says that the revelation by angelic spirits of the doctrine of the celestial life to certain people in Africa, was not only the initiament of the New Church, but the advent of the Lord. He also states plainly the universal truth, that the formation of the church and the heavenly life in the soul constitutes the coming of the Lord; and moreover, that the opening of the interior degrees of life in the regeneration, constitutes the coming of the Lord to the individual.

The better portion of the Christian world turns us a deaf ear when we insist that the coming of the Lord is in a new system of spiritual doctrine, to be promulgated by a new church. It is not looking for doctrines or churches, but for the Lord Himself. It will willingly accept new doctrines and new churches if they are preceded by the personal presence of the Divine man. And in this it is quite right. We want no more authoritative teaching; we question the authority of Authority. We care but little at present for outside church-building; we want the church constructed within ourselves. We want the Lord: we want to hear his voice; to see Him walking upon the troubled waters of our life; to touch the hem of his garment and be healed; to put our fingers into the print of the nails and to believe. We expect Him to fulfil his promises.

*"And when He had spoken these things, while they beheld, He was taken up: and a cloud received Him out of their sight.*
*"And while they looked steadfastly toward heaven, as He went up, behold, two men stood by them in white apparel:*
*"Which also said, Ye men of Galilee, why stand ye gazing up into heaven? this same Jesus which is taken up from you into heaven, shall so come in like manner as ye have seen Him go into heaven."*

Now, my dear sir, the assertion of the two men, who were two angels, that Jesus would come again from heaven, "in like manner" or under precisely similar conditions, as those under which He ascended to heaven, was absolutely and literally true. But what was the manner? What were the conditions? All depends upon a correct conception of the manner and the conditions. If our Lord was in the same organic state He occupied before his crucifixion; if the disciples were in their normal, closed condition of life; if a material body really disappeared in a material cloud; then is the Christian world perfectly justified in expecting the Lord to descend through natural space in a material form, and meet us and judge us on the lowest or sensuo-corporeal plane of life, however preposterous and incomprehensible such a proceeding might appear.

But there is a very different and perfectly rational way of interpreting the phenomenon. There is a coming from within far more sublime and effective, because universal and special, than any coming from without, like a king marching from one country to another, ever could be. He is to come from within, because He passed from without inwards. Our Lord's glorified body was never seen by the natural eyes of men; but all his appearances or manifestations after his resurrection were projections from and through the minds of his disciples into apparent time and space, made according to spiritual laws, with which the experience of Swedenborg and others have now made us familiar.

The disciples, no doubt, told the story precisely as it appeared to their senses. They knew nothing, however, of the difference between spiritual and natural senses. They did not know that their spiritual senses were open, and that they were witnessing a scene which was transpiring in a spiritual sphere and not in the world of nature. They thought, no doubt, that if all the Jews and Romans had been present they would have seen the same things. They had forgotten the Lord's words—"in a little while the world shall see me no more; but ye see me."

The disciples were held in comparatively open or internal states by the angelic spheres about the Lord, for the purposes of divine manifestations and revelation. But when their own hereditary sphere reacted against the internal sphere, it receded, and the disciples were left in their natural and external states. Our Lord disappeared from them because their states of affection and thought were too gross and material to maintain that spiritual rapport which induces presence. He seemed to ascend up, because they were not able to follow Him into the high spiritual state into which the glorification of his human nature had lifted Him. "Whither I go," He said, "thou canst not follow me now; but thou shalt follow me afterwards."

He was concealed from them by a cloud, because it is the cloud of our own natural thought and life, which conceals the spiritual world with all its transcendent issues from us. It is the cloud of the letter of the Word which to-day conceals the infinite treasures of divine truth from the church and the world. When He comes again, therefore, He must come into these clouds. "Behold, He cometh with clouds." He has so come again; He has illumined the clouds of the letter of the Word with the radiance of heavenly wisdom. He is even now descending into the clouds of our natural and sensuous life, bringing us into judgment, revealing Himself to us in innumerable ways, according to our faith and our own states of reception, and thus preparing a new heaven and a new earth, or entirely new spiritual conditions both internal and external, for his presence and perpetual reign among men.

Returning now to the first paragraph in this letter, you can see its assertion in a better light. It was the closing or shutting up of our souls to influx from within, that has sunk us into our present closed natural and sensuous states. The supreme condition of our Lord's reappearance, or second coming, is the reopening of the degrees of our spiritual life as to its affections, its thoughts, and its sensations. It is, therefore, always a matter of personal experience. The possibilities of the unfoldings from within in each of these discrete degrees, are incalculable. They constitute the new things of the coming era, when the Lord will "make all things new." The opening of the spiritual degree of the understanding in Swedenborg has given us a flood of new and precious light from the Divine Word, and tapped a vein of spiritual truth which is absolutely inexhaustible. The opening of the sphere of the affections to the divine influx ("behold, I stand at the door and knock!") will bring the life of the heavens down upon the earth. The opening of the spiritual senses is a subject too vast and solemn, and too little comprehended, for vague speculation. We must patiently await its evolution and development. The opening of these interior degrees of life to the reception of the Divine influx, will constitute the real and special coming of the Lord, which, when universal, will be his living presence—something like a re-incarnation of Himself—in the Body of Humanity.

That innumerable Herods professing to be in search of the true King, will endeavor to strangle this revolutionary Christ, there cannot be a particle of doubt.

Yours, truly,

W. H. H.

3*

# LETTER II.

### *THREE DEGREES OF HUMAN LIFE: CELESTIAL, SPIRITUAL, AND NATURAL.*

MY DEAR SIR:—It will aid you immensely in comprehending both the individual phenomena and the historical phases of the religious or spiritual life, if you will master (and it is easily done) the meaning of the three terms, celestial, spiritual, and natural, in the Swedenborgian philosophy. I will, therefore, give you a few hints on the subject.

First, notice hastily how the law of three degrees runs through all things. In every object we have the degrees of dimension, length, breadth, and thickness. In natural substances there are solids, liquids, and gases; and again land, air, and water. Organized forms are in three kingdoms, mineral, vegetable, and animal. In philosophy there are three terms which include all things, end, cause, and effect. In man there are will, understanding, and conduct; affection, thought, and sensation. In the Divine, there are Love, Wisdom, and Power, signified by the Father, the Son, and the Holy Ghost. There are three heavens with entirely different phenomena; and three senses of the Divine Word within and above the letter, each sense adapted to its special heaven. These trines and their relationships involve and include all things. The doctrine of three degrees and their organic connection with each other, is the key to the philosophy of the universe.

It is a trite saying that human nature is everywhere and at all times the same. It is true that all men differ in the same respects from animals. All men have similar appetites also, and similar faculties of observation and reason, and a similar natural basis of affection, thought, and sensation. But the interior structures and operations of the souls of men differ so immensely, that we may say there are three different kinds or grades of human nature. These three degrees of human life stand so far apart from each other, that after death when similar spiritual affinities draw souls together, and dissimilar qualities drive them apart, men and women who even seemed alike in the natural world, are separated by impassable gulfs of organic incompatibility. They go into different degrees and different societies of heaven or hell; and the question is so purely one of acquired spiritual organization, that one soul can no more permanently change places with another, than a fish can take a bird's place in the air, or the bird take the fish's place in the water.

Every man has three degrees of life, or rather the organic forms capable of receiving and manifesting it, concealed within his external organization. He is, therefore, an image of all the heavens, differing therein entirely from animals, which have only the external organization and a sensuo-corporeal life with its various instincts and appetites.

Man begins with a merely animal life, and the interior degrees are gradually opened and formed in him by instruction, education, revelation, and the spiritual experiences of the regenerating process. The differences between men and races of men, and between ancient and modern men and races, depend largely upon the extent to which these three human natures have been unfolded within them. This is a chief cause of sympathies, antipathies, coalitions, and misunderstandings among men. One person does not understand another nor sympathize with him, not only because of the obvious differences on the same plane, but because interiorly he stands upon an entirely different plane of life. The natural man judges all other men from his own standpoint. The motives, principles, affections, thoughts, and conduct of the spiritual and the celestial man are mysteries to him. The former he frequently calls a fanatic and the latter a fool, and both are objects of his incredulity or his contempt.

The natural man derives his wisdom from the light of nature alone, and is governed by the evidence of his senses. He loves himself supremely, whether he knows it or not, and even his love for his children, relatives, neighbors, and country, is another form of self-love. He loves the world, its pleasures, and its possessions. He desires to be elevated in all respects above his fellows. Pleasure, fashion, reputation, wealth, power, are his idols. His motives are all interested, his ends are thoroughly utilitarian, having reference only to the things of this life. If he is civil, honest, temperate, chaste, industrious, as he often is, it is because he feels it is safest, wisest, and best for him to be so. When the general interest coincides with his own interest he is capable of being an admirable neighbor, philanthropist, and patriot. The evolutions of social and civilized life may make him a gentleman of the most delicate sentiment and refined culture. He throws his weight into the scale of law and order, because there is peace, comfort, and progress under their powerful protection.

Now these states of life and character, evolved and evolving upon the natural plane or degree of the human mind, have nothing whatever of a spiritual quality about them. It is not only possible, but highly probable, that the evolution of an advanced grade of civilization on these natural principles will take place finally in all the hells. It is the assertive, aggressive, self-derived, competitive civilization of the selfhood or proprium. Its spirit, at the bottom of all appearances to the contrary, is the spirit of hell—for the hell hereafter is only the consociated states, and the corresponding environment, of all those who have loved themselves and the world instead of the Lord and the neighbor.

You will perhaps understand me better when I say, that we repudiate entirely the old ecclesiastical idea that hell is a place prepared by God for the punishment of sin. Every man makes and voluntarily seeks his own hell. Men after death as well as before it, and according to the same spiritual laws, enter into social and governmental organizations; selfish and unregenerate men gravitate together, and form societies as they do here, each individual striving to rule or exploit the rest, and their punishment is nothing but the continued miseries which their own evil natures inflict upon themselves and each other. They are in the same interior states there that they were here, and so far as living men are in the love of self and the world, so far they are virtually in hell, whether they know it and feel it or not. The business of religion is not so much to prevent us from going to hell, as to deliver us from the hell we are already in.

Do not be astonished, my dear sir, when I tell you that this natural man is sometimes exceedingly religious (without a spark of genuine spirituality), and spends an enormous amount of money, enough every year to relieve all the real distress in the world, on churches, ministers, missionaries, agencies, books, papers, etc., etc. But, in becoming religious, he does not rise above his old level. He is as selfish, dogmatic, ambitious, and competitive in his religion as in his business. The hope of reward and the fear of punishment are his chief motives, those selfish motives which we bring to bear successfully in the training of animals and children. He yields willingly and gracefully, as if he was performing the chief duty of man, to the combined pressure of ecclesiastical authority, social demands, and hereditary usages. He does not seek for truth to illumine his understanding, but for miracles to compel belief. If Christian, he is perfectly satisfied with the literal sense of the Word of God, because he cannot think of spiritual things in any but a natural or literal manner. One form of this natural mind contends vigorously for purity of doctrine, and is exceedingly zealous for the church and its ordinances; another form aspires after distinguished pieties and sanctities, striving, like the sons of Zebedee, to be first in the kingdom of heaven.

Now this ecclesiastical religion, this professional morality, this righteousness of the Scribes and Pharisees, is the religion, under a thousand different forms, of nine-tenths of the human race. It involves no fundamental organic change of character, but is a life of compelled obedience and of suppressed, not renovated, selfhood. Yet the sincere, natural Christian is capable of unfolding, after death, into the spiritual man. The organized institutions of this natural religion, claiming to be spiritual, are the greatest obstructions to the Coming of the Lord and the development of the new life in the world. They have the advantage of enormous majorities and the prestige of many centuries of intense literalism. They will cling with the tenacity of self-preservation to the old formulas and the old issues, until the imaginary heavens in which they have entrenched themselves shall flee away forever from the face of the Lord; "for He cometh, for He cometh to judge the earth."

So much for the natural type of man, religious and irreligious. Now there are some celestial men in the world, and a great many more spiritual men, and always have been; and the number of both is about to increase in a wonderful manner. But engrave, my dear sir, very deeply upon your mind this fundamental fact in regard to spiritual evolution: that no possible extensions or amplifications of the goodness and wisdom of the natural man, on his own plane of life, can ever develop the spiritual or celestial type of being. Paul understood this very clearly when he declared that a man might be perfect in all knowledge, have faith which could remove mountains, benevolence to give all his possessions to the poor, and the courage of martyrdom for his religion, and yet have nothing of that true charity or divine love in the soul which constitutes the life of heaven.

Now what is the key to this seeming paradox? It is the wonderful secret of the New Birth. When a man from natural becomes spiritual, he passes from death into life; he is born again; he has a new nature, not his old natural disposition modified this way or that, but absolutely a "new creature," given to him from above. This new, higher, discretely different grade of human nature lives and works from standpoints of affection and thought unknown to the natural man. A divine altruism or love of others has displaced the self-love of the "old man." He is no longer governed by self-interest and natural conceptions of duty, but by conscience or spiritual conceptions of duty. Natural appetites and passions have no power over him. On the contrary he has absolute power over them, and subordinates the natural entirely to the uses and service of the spiritual life. His neighbor, the church, the country, the Lord's kingdom, are always first and foremost in his affections and thoughts; self and self-interest being always remanded to the last and lowest place.

Now this spiritual man is not born of flesh and blood, but of the will of God. It is a new conception, between the love and obedience of a man to natural truth as a mother, and spiritual good inflowing from above as a father. This new birth is the product of the conjunction between a lower and a higher discrete degree of life. There was a point somewhere in the mineral kingdom, when some form of it was impregnated by the vegetable soul above it, and the plant evolved into being. There was a point somewhere in the vegetable kingdom, when forms were prepared for the influx of the animal soul, and animated nature was the result. There was a point in the animal sphere, perhaps now undiscoverable, when impregnation from a higher, living, loving, reasoning degree of life (the human) took place, and Man was created.

This first man or first Adam is the natural man whom I have described. The new man or the second Adam is "the Lord from heaven," because it is the divine life communicated to us from a higher plane, and making us "Sons of God." We here approach logically that solemn mystery, the birth of Jesus from the virgin Mary. It was only through a virgin form that the divine uncreated life itself could become immanent in the world as a human being. Then by successive openings of the interior degrees in Himself, by successive new births or ascensions, progressive unions of the Son with the Father, from sensuo-corporeal He became natural, from natural spiritual, from spiritual celestial, from celestial Divine—and so, neither Father nor Son, but a Divine Man, from beginning to end, from first to last, the Alpha and the Omega, including and involving all degrees of life in his own divine-human person.

The natural man finds it difficult to understand the unfolding of the spiritual nature; but the celestial nature, born of spiritual truth as a mother and of celestial good as a father, is something still more incomprehensible. Even the spiritual man finds it difficult to comprehend the celestial character. The natural man is in the sphere of science and its practical utilities; the spiritual man is in the sphere of truth, and especially of the spiritual uses of the Divine Word; the celestial man is in the sphere of love, and its outflowing activities towards the whole human race. The natural Christian delights more especially in the church, its ordinances, and its influences: the spiritual man delights more especially in the Word, its correspondences, and its infinite applications to the needs of the spiritual life: the celestial man lives in the personal atmosphere of the Lord, and in a state of perfect coincidence of his own will with the Divine will. His life is truly "hid with Christ in God." All these forms or degrees are necessary to a perfected world upon which all three heavens may rest.

The natural and the spiritual man are in states of combat and temptation, resisting evil, organizing for good, with more or less of the old selfhood or proprium mingled and perhaps concealed in their best feelings and best works. The celestial man has laid down the life of self, and is clothed upon with the spirit of Christ. He is in states of supreme peace, and is always the peacemaker. He thinks no evil, does no evil; "for whosoever is born of God doth not commit sin." He has no sense of interest, or duty, or conscience, such as men in the lower degrees have. The law of the Lord is written on his heart, and he lives out all the divine commands as spontaneously as the bird sings. He has no concealments, no prevarications, no self-interests to serve. His life is a simple yea, yea, or nay, nay. He has no enemies to forgive, for he regards every human being with unchangeable tenderness and love. He perceives truth by a certain intuition unknown to others; for he that doeth the will of the Lord shall know of his doctrine. He is in that heavenly state of life, the innocence of wisdom, typified by Jesus when " He took a little child and set him in their midst." His coming is predicted in many wonderful and beautiful passages in the prophets.

Ancient history, as distinguished from modern history, cannot be understood, unless it is known that three successive manifestations of the religious life, celestial, spiritual, and natural, succeeded each other from the creation of man to the time of Christ. The laws and phenomena of those different dispensations, the causes and effect of their decline and termination, are all unfolded in the voluminous works of Swedenborg, which contain treasures of knowledge for the philosopher and the Christian, to which the unearthed relics of Troy and Babylon and Egypt are mere baubles. And yet they lie undiscovered or ignored, mainly because men stand at the threshold, and in the irrational spirit of the dead past exclaim, "We will not accept or even examine his teachings, unless he first gives us some miraculous attestation of his authority."

The Incarnation of Jehovah in the person of Jesus Christ is the central fact of human history, organically connected with everything that preceded and with everything that has followed it. It was the successive closure of the interior degrees of the human mind, celestial, spiritual, and natural, successively cutting off the influx from the heavens, and the impending descent into animalism and destruction, which necessitated the assumption of our infirm and finite humanity by the Divine Being. Jesus Christ, necessarily conceived at the time as "the Son of God," was a prepared human form into which the Divine life, called the Father, flowed in such a manner, that, starting from our own sensuo-corporeal basis, He opened successively all the interior degrees which had been closed, and by successive unions of the lower with the higher degree (the Son ascending to the Father), He became a divine-natural, divine-spiritual, and divine-celestial Man, having all power in heaven and earth. Henceforth the reopening of the heavens to man became possible. By rapport with this Divine Man, through faith, prayer, love, obedience, and perfect coincidence of wills, we may become spiritual and celestial again.

This is a good opportunity to explain more clearly what is meant by the descent of the Lord into ultimates. Ultimates are not the last things in a series on the same plane, like the last object in a row of objects, or the last country reached in a course of travel. Ultimates, in philosophical language, are the last or lowest things which contain within their forms all the superior and prior things of the series. Thus a man's conduct is the ultimate act which includes the causes of the act and the motives which induced the man to set the causes into operation. Affections and thoughts are thus ultimated into actions. The physical universe is the ultimate of the spiritual universe concealed within it. The body is the ultimate of the soul concealed within it. The literal sense of the Word is an ultimate containing spiritual and celestial senses concealed within it.

The descent of the Lord into ultimates means, therefore, that the divine life is now strongly influent into the celestial, spiritual, and natural degrees, awakening, vivifying, and harmonizing the affections, thoughts, and conduct of angels, spirits, and men; so that finally the church in heaven and the church upon earth will make one, and the Lord's will be done upon earth even as it is in heaven.

Believe me, my dear sir, the Lord Jesus Christ with his holy angels, which mean heavenly states of life such as angels enjoy, is now immanent in the world.

Yours, truly,
W. H. H.

# LETTER III.

## THE THREE-FOLD APPEARANCE OF THE LORD.

MY DEAR SIR:—The idea of a triune God, which pervades most ancient religions, and which appears as Father, Son, and Holy Ghost in the Christian system, was generated in the three-fold structure of the human mind by the influx of the one, indivisible, divine life into it. In the celestial degree God appears to us as the divine love, a divine presence in the heart and the affections. In the spiritual degree He appears as the divine wisdom, the eternal truth, the sleepless intelligence governing the universe by immutable laws. In the natural degree He appears as the divine power ultimating itself in all the forms and forces of the physical world.

When the ancients, through successive degradations of the religious life, lost the interior light of truth, they sank into the natural degree of affection and thought, and deified the powers of nature, the sun, moon, stars, light, fire, etc., etc. The gods and goddesses of antiquity were the Divinity dissected into parts and invested with human shapes, the consequence of the loss of the great spiritual idea that God is in the Human Form. The Human Form is as different from the human shape as the form of government is different from the form of the man who rules, or as the body politic differs from the body of an individual. Our Lord laid aside the human shape with the infirmities He derived from the mother, but

He exists in an infinite divine-human form, the absolute expression of the divine love, wisdom, and power. That the entire Godhead is immanent in the glorified person of Jesus Christ, is the last, highest, most fruitful result of the evolution of theological truth.

This one God manifests Himself to all his creatures in the universe under an infinite variety of forms, names, and circumstances. In other words, God always appears to us according to our own states. There is no such thing as a false God or an idol, but only mean, false, inadequate conceptions of God in the minds of men. God is as truly present in the Chinese pagoda and the Hindoo temple, as He is in the Catholic cathedral or the Quaker meeting-house. He accepts all worship from the heart, and accommodates Himself alike to the highest and the lowest states. The idols of wood and stone which we are all even now worshipping, are self, the world, pleasure, money, fashion, and power. The heathen are in far more salvable conditions than we; and alas! for the self-righteous that think otherwise. Beautiful and tender are the utterances of Swedenborg about the heathen. The doctrinals, the morals, and even the idols of the upright gentiles, are accepted by the Lord, and left whole to them as the vessels of celestial things which they are qualified by charity to receive.—A. C. 1832, 4211. Those who have worshipped idols and yet lived in charity, easily receive the goods and truths of faith in the other life; and they are not instantly deprived of what they have esteemed holy from infancy, but are weaned from their delusions by degrees.—A. C. 1992, 9972.

In God there is "no variableness or shadow of turning," but we ourselves form different conceptions of Him and invest Him with different qualities and attributes according as our standpoints are natural, spiritual, or celestial. Let us glance a moment at the different forms which the Divine Being is made to assume by transmission through the different degrees or planes of the human soul.

If the interior degrees, spiritual and celestial, are closed, and the influx is only into the natural degree, man conceives of God as a being like himself, only vastly greater and more powerful. He is a mighty King, conservative of his power, jealous of his authority, who rewards his friends and punishes his enemies, who makes laws for the government of his people, and who opens heaven or hell according as his compassion or his indignation is excited. This kind of a God builds churches or temples wherein He demands that He shall be worshipped; issues commands to be obeyed, and promulgates creeds which his people are to believe, ordains priests and other ecclesiastical powers which are to be duly respected, extends his conquests and condemns to hell all who reject Him as the supreme ruler. This was the God of the Jews; and the Christian religion, as interpreted by many of its disciples, retains some melancholy traces of this anthropomorphic deity.

When the rational degree is opened, which is intermediate between the natural and the spiritual, the mind rises into the conception of inflexible laws and immutable order. It sees God in an abstract manner, and shrinks from any personal or concrete conception of Him. If the rational man leans to the natural side, he generates the natural utilitarian religion of Spencer or Comte. If he leans to the spiritual side, he views God as the Supreme Intelligence, governing the world with love and wisdom; and if he accepts revelation, he beholds God as the Divine Truth, unveiling itself more or less clearly to the human understanding in a written Word. If this degree is freely opened, without a corresponding opening of the celestial degree above it, we have a cold, hard, barren, intellectual religion, based upon rigid conceptions of right and duty.

The God of the celestial man, or to speak philosophically, God as seen from the celestial degree, contains within Himself all that is true and beautiful in the lower degrees, and a great deal more. He is "the way, the truth, and the life:" the way, because He governs in the least of external things as in the greatest; the truth, because He is the divine wisdom, the source of all intelligence; the life, because his divine fatherly love is the uncreated life which He gives freely and abundantly to all who seek Him.

This God will hide Himself from you if you try to make Him a King, because He wishes to be your Father and to give you the kingdom. He never judges or condemns even the most wicked. He never punishes, or resents, or revenges. He is always "meek and lowly of heart." His constant, unceasing effort is to give and to bless. He will reveal Himself, He will explain Himself to you in the sweetest, humblest manner. He will take your children in his arms; He will weep with you at your friend's grave; yea, if He can instruct you even in little things, he will gird Himself and wash your feet. He will suffer and die for you, and bear your infirmities forever, if He can only have you where He is, and crown you with his love.

This, my dear sir, is the God of the New Jerusalem, "the same Jesus" who is now returning to the earth by opening the interior degrees of our life. He is now moving from inmost to outmost, and He will eventually fill the tabernacle of our lives, the temple and its outer court, and even the whole city with his presence.

Yours truly,<br>W. H. H.

# LETTER IV.

*THE LORD AS PHYSICIAN: "WHO HEALETH ALL THY DISEASES."*

MY DEAR SIR:—I said in one of my letters that the Lord at his second coming would reorganize society, and reconstruct even the elements of nature; that He would direct all enterprises, transact all business, and cure all diseases; and this without infringing in the least upon the free agency, rationality, and individuality of any human being. You are deeply interested in the so-called "faith-cures" and "mind-cures," and desire some more explicit declaration of opinion as to the operation of the Lord in the cure of disease.

In the first place, let us understand clearly who this Lord is, from whom these wonderful things are to be expected. He is not the infinite, omnipotent, omnipresent God, conceived of as a Supreme Being separate from the person of Jesus Christ. Nor is it Jesus Christ as a vastly superior Man, separate from the infinite, omnipresent, omnipotent God. The coming Healer of the nations is God revealed and manifested in the person of Jesus Christ. "No man hath seen God at any time: the only-begotten Son which is in the bosom of the Father, He hath declared Him." We know nothing whatever of God outside of Jesus Christ, who has made Him visible to us. "He that seeth me, seeth Him that sent me."

The second coming of the Lord is therefore a reappearance of the Divine Man to us; the coming from heaven, under certain conditions, of "this same Jesus" who was taken up into heaven from his disciples. He never would have disappeared from his people if their interior states of affection and thought, or of love and wisdom, had been such as could have retained and utilized his presence amongst them. So long as they kept to their first love, and the strong, personal faith in Him as a Divine Man having all power in heaven and earth, they cured diseases, performed miracles, and were blessed with interior vision and spiritual gifts of a marvelous nature. These things all disappeared, not because they were no longer needed, but because the church sank into dead, natural, closed conditions in which they were impossible.

The Lord, who has been dead and buried in the church for so many centuries, has risen again. It is the same Jesus who healed "every sickness and every disease among the people," in the towns and villages of Judea and Galilee. The Mary of our hearts, ransomed from her degradation, hears his voice and recognizes the Master; and some have "seen a vision of angels," who have told them that He is not only living, but is here in our midst. He has made Himself known to some of us in the breaking of bread, when we received Him into the house of our soul and prayed Him to abide with us. Some of us have witnessed that miraculous draught of fishes, and seen the great net of the Word unbroken. Many, shut up in their own minds for fear of the unbelieving, scornful world, have felt Him enter from within, and reveal Himself to them as a Man—divine even as to his flesh and his bones, to whom all things were possible—and breathe upon them the Holy Ghost, or the living spirit of his own divinely human love.

Christ is within us or nowhere. "Neither shall they say, Lo, here! or lo, there! for behold! the kingdom of God is within you." Christ, immanent again in the sensuo-corporeal sphere of humanity, can cure all diseases, forgive all sins, renovate all natures; because He occupies the inmost standpoint to work from, and can move downwards and outwards, from centres to circumferences, moulding all things to his heavenly will, according as the interior doors of the heart are opened for his admission, and the organic conditions are provided for the manifestations of his power.

Our Lord, by virtue of his own Divine Humanity, is now opening the interior doors of the three degrees of the human mind, celestial, spiritual, and natural, and descending through them into the Body of our Humanity, in such a manner that He will manifest Himself in innumerable forms of love, wisdom, and power, according to the organic states and receptivities of his creatures. He is immanent in all the progressive movements of the age, good or evil, for He comes like the sun to all alike. He is in the grand cathedral, in the faith-cure, in the Methodist camp-meeting, in the merchant's exchange, in the Salvation-army, in all places alike. He is with the temperate and the intemperate, with the chaste and the unchaste. He is with the agnostic, the rationalist, the sensualist, the nihilist. He is no respecter of persons—He is the same to all. But He comes for judgment, and He permits every man to judge himself and to choose his own final condition. To those who receive Him, and assimilate his flesh and blood to their own organisms, He is a revelation of life and salvation. This is the "manifestation of the sons of God." To those who repudiate, reject, and pervert his influent sphere, He is a revelation of death and destruction. The outcome of every man's life and thought at this moment, whether he knows it or not, is the life of Jesus Christ modified in his passage through the structures of the man's mind and the tissues of his body; for "in Him we live and move and have our being."

The Lord now stands in the ultimates, or the last and lowest things of the human mind, in such a manner that the evil spheres, which are the causes of all moral and physical disease, can be made to recede from his presence. The sensualist and the drunkard, convicted of sin and full of self-loathing, may now come to Him with supreme faith that He will take away all their evil appetites, and give them absolute power over the lusts of the flesh. There is no sin, no infirmity of spirit, no frailty of temper, which will not pass away when He enters to abide in the hearts of his children. The state of Christian perfection is no idle dream. It is the simplest and most feasible of all realities. It will soon be a supreme necessity with us; for, as the sphere of judgment descends, the conjoint worship of God and Mammon will no longer be permitted.

When our Lord was upon earth in a material body, He cured diseases by taking on or assuming the spiritual state of the diseased persons. This was done in the infirm humanity derived from the mother. From that standpoint He entered into spiritual combat with the evil sphere which caused the disease, and cast it out into the hells, leaving the released victim free from the infestation, and restored to physical health. It is commonly supposed that Christ had merely to speak the word of power and the miraculous changes took place. But it is not so; every step of his victorious progress was achieved by assuming the spheres of the afflicted, and contending for them against the combined power of the hells. This was the end of the incarnation, and this is the method of our salvation. We cast ourselves in faith upon Him: He assumes our interior states: He fights and conquers for us, removes the causes of our trouble, and restores us to conditions of moral and physical order.

*"When the even was come, they brought unto Him many that were possessed with devils, and He cast out the spirits with his word, and healed all that were sick:*

*"That it might be fulfilled which was spoken by Esaias the prophet, saying, Himself took our infirmities and bare our sicknesses."*

The Lord in his glorified body cannot be directly approached or tempted by evil spirits; but as He descends through prepared vessels into the body of humanity, He will obtain through his mediatorial children such an organic foothold in the world, that He can repeat mediately through them the wonderful works which He performed immediately from his divine sphere when He walked the earth. *"He that believeth on me, the works that I do shall he do also."*

When our Lord, Himself an infinite and divine Man, enters into our mental sphere to abide and to reign, transforming us to his image, so that we are truly "clothed upon with Christ;" then, my dear sir, "the redemption of the body" for which the whole creation groaneth, is a logical and inevitable necessity. The body in its largest sense is the physical universe, of which the spiritual universe is the soul. In its restricted sense it is the sensuo-corporeal sphere of our life with its external environments. As the Lord enters into these, through the regenerated souls of men, all things in the lower sphere will be brought into rapport and correspondence with all things in the higher sphere; for the regenerate forms of the human mind are, as Swedenborg expresses it, "the gateway between the Divine and nature."

Swedenborg says that the soul creates its own body, shaping every one of its tissues and organs to its own spiritual forms and uses, moving the atoms as it pleases, even as the chess-player moves the figures on his board. Physiologists, who cannot comprehend or accept this great general truth which involves and explains a thousand minor truths, still acknowledge that the soul has a most extraordinary influence on the body. The emotions not only produce muscular contractions and blood changes, but they modify all the secretions and organic functions as powerfully as any medicines have been known to do. In this way the scientist explains the miracles of Christ, the faith-cures of all ages, and many inexplicable spiritual phenomena. "They are," he says, "the physiological effects of mental states, faith, hope, imagination, and expectation."

When to these effects of the soul upon its own body, we add the wonderful power of the mesmeric or magnetic operations of one mind upon the mind and the body of another person, we begin to simplify our conception of the spiritual cure of disease. The divine life flows to us through the media of angels and spirits. When the interior structures of our being are in harmony with the media, the divine life passes through into us; and being the great constructive and preservative force of the universe, it adapts itself to the little universe within ourselves, and proceeds, as far as possible, to repel heterogeneous or evil influences, and to rebuild, as it were, our organic structures into the form and order of the interior life. This would bring all our external forms into perfect anatomical and physiological relations, the result of which would be perfect health. And this would be no miracle or violation of natural laws, but the effect of forces moving from within, and acting strictly according to the most beautiful spiritual laws of which we have hitherto been ignorant.

Laws, both spiritual and natural, are always potential, but conditions must be provided for their manifestation. God is Law, and never acts outside of it or against it. What are called the divine laws or commandments are really the organic laws of his own being, the modes of his existence; and we are obliged to keep or obey them, if we would grow like Him and be where He is. They are the conditions of our union with Him. The laws of nature are only spiritual laws translated into natural terms or forms. Obedience to spiritual and natural laws is therefore the first absolute condition to the manifestation of the divine life or health in both soul and body. Every deviation brings spiritual and natural disease. Spiritual sanitation is obedience to spiritual law, as natural sanitation is obedience to natural law. When these laws and their mutual organic connections are discovered and universally obeyed, the race will attain its maximum of moral and physical health, and our bodies become prepared for the indwelling of the Holy Spirit.

But we are still in the region of general principles, and you ask for special applications. Can the Lord Jesus Christ, entering from within, cure diseases to-day, just as surely and promptly as He did by the external touch when He lived in the world? Those who believe that He cured diseases upon earth, will find it exceedingly difficult to give any good reason why He cannot cure them now, when He is "the same Jesus" raised to higher states and more interior powers. The radical cause of their doubt or unbelief seems to be their false impression, that heaven and the Lord are far off, separated from us by some impassable gulf, bridged only by prayer. Nor do they know that the kingdom of heaven within us is founded upon the solidarity or organic connection of all created intelligences: nor that the Lord as an infinite divine Man, holds the central place in the inmost forms, above our consciousness or comprehension, of all human beings in this and all worlds, infusing into them a vital force as real and powerful as the virtue He felt go out from Him when the diseased woman so trustingly touched the hem of his garment.

You must, however, carry along with you the fact, that the Lord has been always the vital agent at the bottom of every cure of disease from the beginning of the world. Natural laws, as I have said before, are only the expressions of the Divine Mind in the physical sphere. Their operation is for an infinite series of uses, or useful ends, guided by the divine love and wisdom. The same infinite foresight which provides the seed for the food of man, provides the medicinal plant for his cure. The Lord works in two ways, immediately and mediately: immediately when He flows with his own divine human sphere under fixed conditions into prepared forms: mediately, when He flows through the forms and forces of nature, including the operation of one living being upon another; for, as a great writer has observed "the physician begins to medicate his patient by his personal influence, so soon as he enters the room." We may therefore safely say that the Lord "healeth all our diseases," and there is no exception to the law; for although his personal presence is the supreme and perfect means of cure, He has provided many natural and spiritual agencies which men may learn to utilize for the same beneficent purpose.

The conditions of cure by his immediate presence seem to be humility, obedience, faith, and expectation. The deeper the humility or self-abnegation and self-surrender, the more certainly can the divine sphere operate on the soul; for the Lord enters as self recedes. The more absolute the determination to obey the divine commandments and to submit to the divine will, the more surely will the evil influences of the opposite character, which are the spiritual causes of disease, be repelled from the spiritual life. Faith in the Lord implies a knowledge of his character, "whom to know is life eternal," and a perfect assurance of his power to heal. Expectation is a tension of the mind and the body towards the realization of the change hoped and prayed for—a fixed belief that the prayer of faith is about to produce its promised result. These conditions, no doubt very imperfectly developed, have been uniformly present, either with the patients or with those who prayed for them, in all the wonderful cases related of the cure by faith and prayer. And could these conditions be perfectly fulfilled, I believe there is no limit to the possibilities of the manifestations of the Lord in the souls and bodies of men.

And yet, my dear sir, we may here expect too much, a great deal too much, by understanding too little. The above conditions might be apparently perfect, and no cure follow. The whole Christian world might concentrate its prayers on one object, and no result be obtained. The faith-cure and all other spiritual exaltations may die away and disappear. The faith and love of the church may be utterly darkened like the sun and the moon of the last days, and yet the Lord will continue to descend into ultimates, to imbue the sciences with new light and greater uses, to illumine the minds of men

5 *

with spiritual truths of higher and higher degrees, and to inspire their hearts with a new, perfect religious life, immeasurably nearer to Himself than all the righteousness of the Scribes and Pharisees. And so, working from within, removing obstructions, striking at the very roots of causes, moving downwards and outwards, He will finally eliminate all the elements of disease and disorder from the physical universe.

Of one thing, my dear sir, we may be perfectly certain, viz.: that there are some hidden elements at work in the faith-cures besides the faith and the prayer, or that faith and prayer have some deeper meaning than those which are usually attached to them. If an infinitely merciful and all-powerful God could relieve suffering and cure diseases outside of fixed laws, why should He wait to be begged and implored for help before He is willing to give it? and why should He confine his beneficence to those who had the good fortune to know of Him and to believe in Him? It is plain that God operates always according to law and through definite media or agencies. Prayer then is not mere supplication. No amount of supplication can open heaven to a man. The only key that opens heaven is a heavenly character. Prayer is a state of the heart and the will, a state of humility, submission, expectation, receptivity. It is the law of the mode of union with God in operation. Faith is a similar attitude of the understanding. The two in active exercise constitute and imply the accommodation of the whole man to divine influences. This state puts the soul into rapport with good spirits and angels and all the great organic media which are posited between God and nature and connect one with the other. The question of what results are attainable and how attained, must be infinitely complicated and difficult of solution. We can readily imagine that under perfect conditions all the miracles of Christ might be repeated, while under imperfect conditions nothing whatever would ensue.

Reflect also, if you please, upon the exceedingly complex nature of the problem on the physical side. There are three great classes of disease. 1st. Those that belong to the individual and his surroundings—diseases caused by his situation, business, habits and conduct, in his struggle for existence against both man and nature. 2d. Diseases whose germs are constitutional inheritances from innumerable ancestral sources. 3d. Diseases which flow from the solidarity of the race, concrete spheres of evil, epidemics, contagions, that come and go like malignant comets, visiting with destruction places and persons who have not originated them, and who do not seem to be in any way spiritually responsible for their appearance.

Now, if we knew the spiritual causes of all these complex phenomena and their relations to each other, as well as their bearing upon each individual case, we would perhaps discover why some people are easily cured by prayer and faith, others with difficulty, and the majority not at all. We might also learn why the good so often suffer and the evil escape. We might explain that painfullest of all enigmas, the sickness and death of children. Perhaps also we might grasp the spiritual ministry of disease and suffering, and perceive that nothing could be more disastrous to the race than their sudden abolition, whether it was effected by the measures of the scientists or the prayers of the saints.

Yours truly,

W. H. H.

# LETTER V.

*REMAINS: "THE REMNANT:" THE OLD AND NEW PROPRIUM.*

DEAR SIR:—You relate two remarkable cases of apparently total change of character in old age, and ask me to explain them. I feel that this is an excellent opportunity of unfolding to you one of the most wonderful and beautiful doctrines of Swedenborg, the doctrine of Remains and their vivification, and incidentally of casting a strong light upon some of the most mysterious things in the religious experience of Christians.

You tell me of a man who had lived an irreligious and sinful life for sixty years, scoffing at sacred things, and apparently hardening himself in vice. This man, the terror and annoyance of his neighborhood, accidentally (but there is no accident) attended a Methodist camp-meeting. He became convicted of sin, and as the good Methodists say, "powerfully converted." He lived some years after, and never relapsed into his old evil states. On the contrary, he was a model of humility and sanctity, led a truly Christian life, and professed always to enjoy the light and peace of God in his soul.

The other case, which happened many years ago, filled a large religious and social circle with amazement, pain, and sorrow. A clergyman, far advanced in years, of high standing and character, was detected in the commission of a most revolting crime. He was expelled from his church, ostracised by society, and died in the utmost obscurity and wretchedness, apparently deserted by God and man.

Now what shall we think of these two men? Is it possible that evil can be turned into good, and good into evil, in this sudden and unexpected manner? Can the prodigal and the elder brother instantly reverse conditions? Can the leopard thus change his spots, and the Ethiopian his skin? The psychologist would explain the first case, by the power of one grand emotion to displace another, and the second case by the sudden maniacal impulse to crime, due to a diseased heredity. Neither hypothesis is altogether satisfactory. Swedenborg gives the key to both cases, and with it the key to many wonderful things in the experiences of the religious life.

It is an astonishing fact that every impression made upon the human soul, and every state induced upon it, remains to all eternity. Nothing is effaced, nothing is effaceable: all remains, and under proper conditions can be reproduced. The intellectual or mental part of this fact has been long known to physiologists.

"The reproduction," says Dr. Carpenter, "of past states of consciousness induced by either of the forms of suggestive action already described (observation and introspection), constitutes what is known as memory. There seems much ground for the belief that *every ideational state* which has even transiently occupied the consciousness, is registered (so to speak) in the cerebrum, and may be reproduced at some subsequent time, although there may be no consciousness of its existence in the mind during the whole intermediate period."

Now this fact is equally true of all the emotions and affections which the soul has ever experienced, even from the moment of birth. Every good or evil state, every appetite, every passion, every temper, with all their infinitely varied degrees, phenomena and attendant causes and effects, are perfectly registered upon our moral being. Their reproduction in the spiritual world according to spiritual laws and processes, brings us into judgment. No concealment is there possible. Every thought of the mind, every wish of the heart, every iota of the conduct will reappear, according to uses or necessities, and be unfolded and revealed to ourselves and others.

Swedenborg condenses the doctrine of "remains" and their uses in a very interesting paragraph.

"Remains are not only the goods and truths which a man has learned from his infancy out of the Lord's Word, and which are thereby impressed on his memory, but they are likewise all states thence derived; as states of innocence from infancy; states of love towards parents, brothers, teachers, and friends; states of charity towards the neighbor, and also of mercy towards the poor and needy; in a word, all states of goodness and truth. These states, with their goods and truths impressed on the memory are called *remains*, which remains are preserved in man by the Lord, and are stored up in his internal man, and are carefully separated from the things of man's proprium, which are evils and falsities. All these states are so preserved in man by the Lord that not the smallest of them is lost, as it was given me to know by this circumstance, that every state of man, from his infancy even to extreme old age, not only remains in another life, but also returns, and that in their return they are exactly such as they were during man's abode in this world. Not only the goods and truths as stored up in the memory remain and return, but likewise all the states of innocence and charity. When states of the evil and the false, or of wickedness and fantasy recur, which also both generally and particularly as to every least circumstance remain and return, then these latter states are attempered by the former through the divine operation of the Lord. Whence it is evident that unless man had some remains he could not avoid eternal condemnation."—A. C. n. 561.

The implantation of "remains" should be the chief end in view in the treatment and training of the young. The more tenderly we love and rear our children, the more we do to call forth the gentleness, sweetness, goodness, innocence, love, peace, and joy, which the Lord, through attendant angels, is perpetually endeavoring to infuse into them, the more richly will they be dowered with "remains," the more easily and rapidly will they progress in the work of regeneration, and the better and more beautiful will be their lives as men here and as angels hereafter. O, my friend, what shall we say of those who neglect, or maltreat, or badly train their children? Who repress the good that is striving to unfold, and encourage the hereditary evil of their natures? Who introduce them, by example if not by precept, into atmospheres of deceit, fraud, selfishness, pride, cruelty, and violence? Alas! what can we say, except to repeat the words of the Master, in allusion to those who murder the states of innocence and faith in themselves and others:

*"But whoso shall offend one of these little ones which believe in me, it were better for him that a millstone were hanged about his neck, and that he were drowned in the depths of the sea."*

But the remains of good and truth are not insinuated into infancy and childhood by parents and teachers only. There are remains of good and truth—genuine states of affection and thought, implanted by the Lord through his angels, in the inmost recesses of our being, which may have never come to the surface where our consciousness resides, and which are the fountains and storehouses, the potential germs and possibilities of an eternal life. This great truth is illustrated by a curious fact cited by Dr. Carpenter in his Physiology, which will perhaps enable you to understand more clearly what I mean.

"There was a congenital idiot who had lost his mother when two years old, and who could not subsequently have been made cognizant of anything relating to her. And yet this man, when dying at the age of thirty, suddenly turned his head, looked bright and sensible, and exclaimed in a tone never heard from him before, 'Oh, my mother! how beautiful!' and sank round again, dead."

Whence did this poor creature, born in utter darkness of soul, and evincing no ray of external intelligence through thirty years of idiocy, whence did he suddenly derive the light of thought in his countenance, the tones of affection in his voice, and all the tender and glorious associations which cluster around the composite ideas of mother and beauty? Truly, "a man can receive nothing except it be given him from heaven"—the motto of a philosophy of nature, which was the oldest and is yet the newest and the least understood in the world.

Now, my dear sir, our thoughts or mental impressions, and our feelings or emotional impressions, are not piled together in the spirit like a confused heap of stones or lumber. They are arranged by spiritual laws, of which we know almost nothing, into groups and classes and genera, and with such exquisite accuracy and order that all relationships are exactly maintained, and the whole understanding of the man, and his whole will-principle, are organized into forms as absolute and perfect as those of the human body.

Moreover, the good and true thoughts and the good feelings or states of the will are kept entirely separate from the evil states of the will and the false states of the understanding. The remains of good connect us with the Lord and the angels, for the heavens flow into them with a ceaseless conatus or endeavor to animate them into a heavenly life upon earth. The remains of evil, both acquired and hereditary, connect us with the hells, and are the sources of all our wickedness and fantasies. Thus we carry both heaven and hell within us, and we make our own heaven and our own hell by voluntarily inclining to one or the other of these interior departments of our own being.

Between these two great lines of force we are held in perpetual equilibrium by the mysterious operations of Divine Providence, so that our free agency and liberty are always preserved, and we can choose which life to appropriate and make our own, the good or the evil. According as we incline this way or that, we create our spiritual day or night, our spiritual summer or winter, our spiritual heaven or hell. In proportion as we die to one sphere, we live to the other. One life is that of the old proprium, the old Adam; the other life is that of the new proprium, the new man "created in Christ Jesus." When we sink into the old life, the angels of the good life (the angels of our better nature) plead with us and strive for us. When we return into the remains of good and truth, the spirits of the evil life assault our positions, and we are led into grievous temptations, in which the goods and truths of the Word assist and defend us. And thus we fluctuate to and fro, up and down, until we lay aside forever the life of self and the world for the sake of Christ and his gospel; or until we suffocate and destroy the angelic remains within us, so that the Holy Spirit is grieved away and the heavens are closed against us, and we sink into obdurate states of unbelief and sensuality.

These states of goodness and truth are stored up in the interiors of our being for use in the subsequent work of regeneration. They are represented in the Word by the corn which was stored up in the granaries of Egypt during the seven years of plenty, and which was distributed to the people according to their vital necessities during the seven years of famine. This spiritual work is done by the Lord for every man. No matter how near we are to the angels in infancy and early childhood, we are sure to recede from their heavenly influences, to become entangled in the snares of the world, to fall into temptation and sin, to wander away from our Father's house, and sink into states of spiritual famine and wretchedness, contending with the swine for their husks, which are the vanities and ambitions of this life. But into whatever depths of evil and infamy a man may fall, he need not perish; for the "remains" of goodness and truth implanted in early life will reach him even while he grovels in the dust. The memory of "bread enough and to spare" in his Father's house, will be stirred, and the desire to arise and go to his Father will be awakened in his bosom.

It is a wonderful fact that the goods and truths of our life are never mixed or amalgamated with our evils and falsities. They are kept separate, and we do not live in both at the same time, as it appears, but we pass, however rapidly and imperceptibly to ourselves, from one to the other. In proportion as men become worse and worse, and seem to be irreclaimably evil, the remains of good and truth are indrawn and more deeply concealed by the Lord to save them from profanation or destruction. So when men seem to be holy and saintly beyond temptation, the indestructible hell is only covered over within them, ready to burst forth on some unfortunate opportunity.

*"For man also knoweth not his time: as the fishes that are taken in an evil net, and as the birds that are caught in the snare, so are the sons of men snared in an evil time, when it falleth suddenly upon them."*

So long as we live in this world, in equilibrium between heaven and hell, we fluctuate between good and evil; but after death and the judgment we enter into the relatively fixed conditions of one or the other. That these two opposite lives are evolved and developed within us simultaneously, is illustrated by a very curious fact which often occurs in the experiences of the religious warfare. The Christian who falls back into open sin, and the reformed drunkard who returns to his cups, do not hold their good state and gradually lose their virtue and their self-control as they did at first. They drop at once, or very rapidly, into all their old iniquities. They seem to take up the thread of the evil life exactly where they left it. It is the same old sinner, the same old drunkard. This is equally true of the good life. When a man repents and returns, self-loathing, into states of obedience and faith, he also takes up the thread of the Christian life exactly where he had dropped it. He does not have to begin it all over again with feeble, uncertain steps. Everything once gained has been carefully and tenderly preserved for him, and he re-enters upon his spiritual inheritance, amazed and overwhelmed at the mercy and goodness of God toward such a miserable sinner.

With these general principles in view, you will be able, my

dear sir, to comprehend the phenomena of the two cases you have presented to my consideration.

The first man underwent no such sudden change of character as he seems to have undergone. He simply entered into the conscious possession and manifestation of a different character, which had been early implanted and was long maturing within him. No instantaneous change from evil to good, or from good to evil, is possible. All such phenomena are appearances, and are explained by the fact that good or evil states, which had been long organically registered on the spiritual structures, were revived and brought to the surface. The piety of an old man thus brought into the heavenly vineyard at the eleventh hour, is apt to be childlike, trusting, and tender, for it is a sort of return into the Sunday-school states of his boyhood, qualified by a deep humility from the memory of a long life of sin. He is a babe and not a strong man in Christ. He, too, however, receives the same wages as those who have "borne the burden and heat of the day," which is the full measure and running over of what his own organic states are able to bear and to utilize in the life to come.

As the first man you mention was not nearly so good as he seemed, so the last man was not nearly so evil as he seemed. A long life of religious fervor is no security against the sudden outburst of the hells within us, as many have found to their misery, both in this world and in the world of spirits, when the secrets of all hearts are laid open. But this state, imposed from within, is always transitory. The poor criminal minister, who was hounded to death by the self-righteous church and world around him, was no doubt delivered from the evil spheres which infested him, and re-entered into the peaceful, happy, useful life, for which his spiritual struggles of so many years had prepared him. His great fall was perhaps one of the strongest means of his regeneration; for there is no spiritual experience so valuable to us, as that which reveals plainly to us the unfathomable hells within ourselves, and so convinces us of our lost condition. Never until we reach this true estimate of our own natures, can the selfhood be radically subdued and the Lord enter to abide.

Do you say that I condone the crime of this man and wink at evil. I tell you, nay; but I say that we are all in the same organic conditions, with the same hells within us, and that this man in his own nature was no worse than the best of us. I answer you in the precious words of our Lord:

"*Suppose ye that these Galileans were sinners above all the Galileans, because they suffered such things?*

*I tell you, Nay; but except ye repent, ye shall all likewise perish.*

*Or those eighteen, upon whom the tower of Siloam fell and slew them; think ye that they were sinners above all men that dwelt in Jerusalem?*

*I tell you, Nay; but except ye repent, ye shall all likewise perish.*"

The surest, indeed the only way, to vivify the remains of good and truth, and to bring them into external activity, is to reach and touch and arouse the affections. The camp-meeting and the salvation army, in their rude, rough way, and with a false system which can never be anything but ephemeral, hold the secret of secrets, which it would be well for the more enlightened Christian element to discover and to utilize. This secret is, that a man's life is in what he loves and not in what he believes, and his affections are the hidden springs from which his thoughts and his actions proceed.

Truth by itself is cold and dead; and a doctrinal sermon, with all its finely pointed lessons, is about as useful to the soul as a polished essay on history or astronomy. The tender voice of earnest prayer, and the touching music of beautiful hymns are the strongest elements for good in our ordinary church service. But there will no flesh grow upon the skeletons of our religious life, until the affections are vivified and the emotions ignited; until fear and terror and trembling overtake us; until repentance, remorse, self-loathing, and despair afflict us; until hope, peace, and joy are born in us; and until the love of God and the neighbor burn through us like great fires, consuming the lusts of the flesh, the cares of the world, the deceitfulness of riches, and all the ugly and detestable brood of the selfhood.

The new proprium, or the life of consociated goods and truths, and the old proprium, or the life of consociated evils and falsities, are the two lives alluded to in the Word—one of which must be laid down or lost if the other is saved. There is no compromise between them, but an organic antipathy and perpetual divergence. In the new proprium or the new man, we are in the Lord who is the new Adam. In the old proprium or the old man, the old Adam, we are in hell. In the latter, we are capable of all crimes whenever the circumstances and opportunities of our environment are favorable. In the former, we are capable of being wrought up into the organic structures of the heavens, and of leading that life which is "hid with Christ in God."

Yours truly,<br>W. H. H.

# LETTER VI.

### *ECCLESIASTICAL AND VITAL RELIGION.*

MY DEAR FRIEND:—You have asked me what are the differences and the relationships between what you have heard me call ecclesiastical and vital religion. Are they not one and the same thing? Is not the religion engendered by the teachings and ordinances of the church, the New Church specifically, a vital and spiritual religion? Can there be any vital religion without an ecclesiastical basis? These questions are of vast importance, not only to the aggregate church in its social and historical relations; but also to the individual church, the church within every man's soul, where, whether he knows it or designs it or not, he has either an ecclesiastical or vital religion separately, or both harmoniously combined, or neither—the church in the man being unformed, or perhaps in ruins. I cannot better preface what I have to say, than by drawing upon the supernal knowledge of Swedenborg in relation to the differences between the internal and the external man of the church, and the differences between internal and external worship in general.

"The man of the internal church attributes to the Lord all the good he does and all the truth he thinks: but of this the man of the external church is ignorant, although he still acts rightly. The man of the internal church makes charity the essential of the worship of the Lord, and indeed regards internal worship as more important than external: but the man of the external church makes external worship the essential, being ignorant of what internal worship is, although he performs it. The man of the internal church believes that he acts contrary to conscience, if he does not worship the Lord from an internal principle: but the man of the external church believes that he acts contrary to conscience if he does not reverently observe external rites."—A. C. 1098.

"Internal worship, which is grounded in love and charity, is real worship or worship itself, and external worship without this internal is no worship. To make internal worship external, is to make external worship essential more than internal, which is to invert the true order. . . . The religion of those who separate faith from charity is of such a sort, viz., they give a preference to the things of faith above the things of charity, or to the things which respect the knowledges of faith above the things which respect life; thus they prefer formalities to essentials.

"Supposing a person to live where there is no church, no preaching, no sacraments, no priesthood: if it be asserted that such a person cannot be saved, or that he cannot exercise any worship, when nevertheless he may worship the Lord from what is internal, this is to make worship consist of that which is formal without the essential, and thus to make internal worship external.

"It does not hence follow, however, that there should be no external worship. There are persons who place the very essential of worship in going to church, attending the sacraments, hearing sermons, repeating prayers, observing the festivals, and performing other things of an external and ceremonial nature, talking also occasionally about faith; and who persuade themselves that these things, which all relate to the formal part of worship, are sufficient.

"Now they who make essential worship to be that which proceeds from love and charity, do like the former: that is, they go to church, attend the sacraments, hear sermons, repeat prayers, observe the festivals, and perform other things of a like nature; and they do them very diligently and carefully, but still they do not place in them the essential of worship. In the external worship of these, because it has internal worship within it, there is a holy and living principle; whereas in the external worship of the former there is no such principle." —A. C. 1175.

You see, my dear sir, that the human mind has two states as to religion. One is an internal and vital state, in which the man is organically and spontaneously religious, having reached the second stage of regeneration, a state which exists above, within, and independently of external things. It may, and when opportunity occurs it does, conjoin to itself a corresponding state of external worship. The other is an external or ecclesiastical state which may and always ought to have the former state within it as a vivifying principle, but which very generally exists without it. This external church-religionist persuades himself that what he calls the venerable and precious ordinances and usages of the church, have a genuine efficacy in the generation of the religious life; and he estimates his own religious vitality and that of others by his and their conformity to all ecclesiastical demands. When this state exists without any regeneration of the will-principle, the man is simply a church-idolater, and may be externally devout and righteous, while internally he is estranged from the Lord and the life of heaven.

Now why should the internal man—the man who lives in and near the Lord, and who is really independent of external things—why should he interest himself so "diligently and carefully" about the external or ecclesiastical forms of religion? With the Word and the writings of Swedenborg at home, he never need go to a church for instruction as to matters of faith. He never need go to a church for the worship of the Lord, for he knows that true worship does not consist in religious exercises, but in profound humiliation of heart, in the ingrained spirit of charity in the soul, and in the good deeds of the daily life. The answer is, that the man who has any spark of spiritual or celestial life developed in him, loves and works for the church as a form of eminent use to the neighbor.

This point needs further illustration. The man who supposes that the church was founded for the instruction and salvation of his individual soul, or to draw down the divine influx into forms of praying, singing, preaching, etc., has missed the genuine use of the church altogether. The church was established that each and all may take hold of it to promote the social and spiritual welfare of others. In its highest sense the church is the heart and lungs of the world, deriving its life from the living Word, the Divine Humanity, and distributing the love and wisdom of this Humanity to all creatures. That love and wisdom flow into humble and contrite hearts, into rational and enlightened minds, into hands and feet that are busy with labors and errands of love and charity. The entire associated uses of the world, however remote and impossible it may appear, have their spiritual origin in the activities of the internal church of God. He who most closely follows the Lord in the regeneration, dying most to self and living most in the Master, contributes most to all beneficent results.

Moreover the Church, and every society in it, is a complex body. Like man himself, it is an image of the heavens. The true Church in ultimates must contain within itself all the simultaneous degrees of life, celestial, spiritual, and natural. It is a living, breathing, growing body, containing every degree of life and ever-fluctuating and alternating varieties of states. It must provide spiritual sustenance and active uses for all the stages of the spiritual life, from the sensuo-corporeal receptivities of the child, through all natural, rational, spiritual, and celestial states, up to the highest demands of the inmost life. Every one in a church can in some way help others in it; and the higher and more inward a man has progressed, the greater becomes his obligation as well as his capacity to administer to the spiritual advancement of others.

And right here, my dear friend, let me correct a false impression which prevails in relation to my views of the external church, unimportant as they are to any one else but myself. I saw a letter the other day in which a New-Church minister asserted, that we who believe in a celestial movement from the interior, repudiate the external church and even the holy Sacraments! If I have ever said or written anything to justify this charge, I assure you that my remarks were addressed, not against the Church itself, or the principle of organization—but against the defective forms, modes, and measures of our New-Church bodies, which have seemed thus far to have produced so much more ecclesiastical than vital religion. The following admirable extract from Swedenborg I accept unreservedly as a statement of my faith on this subject:

"By worship, in the internal sense, is signified all conjunction by love and charity. Man is continually in worship, when he is in love and charity, external worship being only an effect proceeding from the former. The angels are in such worship; wherefore with them there is a perpetual sabbath: whence also the sabbath, in its internal sense, signifies the kingdom of the Lord. Man, however, during his abode in the world, ought not to omit the practice of external worship, for by external worship things internal are excited (not created but called into activity): and by external worship external things are kept in a state of sanctity, so that internal things can enter by influx.

Moreover, man is hereby initiated into knowledges, and prepared to receive things celestial. He is also gifted with states of sanctity though he be ignorant thereof; which states are preserved by the Lord for his use in eternal life."—A. C. 1618.

Moreover, it is to be remembered that any criticisms I may have made against the external church, are especially applicable to the external church within ourselves, that old ecclesiastical proprium which we all inherit, which delights in church matters and in artificial exaltations of the religious life ; which, as Swedenborg says, persuades us that the zealous performance of church duties is sufficient, which engenders the spirit of self-complacency, self-merit, and self-righteousness, and which, ignoring the new birth, conceals from ourselves and others the evil and false things which constitute our interior life. This old ecclesiastical proprium is such a cunning, persuasive, secretive devil, that it takes the touchstone of the living Word to discover whether he does not underlie all our courtesies, our charities, our tolerations, our prayers, and every movement of our religious life. It is always self-love masquerading in the garb of love to the Lord and the neighbor.

Now what is this vital religion which ought to pervade, vivify and sanctify the external things of the church ? Is it an ardent zeal acquired by the long and conscientious discharge of our duties as members of the church ? Is it a high state of religious culture, attained by sedulously keeping the commandments and modeling one's life after the purest and loftiest standards? No! it is something entirely different. There is no possible outcome to these ecclesiastical modes and measures, but a gentle, delicate, and refined Phariseeism, a thoroughly concealed and suppressed proprium, such as adorns the beautiful and cleanly pages of church history from beginning to end. We instinctively gasp and shudder at the thought that David and Paul may possibly be found in the hells; but such things become comprehensible, if not credible, when we learn the difference between ecclesiastical and vital religion.

Vital religion is the birth and growth of the Divine life and character in the soul, in proportion as the evils and falsities of the old proprium are seen, acknowledged, deplored, dethroned, and removed from the conscious sphere of life. It is indeed the Lord in the man. The Lord enters only as the selfhood, with all its vanities and follies and its ambitions and aspirations, recedes and disappears. The new will cannot be born into a man until the old will is broken and subdued by suffering, temptation, conviction of sin, humiliation, self-loathing, and despair. The inflowing new life is the Lord's life, which man is permitted to feel as if it were his own—but which effectuates the Lord's will from the centres to the circumferences of his organic being. This new proprium, this new Adam, never did and never can sin; and in proportion as it displaces the old proprium in the organic life of the church, the Lord Himself will enter the body of humanity, and stand in ultimates, constituting the life of the world as He is now the life of heaven.

Now, my dear friend, you have preached for many years to a large congregation. Have you kept another record beside that of baptisms, marriages, deaths, removals, admissions, how many sermons preached, how often the sacrament was administered, how much money received, how much spent, etc., etc.? Have you watched carefully the birth and growth of vital religion among your people? Have you seen enemies reconciled, breaches healed, and the spirit of brotherhood and sisterhood steadily advancing? Have you seen that sordid man grow liberal, that proud man grow humble, that choleric man become meek and patient, that self-opinionated fellow grow silent and lowly? Have you seen the tattler cease to gossip, the busybody stay at home and make no mischief, the ostentatious person become simple and unpretending, the exaggerator and prevaricator subside and tell the unvarnished truth, the tricky tradesman become thoroughly honest even to his own injury? Have you seen that your people grew deeper and deeper into the spiritual life, and more and more active and zealous in all the works of love and charity? Or do you find things to-day pretty much as they were in the beginning—no progress, no living experiences, no vital changes —the people quietly growing old in all their moral infirmities and vices, with no genuine self-knowledge or reformation, self-complacent, and satisfied with the cheap moralities that are imposed upon or engendered in us by self-respect, self-interest, and the outside pressure of law, social usage, and public opinion?

Who is to blame for the lukewarmness and deadness of the church,—the people, the preacher, the doctrines taught, or the methods employed? However these questions are answered, one thing is certain: the great need of the church is vital religion. Internal worship first, external worship afterwards. If the old methods and forms and liturgies, so venerable and precious to some people, produce no better results than we have seen, let us abandon them. We need not regret the old garments and the old bottles, assured that the inspirations of internal worship will lead us to something new and better.

The history of the human heart, from Buddha to John Wesley, reveals many yearnings after a true and vital religion.

The celestial seed, however, would scarcely be planted, before some towering Babel of ecclesiasticism would overshadow and destroy it. Before Swedenborg, moreover, no opening of the celestial degree could have been anything else but premature, imperfect, and even hazardous. If planes are not formed in the spiritual degree of the mind for the reception of celestial influx into its corresponding truths, the influx passes through into the natural plane, where it falls into the old proprium, and is turned into fantasies, follies, and even abominations. By the opening of the spiritual sense of the Word, those receptive planes of spiritual truth are formed in the mind, and the celestial life, which is *vital* religion, becomes possible— yea, imperative to the man of the New Church; for our Rachel is even now crying, "Give me children, or else I die."

The vital religion which will inevitably, sooner or later, be developed in the bosom of the New Church, will exceed in strength, purity, and perfection anything which has hitherto been witnessed, taught, or dreamed of in the world. It will have the true spiritual basis, and will finally organize for itself its true and perfect externals. The Church is the heart and lungs of the world—the central, vivifying force in human society. When its breaths and its pulsations are brought into harmony with those of the heavens, the fire of divine love and the light of divine wisdom will pour in living streams through the social fabric, and their regenerating influences will be felt in the uttermost parts of the earth. When the augean stables of our own souls are cleansed of all sin, the power of the Lord passing through his church, will pervade all nations and will reach the slums of New York, Paris, and London, the brutal and dangerous classes everywhere, and even the serpents and wild beasts—those hideous outbirths of the evil principles in our own hearts.

O my friend—my brother! Let us forget all that is behind and press forward toward this great light. Study these interior truths of Swedenborg: preach them to your people. Awaken their consciences: convict them of sin, pointing with the finger, "thou art the man." Cry aloud. Spare not. Lift up the standard. Prepare ye the way of the Lord. Teach the celestial church—the celestial life—the new and perfect life—the life which is "hid with Christ in God."

Yours affectionately,<br>W. H. H.

# LETTER VII.

*THE NEW LIFE.—MADAM GUYON.—THE RELIGIOUS PROPRIUM.*

MY DEAR FRIEND:—Your photograph arrived the other day, and I submitted it to my friend G. W. C., without informing him whose it was. He gazed at it intently for several minutes, and then made the following remarkable utterance:

"This man is so thoroughly good, so absolutely and utterly *determined* to *be* right and to *do* right, from centres to circumferences, that he has no genuine conception whatever of what is right, or of what it is to follow the Lord."

"Explain your paradox," I said.

"It is no paradox," he answered, "but a simple New-Church truth. He is like the young man who had kept all the commandments from his youth up, and who was as lovely as possible in externals, and no doubt a splendid specimen of the good man of his times, but who was entirely unwilling to sell all that he had and follow Jesus."

I reflected upon that incident, related in Matt. xix. 16-22. This was the young man who called our Lord "Good Master," and to whom He answered, "Why callest thou me good? There is none good but God." If our Lord's human nature derived from the mother, which endured the most terrible temptations, and yet never yielded to a single sin in wish, thought, or act, could not be called good, and Jesus expressly says so, how inconceivably absurd, thievish, wicked, and offensive to God must be our personal pretensions to any inherent or acquired goodness of character!

To sell all that we have, Swedenborg says, means "to alienate all things of the proprium"—to get rid of our own wishes, desires, ambitions, conceptions, pretensions, etc. In this way we all have "great possessions," and we are exceedingly unwilling to give them up. And our greatest possession, and the most necessary to be abandoned, is our sense of ownership in our virtues. The more we strive and struggle for the good life, the more we labor and pray from our own resolute determinations, the farther off are we from the new life, which is that of the angels—free, spontaneous, without struggle—a life of total and absolute self-surrender, and therefore an organic evolution of a new proprium, which is God's life in us.

"What do you think," I resumed to G. W. C., "of this man's spiritual condition?"

"He may be a much better man than you or I," he said; "that is, the Lord may manifest Himself more powerfully and usefully through him. Whether the Lord manifest Himself through a man as a prophet or a boot-black, is the Lord's business and not the man's, who in either case is nothing, and should feel and know that he is nothing.

"Your friend," he continued, "is in a state of *suppressed* proprium, or of temporary elevation above the proprium, with a partial opening of the spiritual senses. He is a phenomenon to be studied; and a great many phenomena will appear of a still more astounding character. He cannot teach. He can never realize the new life until the sphere of ecclesiasticism in which he is encased, is entirely broken up."

"You say there is a strong methodistical sphere about my interiors," I suggested.

"So there is," he replied, "and you are maintained in it at present for purposes of use; but when you are delivered from it, you will discover how poorly and feebly you have ever understood or realized the 'newness of life' in which the Christian of the New Age is to walk."

"Your conceptions of the new life are very surprising to me," I said, "and I cannot fully comprehend them. I have never heard or read of anything like them but in the Spiritual Torrents of Madam Guyon."

"Ah," he answered, "how can the new life be comprehended until it is unfolded? It has very seldom existed in the world since the Most Ancient Church. It is coming, however. The seed is planted, and it must grow. As to Madam Guyon, I have gone through every one of her spiritual states hundreds of times. I have experienced the truth of all she has said, but she is imperfect, inchoate, and has left a thousand things unsaid. You will find the key to her experiences, and mine, and probably all others, in Swedenborg. And yet many good people will read Swedenborg over and over again, and never find it."

Now, my dear friend, that little book of Madam Guyon, edited by Rev. A. E. Ford, with illustrative extracts from Swedenborg, would be very useful to you. It was published by Otis Clapp of Boston in 1853, and is such a genuine stimulus to the truly regenerate life, that it is a wonder and a pity that it is not better known to our people. Madam Guyon, under the title of *proprietary* things, reveals to us the dangers, subtleties, and concealments of the proprium, "the depths of Satan," in a most striking manner, and in perfect accordance with the doctrines of the New Church on that subject.

We all understand the movements of the proprium in the

sensual, social, and civil spheres of life, but few of us have ever comprehended its immense strength and subtlety in moral and religious matters. The selfhood often busies itself intensely in spiritual things. We compel ourselves firmly and bravely to abstain from evils and to do goods, we infuse our whole will into the discharge of religious duty, and make great progress in the religious life, and seem to ourselves and others to be wonderfully endowed with heavenly gifts and graces; and yet all this is only what Swedenborg calls "the life of truth from itself" (A. C. 3607); and the utter privation of such a life is not, as he goes on to say, "the extinction of truth, but its vivification."

This is only the first stage of, or ascending movement toward, the new life. It is not the new life which descends altogether from above. The selfhood is unbroken: it is only elevated above sensual matters and enlisted powerfully in the service of the spiritual life, but really for its own benefit. As Swedenborg says: "In doing good, they do it not from the affection of good, but from the affection of somewhat blessed and happy in regard to themselves."—A. C. 3816. "You love God," says Madam Guyon to this class, "not only because He is lovely, but you love also for the pleasure you find in this exercise of loving." God, however, does not always leave these good souls in the peaceful delights of their own sanctity, but leads them gently on to that mystic death, which is the laying down of their own life for Christ's sake.

"The poor soul sees well that it must needs *die*, for it no longer finds life in anything. Everything becomes to it, death and the cross. Prayer, reading, conversation, all is death. It no longer has a relish for anything, neither for the practice of the virtues, nor for aiding the sick, nor for anything else which constitutes a virtuous life. It loses all this, or rather it dies to all these things; doing them with so much pain and disrelish, that they become a kind of death to it. At length, after having fought long and ineffectually, after a long succession of sorrows and reposes, of dyings and livings, it begins to perceive how it has abused the mercies of God, and how much more profitable this state of death is to it than that of life."—Spl. Torrents, p. 86.

Now, my dear friend, this is not a mere state of very severe temptations from which a man emerges into a renewed enjoyment of the sanctities of his former experience. It is the process by which the Lord breaks the force of the human will, which infuses itself into holy things and appropriates them to itself. It is a renunciation of all the splendid and imposing spiritual gifts for what Paul calls "a more excellent way" —the way of simple charity—the charity of the 13th I. Corinthians. Of the life which follows after these experiences, Madam Guyon says:

"The soul on leaving the tomb finds itself, without knowing how it came to pass and without thinking of it, clothed with all the inclinations of Jesus Christ: and this, not by distinct views or practices, but by *states*, finding them all on any occasion when they are necessary to be acted, without thought of its own. Then it is truly clothed with Jesus Christ. It is properly He who is then acting, speaking, and conversing in the soul: our Lord Jesus Christ being the principle of all its movements."

Do we know anything about these states? Have we ever experienced this death and life? Only by the death of the religious proprium can our Lord descend into the body of Humanity.

Yours truly,

W. H. H.

F

# LETTER VIII.

### SHALL WE KNOW OURSELVES, OR NOT?

DEAR FRIEND:—In the interest of genuine New-Church doctrine, I must protest against the spirit and matter of the article entitled "Keep your eye on the Lord Jesus, and not on your old proprium." Mr. P. is evidently a gentleman of excellent intentions, earnest convictions, and enthusiastic piety, and has been for nearly two years the subject of conscious influxes from the interior into the sensories of his body of the most remarkable character. But all these do not constitute a man a judicious teacher of a New-Church public, and we must bring his utterances to the test of that high standard of truth which we believe has been revealed to us from heaven.

The gist of his article is this: that it is useless and even harmful to bother ourselves in the least about the old proprium and all the evils and falsities it contains; that the true road to Christian felicity is to dismiss self entirely from the mind, and fix your eye upon Jesus, the author of our faith and the finisher of our hope.

To strengthen this position, which has a strong resemblance to the "faith-alone" teachings of Moody and Sankey, he makes some extraordinary assertions, which we of the New Church cannot permit to pass for genuine truth.

He says the devil delights to have us turn our attention exclusively upon himself, to make a great deal of him, to watch him, explore him, expose him, and make ourselves unhappy about everything he is doing in us, satisfied that in that way he can keep us from fixing our eye upon Jesus. How strange and untrue this sounds to us who learn from Swedenborg that the evil spirits within us are tortured when the searching light of divine truth is turned upon them, and that our self-examinations, leading to true self-knowledge, beget states of humiliation and repentance, which bring the angels and the Lord nearer and nearer to us, until after severe combats, the evil spirits are thrust down and cast back into the hells, into which, during our states of self-ignorance or suppressed proprium, they were dragging us.

Again he says, that although the devil may appear as an angel of light, he can never put on the garb of an angel of love. Another terrible mistake! Swedenborg says that evil spirits, especially the sirens, imitate our good affections so closely, present such aspects of purity, loveliness, and goodness, as to seem like the very angels of heaven. These insinuate themselves into all the good works we do, and as Henry James clearly shows in his "Substance and Shadow," have been, through our suppressed propriums, the most active and prosperous churchmen and churchwomen from the beginning of the world. This class are truly happy when we give ourselves up without analysis to their leading, and build our hope of salvation on faith and religious exercises and enjoyments.

Mr. P. thinks that the Christian who looks perpetually to Jesus, has no right to be anything else but blessed, blessed, blessed, continually blessed, for so run the promises. He has not noticed that the Word bestows all these blessings, not upon those who only look to Jesus, but always upon those who have contended with and vanquished the old proprium. "To him that overcometh" is the word of promise in all the seven churches. "Blessed is the man that walketh not in the counsel of the ungodly," etc. "Blessed is he whom the Lord chasteneth." "Blessed is he that watcheth and keepeth his garments." "Blessed are the poor in spirit." "Blessed are they that mourn." "Blessed are they that hunger and thirst." "Blessed are the reviled and persecuted." "Blessed is he that endureth temptations." "Blessed are the dead which die in the Lord," or who die like their Lord to all the life of the old proprium. They "rest from their labors" only because the old proprium is conquered and fights no longer.

So convinced is Mr. P. that all Christians should be always happy, as angels are supposed to be, which they are not (see H. & H. 155), that he objects seriously to the words of the Litany, "Be merciful unto us, miserable sinners." He thinks a man has a good excuse for staying outside of the church, when those inside of it consider themselves and each other "miserable sinners." Has he forgotten the publican who smote upon his breast, using those memorable words, and "went down to his house justified rather than the other"?

This writer seems to have no clear conception of the regeneration of the soul, as an organic process of continual death and resurrection, life-long and indeed perpetual, whereby the selfhood is continually being subordinated to the influent goodness and wisdom of the divine life. It is not a question of looking to Jesus or believing in Jesus, but a question of cleansing the foul chambers of the heart, of scourging the thieves out of the temple, so that the Lord Jesus can enter in and abide. The Lord can only enter into a man in proportion as the selfhood or proprium goes out; and the only sure way to receive the kingdom of heaven within us, which alone is religion, is to explore "the depths of Satan" in our souls, to expose him, repudiate him, and cast him out so far as it is possible.

The regeneration of man is a continual putting off of the old carnal nature, analogous to the progressive glorification of the Lord by his renunciation of the life derived from the mother. And he who is continually sounding the depth of his nature, and still finding some lower and more hideous depth, until he sinks in humiliation and despair, is more surely following his Lord in the regeneration, than the man who insists upon building a tabernacle on the Mount of Transfiguration, and gazing forever on the heavenly vision.

The way of the Christian, however, is not all warfare and darkness. The nights are alternated with glorious days, the winters with beautiful and prolific summers. We have little sabbath states scattered all along, sometimes every day, full of peace and love and prophetic insight. Sometimes these states are of long duration, and we are fed with "the hidden manna." But all these are the legitimate, organic fruits of battles fought and victories won.

Mr. P. gives the worst possible advice. It is the voice of them that "prophesy smooth things." It is the voice of them that cry, "Peace, peace!" when there is no peace. He has not touched the true cause of the languor and unfaithfulness of the Christian world. Old-Church people are looking faithfully to Jesus, each in his own way: New-Church people are looking, amid a blaze of spiritual light, to the Divine Humanity, and yet matters apparently grow worse and worse. What is the reason? It is because they are all moving in a vain show; having no genuine interior self-knowledge, and shrinking from its acquisition; with covered up and concealed propriums, and no consciousness of the hells within: thinking they are increased with goods and have need of nothing, when they are poor, and miserable, and blind, and naked.

We do not want religious ecstasies; but self-discovery, contrition, repentance, humiliation, despair, and that death which leads to resurrection and the new life. We cannot exchange the pure gold of Swedenborg's teachings for the inflated currency of modern revivalism.

Yours truly,

'W. H. H.

# LETTER IX.

*SWEDENBORG AND PAUL ON THE NEW BIRTH, AND THE GRAND MAN.*

MY DEAR MADAM:—I am glad that you have discovered the beautiful truth that Paul and Swedenborg are very, very near together on all the vital questions of the religious life: and that the Epistles of that great Apostle, picturing, as they do, the life and faith of the infant Church of Jesus, are inexpressibly dear and valuable to you. I always feel sorry when I hear a Newchurchman depreciate these excellent writings, because it displays quite as great ignorance of Swedenborg as it does of Paul. I expect in this letter to show that Swedenborg, on the subject of the new birth and the new life, is more thoroughly orthodox or in harmony with Paul, than all the commentators who have formulated the doctrines of the old church from the teachings of that great authority.

When a sinner in common parlance becomes a saint, the appearance is, that, convinced of the folly and danger of his ways, he reforms, compels himself to obey the dictates of reason and truth, and gradually eradicates his evil tempers, habituates himself to good courses, and finally, by the operation of the Holy Spirit, undergoes a thorough and total change of character. It is supposed that there is an organic, radical modification of the very spiritual substance of the man, so that the old being has become a new being. The leopard has changed his spots, the Ethiopian his skin. The bad man has become a good man, in spite of the declaration of the Master, "there is none good but God."

That this is no misstatement of the orthodox conception of the new birth or the new man, is evident from the following quotations:

A great Presbyterian minister defines it thus: "a supernatural change wrought upon the whole nature of the sinner, in the transformation of that inner disposition which gives color and tone to every act, which is brought at once under the controlling power of holiness."

A still greater Methodist divine says: "The new birth is the change wrought in the whole soul by the almighty Spirit of God, when it is 'created anew in Christ Jesus:' when it is 'renewed after the image of God in righteousness and true holiness,' when the love of the world is changed into the love of God, pride into humility, passion into meekness; hatred, envy, malice, into a sincere, tender, disinterested love for all mankind. In a word, it is that change by which the earthly, sensual, devilish mind is turned into 'the mind which was in Christ Jesus.'"

Now this conception of the new birth based upon appearances, is absolutely and utterly false—false according to Swedenborg, false according to Paul. This misconception of the genuine truth has been, no doubt, the cause of a great deal of self-righteousness, spiritual pride, and ecclesiastical bigotry. It leads us to appropriate the goodness of the Lord to ourselves, and makes us spiritual thieves. It is impossible for a man to remain in genuine organic states of humility, who thinks and feels that he is of a peculiarly advanced and endowed spiritual nature (even if it be the free gift and grace of God), and therefore better and wiser than others. The holier-than-thou spirit will insensibly creep in, and with it a subtle, self-complacent sense of superiority, a desire to dictate or control, or even a secret contempt for others. In a highly cultivated nature, this suppressed proprium may go on ravaging the interior life, like "the worm in the bud," entirely concealed from the victim himself as well as from others. This accounts for what John Wesley said of William Law, the great Christian perfectionist, who devoted his whole time to prayers and charities; that Law was a very good and holy man, but if you differed from him in opinion, he would trample you under foot! And this is always more or less true of the suppressed proprium.

Now, dear madam, let us look steadily at the genuine truth. Our natural and sensuous life exists upon a discrete degree lower than the spiritual life. It is not continuous with it, cannot be turned into it, and is only connected with it by correspondence. It is the plane of our earthly existence, of the world of spirits and of the hells. It is the plane of the old proprium, of the old man, the old Adam, the plane of reaction and resistance to spiritual things. It may be made to serve and correspond to the intuitions of the spiritual life above it; but it can never be spiritualized. The heart of stone may be removed, and a heart of flesh may be created in us, but never can the one be turned into the other.

That the two lives, or centres of affection and thought, exist on discrete planes, so that one cannot become the other, is thus clearly taught in the Scriptures.

"*That which is born of the flesh is flesh, and that which is born of the Spirit is spirit.*"—JOHN iii. 6.

"*Which were born, not of blood, nor of the will of the flesh, nor of the will of man, but of God.*"—JOHN i. 13.

"*To be carnally minded is death, but to be spiritually minded is life and peace:*

"*Because the carnal mind is enmity against God, for it is not subject to the law of God, neither indeed can be.*"—Rom. viii. 6-7.

"*For I know that in me, that is, in my flesh, dwelleth no good thing.*"—Rom. vii. 18.

"*The first man is of the earth, earthy; the second man is the Lord from heaven.*"—1 Cor. xv. 47.

"*Flesh and blood cannot inherit the kingdom of God; neither doth corruption inherit incorruption.*"—1 Cor. xv. 50.

"*Though our outward man perish, yet our inward man is renewed day by day.*"—2 Cor. iv. 16.

"*The flesh lusteth against the Spirit, and the Spirit against the flesh; and these are contrary, the one to the other.*"—Gal. v. 17.

"*But the natural man receiveth not the things of the Spirit of God: for they are foolishness unto him; neither can he know them, because they are spiritually discerned.*"—1 Cor. ii. 14.

Swedenborg teaches that the evil and false states of our sensual and natural life, are never changed into good and true states—are only put off or removed and are never destroyed, but remain quiescent even in the angels, like things forgotten but which circumstances may recall. The new states of good and truth—the new life inserted—are not the old states and the old life reformed, but are absolutely a new creation, the opening of an interior degree, the formation from the Lord's Divine Humanity of a new will and a new understanding. This new life born in us from above, and felt absolutely as our own (although it is not ours but the Lord's in us), is pure and holy, the image and life of God in us, capable of sitting "in heavenly places with Christ Jesus," or of inauguration into the order, uses, and felicities of heaven.

"All the evils which man derives from his parents which

we call hereditary evils, reside in his natural and sensual man, but not in the spiritual: hence it is that the natural man and especially the sensual man is opposed to the spiritual, for the spiritual man is closed from infancy, and is only opened and FORMED by divine truths received in the understanding and the will; and in proportion as the spiritual man is opened and FORMED, and according to the quality thereof, in the same proportion are the evils of the natural and sensual man REMOVED, and goods implanted in their place."—A. E. 543.

"Every man is born into two diabolical loves, namely, the love of self and the love of the world, from which loves all evils and falsities flow as from their fountains: and as man is born into those loves, he is also born into evils of every kind. Inasmuch as man as to his proprium is of such a nature, the Lord in his divine mercy has provided means by which he may be removed from it. These means are furnished in the Word, and when man acts in accordance with them, that is, when he speaks and thinks, wills and acts from the Divine Word, then *he is kept by the Lord in things divine, and thus is withheld from his proprium:* and as he perseveres in this, a new proprium as it were, both voluntary and intellectual, is formed in him by the Lord, *which is altogether separated from his own proprium.* Thus man is, as it were, created anew; and this is what is called his reformation and regeneration by truths from the Word, and by a life according to them."— A. E. 585.

Now, my dear friend, see how clearly and beautifully Paul teaches the New-Church doctrine of the new life.

"*Therefore if any man be in Christ, he is a new creature; old things are passed away: all things are become new:*

"*And all things are of God.*"—2 COR. v. 17.

"*Our Lord Jesus Christ, by whom the world is crucified unto me, and I unto the world:*

"*For in Christ Jesus, neither circumcision availeth anything, nor uncircumcision, but a new creature.*"—GAL. vi. 14, 15.

"*For we are his workmanship, created in Christ Jesus unto good works.*"—EPH. ii. 10.

"*That ye put off concerning the former conversation the old man, which is corrupt according to the deceitful lusts:*

"*And be renewed in the spirit of your mind:*

"*And that ye put on the new man, which after God is created in righteousness and true holiness.*"—EPH. iv. 22–24.

"*Seeing that ye have put off the old man with his deeds;*

"*And have put on the new man which is renewed in knowledge after the image of Him that created him.*"—COL. iii. 9, 10.

"*There is therefore now no condemnation to them which are in Christ Jesus, who walk not after the flesh, but after the Spirit.*"—ROM. viii. 1.

Now, Old-church theologians have studied and quoted all these sentences thousands of times, bringing them to bear in illustration and confirmation of their special tenets. The Old-churchman says our good life, or "the fruit of the Spirit," flows from the righteousness of Christ *imputed* to us. The Newchurchman thinks that the righteousness is really *imparted* to us. Both parties, however, remain in the same miserable delusion of *appearances,* and think and teach that some really thorough and heavenly change has taken place in us, and that something has become ours which we had not before—so that there must be various differences as to goodness and truth in our own essential nature. They do not face the stupendous statements made by both Paul and Swedenborg, that goodness is never ours, but always the Lord's in us; that there are no good or holy men, but only men in whom the Holy Spirit is more or less immanent and indwelling. It is an appearance that the Lord gives us good desires and wise thoughts to be *in perpetuum* our actual property. The truth is, that when we open our hearts and minds to the Lord, He enters into our inmost organic life—feels good desires and entertains wise thoughts, according to the media into which He has entered, and permits us to feel and enjoy this, his own finited love and wisdom, as if it were our own and self-originated. How this is done may be forever as obscure to us as the new birth was to Nicodemus; but the fact is revealed by Paul, and statements of great scientific precision are made about it by Swedenborg.

" *Ye are not in the flesh, but in the Spirit, if so be that the Spirit of God dwell in you. Now if any man have not the Spirit of Christ, he is none of his.*"—ROM. viii. 9.

"*But put ye on the Lord Jesus Christ, and make not provision for the flesh.*"—ROM. xiii. 14.

"*But of him are ye in Christ Jesus, who of God is made unto us wisdom, and righteousness, and sanctification, and redemption.*"—1 COR. i. 30.

"*Know ye not that your body is the temple of the Holy Ghost which is in you, which ye have of God, and ye are not your own?*"—1 COR. vi. 19.

"*The first man is of the earth, earthy; the second man is the Lord from heaven.*"—1 COR. xv. 47.

"*Always bearing about in the body the dying of the Lord Jesus, that the life also of Jesus might be made manifest in our body.*"—2 COR. iv. 10.

"*Know ye not your own selves, how that Jesus Christ is in you, except ye be reprobate?*"—2 COR. xiii. 5.

"*It pleased God, . . . . to reveal his Son in me.*"—GAL. i. 15, 16.

"*I am crucified with Christ: nevertheless I live: yet not I, but Christ liveth in me.*"—GAL. ii. 20.

"*As many of you as have been baptized into Christ, have put on Christ.*"—GAL. iii. 27.

"*Until Christ be formed in you.*"—GAL. iv. 19.

"*In whom ye also are builded together for a habitation of God, through the Spirit.*"—EPH. ii. 22.

"*It is God which worketh in you both to will and to do.*"—PHIL. ii. 13.

"*The mystery which hath been hid from ages and from generations, but now is made manifest to his saints;* . . .

"*Which is Christ in you, the hope of glory.*"—COL. i. 26, 27.

"*For ye are dead, and your life is hid with Christ in God.*"—COL. iii. 3.

How utterly have they failed to grasp the meaning of these magnificent sentences, who suppose that the Holy Spirit imparts the virtues and graces of the Christian life to the soul, so that it becomes good and wise and holy, and who do not see that our own life is always utterly evil and dead, and that the new life is not our own, but is Christ formed in us, the Lord from heaven, God willing and doing through us, the Lord Jesus manifesting his own life through our organic media, so that we are nothing, and He is all in all! Swedenborg teaches all this very clearly and beautifully, as the following extracts show. The italics are mine.

"Every one in the heavens knows and believes, yea, *perceives*, that he wills and does nothing of good from himself, and that he thinks and believes nothing of truth from himself, but from the Divine, that is, from the Lord; and that the good and truth which are from himself are not good and truth, because there is not in them life from the Divine."

"Because the angels believe thus, they refuse all thanks on account of the good they do, and are indignant and recede, if any one attributes good to them. They wonder that any one should believe that he is wise from himself, and that he does good from himself. To do good for the sake of one's self they do not call good, because it is done from self: but to do good for the sake of good they call good *from the Divine ;* and say that this good is what makes heaven, *because it is the Lord.*"

" Those spirits who, while they were in the world, confirmed themselves in the belief that the good which they do and the truth which they believe are from themselves, or *are appropriated to them as their own,* in which belief are all those who place merit in good actions, and claim righteousness to themselves, are not received into heaven. The angels avoid them; they regard them as stupid and as thieves; as stupid because they continually look to themselves, and not to the Divine; and as thieves, because they take from the Lord what is his. These are against the faith of heaven that *the Divine of the Lord with the angels makes heaven.*"

"That those are in the Lord, and *the Lord in them,* who are in heaven and *in the church,* the Lord also teaches by saying: '*Abide in me and I in you: as the branch cannot bear fruit of itself unless it abide in the vine, so neither can ye unless ye abide in me. I am the vine, ye are the branches: he that abideth in me and I in him, the same beareth much fruit; for without me ye can do nothing.'* "—JOHN xv. 4, 5.

" From these things it is now evident that the Lord dwells *in his own* with the angels of heaven, and thus that the Lord is the all in all of heaven: and this because *good from the Lord is the Lord with them,* for what is from Him is Himself: consequently good from the Lord is heaven to the angels, and not anything proper to themselves."—H. H. 8–12.

Now, my dear friend, if you would see still more clearly that our own proprium is utterly evil and false, and can never be spiritualized, or made good and true; that it must be separated and put off; that the new life which comes in its place is not the old life reformed, but a "new creature," the Lord Himself formed in us, and abiding with us, and working through us (the very doctrines of Paul), I advise you to consult studiously the following references to Swedenborg.

Every man, spirit and angel, as to his proprium, is mere evil, and left to himself, breathes nothing but hatreds, revenges, cruelties, and adulteries.—A. C. 987.

Man is so entirely evil that he cannot be fully delivered from so much as one sin to eternity; but by the mercy of the Lord, he may be withheld from evil and held in good.—A. C. 5398.

Before regeneration, man is possessed as to his natural part by evil spirits, and all his delights are really infernal *howsoever holy they appear.*—A. C. 3928.

The proprium of every one resides in the sensual and the natural plane of life, not in the spiritual.—A. E. 355, 483.

A regenerate man is altogether another man, a new man, and he is said to be born anew, created anew. This is really the case, though he remains the same as to the features of the body. Nevertheless every evil remains, and is only removed from sight. —A. C. 3212, 4564, 5113.

The procedure of regeneration is similar to the procedure of the Lord when He made his human Divine: indeed so far as man is created anew, *he has the Divine as it were in* HIMSELF, only nothing is done by his own power.—A. C. 3043, 3057.

Good and truth from the Lord cannot be appropriated to any angel or man *as his own*, any more than life from the Lord: hence they are given to the regenerate who receive a heavenly proprium, *as if their own, though not actually so.*—A. C. 8497.

The Lord dwells in his own, thus in what is divine in man, and not in the proprium of any one.—A. C. 9338.

The internal man is the celestial proprium given by the Lord, and therefore spoken of as man's own; but it is of the Lord—yea, *it is the Lord with him.*—A. C. 1594.

The internal man is of the Lord, yea, is the Lord Himself in all men; and when their external is quiescent, the angels know no otherwise than that they are the Lord.—A. C. 1745.

Paul recognized the fact that our righteousness is not our own, something given to us to have and to hold; but that it is the Lord's life in us, manifested according to our reception of it and our organic capacities of bringing it into action. He therefore detected the great truth that the church upon earth, which is the Lord's heaven in ultimates, is spiritually united in all its parts and powers, on the principles that govern the human body. The church with him is the body of Christ, of which the Divine Man is the living and actuating soul. He here also approaches Swedenborg's stupendous revelation of the structure or form of the heavens as a Grand Man.

If our goodness and truth were actually our own, and we used and directed them according to our own desires and our own self-derived intelligence, there never could be any fixed and unitizing principle, or true and perfect bond of co-operative action. It is exactly because we think and act upon this false belief, that there is no unity in our societies or churches; and instead of the supreme order and harmony which the Divine presence must always produce, we have the repulsions and chaos which the selfhood invariably inaugurates. All our very best religious activities are tainted with the proprium, and to celestial perceptions have the smell of the pit about them, until we cease to think and act *of*, and *from*, and *for* ourselves, and recognize the Lord as the only working power for good and truth in ourselves and our neighbor. Then only can we begin to comprehend and realize the stupendous truths taught us by Paul and Swedenborg.

"*For as the body is one and hath many members, and all the members of that one body, being many, are one body: so also is Christ.*

"*For by one Spirit are we all baptized into one body, whether we be Jews or Gentiles, whether we be bond or free, and have been all made to drink into one Spirit.*

"*For the body is not one member, but many.*"—1 COR. xii. 12–14.

"*Now ye are the body of Christ, and members in particular.*"—1 COR. xii. 27.

"*The bread which we break, is it not the communion of the body of Christ? For we, being many, are one bread and one body; for we are all partakers of that one bread.*"—1 COR. x. 16, 17.

"*For we are members of his body, of his flesh, and of his bones.*"—EPH. v. 30.

Now hear some of the similar but more explicit and sublime revelations made through Swedenborg:—

The societies of heaven are innumerable, and they are all various; yet they make one whole because they are led by the Lord as one.—A. C. 1285, 1316.

The heavens are altogether an image of the Lord's external man.—A. C. 1590.

The whole heaven appears before the Lord as a Grand Man, because the Lord Himself is all in all there.—A. C. 1894, 1276.

The Lord is not only in heaven, but He is heaven.—A. C. 2859.

It is the Divine Human of the Lord that flows in and makes heaven and the church.—A. C. 3038.

The angels are in the Lord and in heaven, because the Lord as to the Divine Human reigns universally in all things of their thought and will. They perceive it to be so, and love to have it so.—A. C. 8865.

They who are in heaven are in the Lord, yea, in his body.—A. C. 3637–8.

The church in general also appears before the Lord as one man, and the regenerate individual is a heaven and a church in its least form.—A. C. 2853, 9276-9.

That which makes heaven makes also the church in man.—A. C. 10,760.

The Lord Himself is heaven and the church, thus all in all—dwelling everywhere in his own goods and truths, and not in the proprium of any.—A. C. 10,125, 10,151.

All men who are in the Lord's church, however dispersed throughout the globe, make spiritually one, even as in the heavens.—A. C. 2859.

Now, my dear friend, we can only be partakers of this spiritual solidarity—this perfect body of Christ, by becoming ourselves a miniature church, a miniature heaven: and this can only be effected by the willing and total surrender of the selfhood or old proprium, by that profound humiliation of spirit in which alone the Lord can be present, by a continual acknowledgment of his Divine Humanity, by incessantly opening our hearts and minds to his divine influx, so that, breathing in us and through us, He may enable us always to believe his Word and to keep his commandments.

Let us all earnestly seek to be thus made one with Christ, even as He was made one with the Father.

        Yours affectionately,        W. H. H.

# LETTER X.

### ANSWER TO INQUIRIES ABOUT THE NEW LIFE.

MY DEAR MADAM:—Your interesting letter was duly received and considered, and I reply with great pleasure, hoping to be useful to you and perhaps to others, for sometimes even a hint is of service.

In the first place let us read over what you say about yourself and your experiences.

"I've been happier ever since for meeting you. A shadowy hope has cheered me ever since, that I might yet sometime learn to know the Lord as you do. I suppose you will say there is no doubt about it. I cannot as yet be so sure.

"I am so old—older than you probably would guess—much older than I feel. The habits of a lifetime are not so easily changed. I, who have all these years made self the prominent object of regard (while many times I thought it dying or dead), how can I ever learn to worship at another shrine?

"Three distinct religious phases I have seemed to pass through: First: In my 'teens, 'converted,' rapturously happy to find myself among the blessed few, whom 'God *out of his mere good pleasure* from all eternity had elected to everlasting life'!

"Ah! I was a whited sepulchre, a self-righteous Pharisee! and I never knew it,—I did not dream it.

"Thirteen years ago there came the second change, when, in accordance with the advice of my spiritual instructors, I 'reckoned myself dead unto sin' BECAUSE I CLAIMED THAT

CONDITION BY FAITH, though altogether contrary to my consciousness.

"Then too, self, though I did not know it, was uppermost, and thoroughly alive.

"Eight years ago came the third crisis in my life. It was a genuine and complete change in my modes of thought and feeling. Perhaps it took out of me a little of the hypocrisy, but otherwise I look vainly for such fruit as I should bear. I allude to the beginning of my acquaintance with the writings of Swedenborg, which *intellectually* have been my greatest delight. Can they ever be more to me than that?

"I am amazingly, detestably, horribly selfish. It seems too much to hope that the Lord can or will come into my life and enable me 'to walk even as He walked,' though such a state seems to me blessed and desirable—infinitely beyond any other.

"But admitting one so selfish, so weak, so vacillating, so blinded by the senses, may hope to attain this blessedness, what experiences must be passed through before its attainment?"

Now, my dear friend, you have gone through several phases of religious belief and experience, and find your past and present life entirely unsatisfactory. You have grand and beautiful spiritual ideals, but they seem very far off, and impossible for you to realize. You are thoroughly disgusted with self and selfishness, and would gladly get rid of them, but feel that you are too old in evil ever to hope it. You yearn after a state of Christian perfection, but you are so profoundly conscious of your emptiness and helplessness, that you only wish to be taught how to *begin* the new life. You distrust all unusual experiences as mere outbursts of enthusiasm.

Truly, in my eyes, these are hopeful signs that you are already growing and strengthening in the new life. How can we judge of our interior states which are known to the Lord alone? Is not the new life the leaven which was *hid* in three measures of meal? Is it not the seed which springs up and grows, no man knows how? Is it not the wind blowing where it listeth, of whose coming and going we know nothing? Is it not the child concealed in its mother's womb, and growing to perfection by laws and processes of which we are ignorant? We are commanded to judge not; and especially not to judge according to appearances. This law is as applicable to our judgment of ourselves as to our judgment of others.

Are you not too hasty in saying you are too old for much improvement? What have time and space, which are incident to nature, to do with spiritual evolutions? You never will be old or die. A million years hence, by our earthly computation, you will be younger than you are now. It is not a question of time, but of state. What states of affection and thought do you love, and endeavor to make permanent in your life? Those states which you earnestly seek, you will surely find; those which you repudiate and reject, will certainly recede from you after a while and disappear forever. The providences of life are designed to remove the natural obstructions of the false and the evil, which prevent the "remains" of goodness and truth, stored away in our infancy, from coming down into our external life and conduct. This rarely happens to any one until middle life, sometimes not until old age, and in the vast majority of cases not until the unfoldings of the world of spirits bring the true life to the surface by casting off its externals.

You are discouraged by constantly discovering new traits of selfishness, "the depths of Satan" within you. Now, my dear friend, you may study that old Adam forever, and you will never find any good in him. The leopard cannot change his spots nor the Ethiopian his skin. Selfish? hypocritical? ambitious? of course you are: and if circumstances and surroundings were favorable and the heavenly powers did not withhold you, you would burst out shamelessly and joyously into blasphemy, lying, stealing, murder, and all uncleanness; nor would you be any worse than any other man or woman, or indeed than any angel in any of the heavens, for doing so; for under the same conditions they would all do the same things.

Now this old life of the proprium, which seems so strongly to be your own, is not entirely yours. Indeed it would be yours in a very slight degree, if you did not deliberately receive it, approve it, and appropriate it. Your natural life is the concentrated essence of hell, flowing through your *hereditary* principle, and endeavoring to fasten itself upon *you*. You have a perfect right to repudiate its suggestions, *as not belonging to yourself*, and to say always, "Get thee behind me, Satan!" Happy is the man whose sins are uncovered, so that he knows the hell within him. Still happier is he, when he learns to reject the influx of evil spirits, to separate himself from them, to deny their accusations, repudiate their sentiments, and disclaim all participation in their affections and thoughts. He is then entering into states of true freedom.

But what is this something within ourselves, which resists and repudiates that influent evil life, which seems so strongly to be our own? It is certainly not a part of that evil life. It is certainly not something self-originated, self-created. No: it is the Lord with his holy angels coming down to us. It is

Immanuel—"God with us." It is the new life, "*born, not of blood, nor of the will of the flesh, nor of the will of man, but of God.*"

"*Ye will not come unto Me that ye might have life.*"

"*The bread which I will give, is my flesh, which I will give for the life of the world.*"

Now this "new life" in us never did nor can commit any sin. "Whosoever is born of God doth not commit sin." It is *not* our own life, although we are permitted to feel *as if* it were really ours. But if we *claim* it as ours, and thereby profess *ourselves* to be clean and pure and holy and perfect, we are thieves and liars, robbing God of his glory, and the truth is not in us. The fruit of such a state is self-righteousness and hypocrisy. No man can remain in that state of profound humility, in which alone the Lord is present with man, so long as he imagines that he has been made clean, and pure, and holy. The angels are indignant when called good and holy, and they use no such false compliments to each other. Our Christian obituaries would generally strike them with ineffable disgust. They take no credit for anything they do, for they know all good and truth are the Lord's. Professions and pretensions are utterly unknown to them, and the sphere of merit and self-assertion is hateful. The *true* "new life" is one like the angel's, and the prediction that the Lord will come "with his holy angels," means that the Second Advent will be attended with such organic conditions, that the angelic states of life will be made possible on earth. They are possible now, but they will generally be manifested among those who love and serve most, and who desire and talk least.

Now I want to put you on the rack a little, and perhaps to

surprise you. What is the secret reason of all this religious restlessness and aspiration on your part? Why do you desire to be good and holy and perfect? Is it because you have such an overwhelming sense of guilt, that you are trembling with the fear of hell, and would save your own soul? Or is it because you have such an innate, organic antipathy to sin, that you would fly to the uttermost parts of the earth to escape its hated presence? Or is it because the social rewards of "holiness" are very desirable in your sight? that you would like to be considered sweet and pure and perfect in your circle—a shining monument of the love of God, and a paragon of Christian graces? thus desiring, like the sons of Zebedee, to be first in the kingdom of heaven? Is it not good and noble and right to desire to excel in all heavenly things? Are you sure of it? Sound the depths of your heart and soul with these questions, remembering that the old proprium, in its selfishness and ambition, delights exceedingly to clothe itself in the garb of Christian humilities, aspirations, and activities.

On the other hand, why should you take any care for to-morrow? Why should you wish that any thought or will of your own should enter into, or any way determine, the adjustment or unfoldings of your future life? Why not lay it all down, give it all up, leave it to the Lord alone, and wait patiently upon Him? Why should you desire to excel your fellow-beings, even in goodness? Why not be willing to make your bed in hell, if the Lord desired to manifest his presence and his power even there? Empty yourself of *self*, and put nothing else in. Desire nothing. Simply shun all evil suggestions, ideas, and intentions, as *sins* against the Lord. He will then enable you to do his will. His will in regard to you is presented to you every day. His providence rules over everything that happens, even the most minute. Whatever your hands find to do, your heart to feel, your mind to think, your tongue to say, is *sent to you every day by Him, and is all especially designed* to fit you for his kingdom and to unite you with Himself. No matter whether it is great or small, agreeable or disagreeable, clear or obscure. Bend yourself to service. A child in spirit, a servant in work, looking always to the Lord. That is the way into the "new life."

I congratulate you on having escaped the sphere of Predestination—a subject too hateful to contemplate; and the more plausible but more dangerous sphere of "faith alone," a sphere which begets an exceedingly subtile self-righteousness, calculated to deceive the very elect. I congratulate you on having entered into the large, clear, sweet light of Swedenborg. You will there surely find truth, strength, and peace. You seem at present to need, not so much the exposition of truth, as to be brought more directly into personal relations with the Lord, who now stands in ultimates. This will be best effected by prayer, and the heavenly atmosphere of the Evangelists—especially John.

Now, my dear friend, I have said so little to the point on so vast a subject, that I seem to myself to have said almost nothing. If your spiritual needs require further utterances or expansions of thought, I am at your service for what little help I can render you.

Yours truly,<br>W. H. H.

# LETTER XI.

### THE INNER WAY.—JONES VERY.

DEAR FRIENDS:—I wish to communicate to you and to others some thoughts which occurred to me while reading your review of my little book, "The End of the World," in your serial, *Words for the New Church*, No. XI. Disclaiming all thought or consideration of myself, either as man or author, I propose to survey the matter from the standpoint of the love of truth for its own sake and its uses to the neighbor.

Unlike your New-Church cotemporaries, you recognize the "most important and timely service" the book has rendered, in "dashing away the veil of apparent truth and good, which hides the real state of Christendom, and showing in all their enormity the evils and falses beneath." If all men in all the churches could see and believe this their real condition, and could be thus brought into states of utter humiliation and despair, how soon would the face of the world be changed! How are they to be approached and instructed in these terrible and most unacceptable revelations of their interior states? You believe such states exist, because you find that Swedenborg, or the Lord through Swedenborg, has declared the facts in the most emphatic manner. What an infinitesimal portion of mankind is ready to accept the exposure of the hells within them on the authority of Swedenborg! You cannot even get one in a hundred of the avowed receivers of the heavenly doctrines, to see these fearful truths as applicable to the old church *in themselves*, so that they will take hold upon the life, and make them fight against the old proprium until it is truly subdued.

Now, dear friends, there are two ways to arrive at truth. There is an interior way, whether you have discovered it or not, by which men are brought to a living perception of truths which have lain as dead material in the memory, or which may never have entered it at all. I had often read what Swedenborg affirms about the ineradicably evil state of the proprium, and the hopelessly evil and false condition of the Christian world. It made little impression upon me, and that a painful one; for there seemed to me an air of uncharitableness about it which I did not like. Nor did I attain to a clear perception of the truths announced in the "End of the World" by a further, more assiduous study of Swedenborg, but by a process of introspection and personal experience: for each man is a miniature form of the universe, and all the heavens and all the hells rest upon him and flow into him; and there are ways unknown to your scientific natural man, ignored by you also, whereby he can learn all things from within.

I had been led by a series of providences through many varying states of evil and falsity, and many hideous temptations, being truly in the wilderness with wild beasts, to a culmination of those states about five years ago, in one long, terrible condition of utter darkness, humiliation, and despair. Now I was delivered from this condition in the course of a few days, mainly in a single day (April 16, 1878), not to all appearance by any light of truth from Swedenborg or elsewhere, but by a realization of the presence of the Divine Man in ultimates—a Divine Natural Humanity standing right by me, ready to assume my states, if I would only utterly give myself up to Him, and to display his "power over all flesh" by immediately giving me the power to abstain from all sin.

It is immaterial how you explain this phenomenon, whether as hallucination or fantasy, or the work of enthusiastic spirits, or the rational final issue of many temptation-combats in which I was sustained by truths derived in the past from Swedenborg and the Word. This last is my own interpretation —but it appeared to me a sudden and a divine reality; for I passed at once into an entirely new life, peaceful and luminous, a sabbath state, which, with the exception of a few, brief assaults from the hells, has continued and grown steadily ever since. The Lord enters in proportion as self recedes, and He brings with Him heaven, the church, and the Word. I have learned from my own experience that the Lord Jesus Christ stands organically upon the earth, just as He did immediately after his resurrection, and nothing but our own clouds of evil and falsity hide Him from our eyes. All things are changed, and He comes now into the humble and contrite heart without the aid of any institutions, sacraments, or churches, old or new.

These experiences are open and free to all men; and whoever seeks and finds them, will enter into larger liberty and rationality of thought, a life of more willing and perfect obedience, a tenderer charity, a clearer vision, a finer perception of truth, and a state of illustration from the Word, as Swedenborg calls it, of which he has now no conception. And the way to seek and find them, is to shun all known evils as sins against the Lord.

The light from heaven which convicts us of sin and reveals

the unfathomable hells in our own hearts, renders us intensely sensitive to the spheres of the evil and the false emanating from others, whether from individuals or from associations of our fellow men. That is the process which enabled me to *realize* the truths unfolded in the "End of the World." It is not we who judge in such cases, but the Spirit of Truth flowing into and through us that judges. The conjoined good in us leads us to regard those evil and false spheres with unbounded pity and sorrow, to excuse and palliate them in every possible manner, to see ourselves in them constantly reflected as from a mirror, and to entertain an unconquerable hope and faith that our merciful Lord will lead all men out of these terrible wildernesses into the light and peace of his own heavenly kingdom. In all my experiences, however, and study of the hells of modern life, I find no difference whatever between New-Church and Old-Church people. Myself, my friends, the Convention, the Academy, were all under the same condemnation. Indeed, higher truths and better doctrinals only condemn us more severely, because we have never manifested anything more Christ-like in our lives than the cheap and easy righteousness of the Scribes and Pharisees.

That this interior life, this inner light, this extreme sensitiveness to good and evil spheres, which reveals to us the hells within ourselves and others, and draws us nearer and nearer to the perception of New-Church doctrine, may be developed in the soul, without the ostensible agency of the writings of Swedenborg, but by the interior operations of the Holy Spirit ("if any man will do his will, he shall know of the doctrine"), is amply verified in the biographies of good men and women in all churches and at all times. One instance of recent unfolding is so clear an illustration, and so beautiful in itself, that I must say something about it.

Jones Very, whose memoir and poems were recently published, was what Emerson calls "a detached, that is, a universally associated man." Held by a mere external thread to the Unitarian Church, without any baptism into the New Church, or reception of the doctrines, or any of the paraphernalia of ecclesiasticism which you think necessary to the development of the true Christian character, this man lived an angelic life, entirely free from the selfhood, walking even as Jesus walked, having learned with Fenelon and Guyon that all sin springs from self-will and all goodness from total and absolute acceptance of the will of God—after which the man himself is nothing, and the Christ is all and all in him, directing, guiding and leading him into all the truths requisite for his spiritual states and his uses in life.

Emerson, who was an intimate friend of this rare and delicate genius, and who, half-pagan as he was, appreciated him more clearly than many of his most Christian friends, tells some good things about him, from which I extract a few sentences.

"His position accuses society as much as society calls that false and morbid; and much of his discourse concerning society, church, and college was absolutely just."

"He says it is with him a day of hate (not of persons but of principles), that he discerns the bad element in every person whom he meets, which repels him; he even shrinks a little to give the hand, that sign of receiving. The institutions, the cities which men have built the world over, look to him like a huge ink-blot. His only guard in going to see men is, that he goes to do them good, else they would injure him spiritually. He would obey—obey. He is not disposed to attack religions or charities though false. The bruised reed he would not break, nor quench the smoking flax."

"A very accurate discernment of spirits belongs to his state, and he detects at once the presence of an alien element, though he cannot tell whence, how or whereto it is. . . . When he is in the room with other persons, speech stops, as if there were a corpse in the apartment. . . . In the woods he said to me: 'One might forget here that the world was desert and empty and all the people wicked.' . . . When he was in Concord, he said to me: 'I always felt when I heard you speak, or read your writings, that you saw the truth better than others; yet I felt that your spirit was not quite right. It was as if a vein of colder air blew across me.'"

"Jones Very has gone into the multitude as solitary as Jesus. In dismissing him, I seem to have discharged an arrow into the heart of society. Wherever that young enthusiast goes, he will astonish and disconcert men by dividing for them the cloud that covers the gulf in man."

It is the work of spiritual truth to divide the cloud which covers the infernal gulf of the proprium in ourselves and others, and to bring us all into judgment. When spiritual truth is conjoined to celestial good, they produce the obedient, humble, trustful, loving soul that shone out in the person of Jones Very. "To have walked with Very," said a brother clergyman, "was truly to have walked with God." "I told my people," said an eloquent preacher, "that to see Very for half an hour in any pulpit, and know that such a man existed in the world, was a far greater sermon than any ever preached to them from the lips of an orator."

"He was as good," said a life-long friend, "as goodness itself, as true as truth. With his knowledge and wisdom, he was as simple as a child, transparent, artless. He was at the extremest possible distance from pomposity or pretension. When he believed that the poetry which came to him like the breath of heaven, did actually come from heaven, it was so naturally and simply said, that you felt it was his profoundest conviction. He believed fully and intensely that the Lord of life gave it to him. It was a sacred idea, a divine reality."

"This nearness of the Divine Presence," says his biographer, "was the great fact of his life. He felt it to be so intensely real and vital, that he was inexpressibly grieved as he looked around among his fellows for men who *thus* walked with God, to find how much alone he stood; and he breaks out into a wail of lamentation that men are dead to the glory around them," etc.

"His own intense, contemplative piety had lifted him out of what he regarded as the 'grave' of the senses, above the world, into that condition of 'inward peace, the sweet patience' which the Buddhist calls Nirvâna."

When this beautiful soul, departing like the man who told the Jews that it was Jesus who made him whole, preached the annihilation of self-will as the true road to peace, goodness, and spiritual illumination, to the social and ecclesiastical circles about him, he was pronounced insane by many. He put himself of his own accord into a private asylum, where the physical excitement and consequent prostration induced in so exquisitely sensitive a nature by the opposition and persecution he encountered, were speedily relieved.

He was about as insane as Swedenborg or my friend G. W. C. The Rev. Dr. Clarke, who saw him at that time, declared it to be a case of *mono-sania* rather than *mono-mania:* and Ralph Waldo Emerson wrote that he regarded him as "profoundly sane" and "wished the whole world were as mad as he." Rev. Dr. Channing said: "He had not lost his reason, but only held his senses, his lower faculties, in abeyance. Men in general have lost or never found this higher mind; their insanity is profound, Mr. Very's is only superficial. To hear him talk was like looking into the purely spiritual world, into truth itself. He had nothing of self-exaggeration, but seemed to have attained self-annihilation and become an oracle of God."

Now, dear friends of the Academy, neither this man's biographer nor his friends possessed the key to the secret of his life and character. That is found only in the writings of Swedenborg. Nor is that man capable of finding it in Swedenborg, who can be satisfied with the solution of "enthusiastic spirits," because Mr. Very was not a Swedenborgian. No man encased in the hard shell of doctrine, and believing the life of charity is impossible without an external revealed basis of faith, can ever find that key. This was one of those partial and imperfect cases of the opening of the celestial degree of life into the external consciousness, which are increasing in the world under greatly varied forms, and which are feebly illustrative but profoundly prophetic of the coming of the celestial church—"the Bride, the Lamb's wife."

This man, who was both proof and sample of the descent of the New Jerusalem by the internal way of perception, had no idea of the causes of his intuitions and illuminations. He lived in states of simple faith, absolute obedience, and utter self-abnegation. He evidently thought and cared little about doctrines or forms, because the divine influxes passed through the will directly into the life and conduct. He not only believed, as we do from doctrine, that all good and truth flow from the Lord and are the Lord's in man, but *he felt it sensationally and consciously*, and therefore declared that the Lord lived in him and spoke through him. This state, pronounced insanity by the natural man of the world and the church, is simply the permanent state of angels as described by Swedenborg.

Your position is, that the Lord is not coming by internal influx, but by external revelation and preaching thence: that the interiors of the whole human race are utterly evil and false, and there is no salvation but by the implantation in the external mind of the doctrines revealed through Swedenborg, and the development of the good to which they lead. You are clearly right as to the necessity of the implantation of truths in the external way; but I am sure you are in great error when you ignore the goods and truths descending from the New Church in the heavens, and struggling in all human hearts and minds to find the natural basis of sound doctrine which has been revealed in the writings of Swedenborg. I beg you to study and compare the following general truths which I have culled from our great authority in spiritual things. If any man will reason from them as centres of thought, he will be led by their own light to clear, broad, and beautiful conceptions of the New Church and the Second Coming.

Revelation is internal perception, and is from perception.—A. C. 5111.

All revelation is either from discourse with angels by whom the Lord speaks, or from perception.—A. C. 5121.

They have revelation from perception which is internal revelation, who are in good, and *from good in truth.*—A. C. 5121.

Those who are in good and in the desire of truth, have revelation when they read the Word, and this by illustration and perception derived therefrom.—A. C. 8694.

The Word *reveals itself* by holy influx to all who are in good; and when it is not received, the fault is with those who read it, in consequence of the opposition of their interiors.—A. C. 8971.

Had the man of the Most Ancient Church read the prophetical or historical Word, he would have seen the internal sense without any previous instruction.—A. C. 4493.

The man who is in good thinks spiritually, thus according to the internal sense of the Word, even though ignorant of the fact.—A. C. 5478.

When the good of the rational flows into the natural man, *it produces truths* almost as the life produces fibres in the body.—A. C. 3579.

Men who are in love and charity have angelic wisdom in themselves, but they can only perceive it obscurely whilst they live in the body.—A. C. 2494.

The Church would be one if all had charity, although they should differ as to worship and doctrinals: thus charity constitutes the Church, not doctrinals.—A. C. 1285, 1316, 1798, etc.

The Church (individually or collectively) which commences from faith, has no other regulator than the understanding; but the Church which commences from good, has for its regulator charity and the Lord.—A. C. 4672.

The internal man in the course of regeneration receives truths before the external.—A. C. 3321.

So far as celestial things which are of the internal man, have dominion, truths are multiplied; but so far as worldly things which are of the external man, have dominion, truths are diminished and vanish away.—A. C. 4099.

Truth is the form of good, and is formed in man according to the quality of his good.—A. C. 668.

The multiplication of truth from good with those who are

in charity, is so immense as to be inexpressible.—A. C. 1941, 1997.

Genuine truths with man *flow in* from the Lord alone.— A. C. 8868.

In the process of regeneration by truths, the Lord miraculously adapts apparent truths and even falsities to the reception of the good of charity.—A. C. 1832.

If you will accept these great truths and many collateral ones from the same authority, and push them boldly to their logical issues, you will understand how the New Jerusalem is descending, not only by the way of external doctrine and preaching which at present is an exceedingly insignificant factor, but also by an internal way, by the vivification of the remains of good and truth implanted in infancy in all men; by the interior developments of truth from the good of charity in the midst of exterior falsities; and thus see how the Lord is universally descending from centres to circumferences, by means of a universal church *forming within*, and pressing outward to destroy and rebuild, and to remodel all things after its heavenly pattern. You will then clearly understand the case of Mr. Very, and the thousand-fold more wonderful case of my friend G. W. C., who, by interior openings, was initiated *through perceptions* into the doctrines of the New Church and the spiritual sense of the Word without the aid of Swedenborg. You will understand my experiences and those of many others, which are now incredible or incomprehensible to you. You will accept many things in the "End of the World" which you now reject, including Swedenborg's doctrine of interior illumination and multiplication of truths, whereby the internal sense of the Word is shown to be infinitely extensible and utterly inexhaustible.

You object, on inadequate grounds as it seems to me, to my theories and speculations in the "End of the World." No matter how rational, logical, legitimate, instructive, suggestive, or interesting they may be, away with them, because they are presumptuous departures from the literal statements of Swedenborg! You seem to have forgotten the orderly and rational extensions of thought and multiplication of truths from radical germs implanted in the mind. Swedenborg says that our perception of new truths increases with the extension of our affection and thought into new societies of the heavens.

Truths come into sight, as landscapes do, on motion of the observer. Our motion is the progressive evolution, the infoldings and unfoldings, of the human spirit, individual and collective. "That the science of correspondences," says Swedenborg, "by which the spiritual sense is given, is at this day revealed, is because now the divine truths of the church are coming into the light."—T. C. R. 207. The divine truths revealed through Swedenborg were, of organic necessity, the infinitesimal portions of the spiritual sense of the Word, which could be received into the organic structure of his mind imbedded, as it were, in the organic structure of his age. The New Church is not born into adult conditions. It has its beginning and infancy like all things: and its present powers of expression (even through a Swedenborg), of feeling and action, are all infantile, feeble, and inadequate, in comparison with the things that are obliged to come upon us in the opening futures. This, a man can *see* from Swedenborg himself, without perhaps being able to understand or appropriate the hundredth part of what Swedenborg has revealed.

Swedenborg does nothing to cultivate the spirit of submission to authority. "*Nunc licet*" is his motto. His final appeal is to human rationality. Every man's cry of "Thus saith the Lord" must be submitted to that, even his own. You want us to believe Swedenborg's writings, not because they so clearly and wonderfully reveal the Lord to us, which is reason enough for believing them, but because the Lord has revealed them to him, and they come with a weight of authority that makes the use of our reason out of the question. This is the Roman Catholic position. It is the vicegerency of the pope and the infallibility of the church in another shape; and in your anxiety to plant yourselves upon *authority*, so that you may speak *authoritatively* (which the old proprium *so* loves to do), you give an undue weight to some expressions of Swedenborg on the subject.

By making Swedenborg's authority infallible and final, and by accepting a revelation of spiritual truth as in itself the coming of the Lord, you are in danger of closing the Word to yourselves. (A. C. 3793.) After that, you will certainly deny and reject every movement connected with the celestial life, which is the genuine life of the New Church. You will not understand that our spiritual truths are to be married to celestial goods, so as to inaugurate the celestial life upon earth. Let me entreat you, above all things, to study the celestial life.

You say, in relation to my views of the new life, "the author forecasts a 'holiness state,' the spontaneous regeneration without divine truth. He does not tell us where in the Doctrines this is taught." The holiness state which I teach, is simply Swedenborg's second stage of regeneration, which has been strangely overlooked, misunderstood, or ignored in the New Church. It is *not* "spontaneous regeneration without divine truth." Divine truth implanted in the external mind leads to good, constituting the first stage of regeneration. This good in its turn *produces truths from the interior*, which you reject in toto if they differ in the least from your exterior formulas. I make a few quotations from Swedenborg to illustrate the genuine holiness state of the New Church.

When good and truth are thus conjoined, man no longer looks from truths at what is to be believed and done, but *from good*, because he is imbued with truths and has them in himself: nor has he concern about truths from any other source than he can see from his own good; and *he sees continually more and more*, for they are *produced from good like offspring from their parents*.—A. C. 8772.

Man is not in the heavenly life, nor in the Lord, until he enters into this *second* state.—A. C. 9832.

In the good of love which flows in from the Lord through the angels, *there is all truth* which would manifest itself of itself if man lived in genuine love to the Lord and the neighbor.—A. C. 6323.

The natural man is to be subdued, and all his concupiscences *extirpated*, together with those things that concern them.—A. C. 5647.

The natural man should become *altogether as nothing*, that is, without will, in order that a man may become spiritual.—A. C. 565.

The former life which is of hell, must be *altogether destroyed*: that is, evils and falsities must be removed, in order that new life, which is the life of heaven, may be implanted.—A. C. 9336.

The regenerate man is reduced to such a state that the external man does obeisance to the internal, which it never can do until it is quiescent, and as it were *annihilated*.—A. C. 933.

The Lord removes the proprium of man, and gives from his own proprium in which He dwells with man.—A. E. 254.

The internal man is the celestial proprium given by the Lord, and is therefore spoken of as man's own, but it is the Lord's; yea, *it is the Lord in man.*—A. C. 1594, 1940, '99.

*Heavenly peace* flows in when the lusts arising from the love of self and the world are taken away. No one can be gifted with this peace, but he who is led of the Lord and is *in the Lord.*—A. C. 5662.

These teachings of Swedenborg indicate a "holiness state," as you call it, different from but far transcending in perfection and beauty anything ever taught or realized by the Quietists, or Quakers, or Methodists, or anything yet exhibited in the teachings or life of the so-called New Church up to this time.

You object to my expression, "the Commune of Christ," profaning my idea with the political insanities of communism and socialism. The Commune of Christ is the *communion* of saints, their *common* life in the body of Christ. It is the law and order of heaven, where all are wrought into the most harmonious and loving associations. It is the law of the new church in the heavens, now forming within us to descend upon the earth. "Thy will be done on earth as it is in the heavens," is not only a petition to be offered, but a prophecy to be fulfilled. Soon may it be!

Yours fraternally,
W. H. H.

# LETTER XII.

### THE INTERNAL AND THE EXTERNAL WAY.

DEAR FRIEND:—Swedenborg reiterates over and over that there are two ways by which knowledge is obtained by the human mind, an internal way through individual perceptions of truth from good, and an external way by revelation through others. He also often affirms that the regenerating man is *in the internal sense of the Word* according to the degree of his regeneration, and that the opening of the interior degrees of life would bring him into *conscious* possession of those knowledges without any previous instruction from external sources. How can any serious reader of Swedenborg be ignorant of these general truths?

There are two or three striking passages from Swedenborg, which I have not before quoted, and which may interest the readers of your magazine.

"The man who is regenerating and becoming spiritual, is first led by truth to good; for he does not know what spiritual, or which is the same, what christian good is, except by truth or by means of doctrine derived from the Word. Thus he is initiated into good."

"Afterwards, when he is initiated, he is no longer led by truth to good, but by good to truth; for he then from good *not only sees the truths which he had before known, but also from good produces new truths which before he had not known, nor could know.*"—A. C. 5804.

This is very clearly stated, and one cannot escape from it

by saying that all these new truths from interior sources belong to the celestial church away before the flood, and are not to be expected in men of the present age, in whom the will-principle is totally destroyed, and who can only learn by the external way.  Swedenborg is not here speaking of the Most Ancient Church, but of the natural man being made spiritual, and he enunciates a universal law of regeneration when he affirms that in its first stage we learn from external sources, and in its second stage we have new truths, such as we could not acquire by the first process, given to us by the Lord from within.  And although the first will-principle of the race was nearly extinguished at the flood, the Lord gives us through the intellectual principle a new will which has the same faculty of weaving new truths out of its own substance.

"It is a very different thing to know what is good and true by perception, and to learn what is good and true by doctrine. Those who know by perception have no need of the knowledge acquired in the way of systematized doctrines. . . . To such as are principled in perceptive knowledge, it is given from the Lord to know what is good and true *by an internal way:* but to such as are taught by doctrine, knowledge is given *by an external way*, or that of the bodily senses: and the difference of knowledge in these two cases is like the difference between light and darkness."—A. C. 521.

Swedenborg is here speaking of the celestial man of the Most Ancient Church, of whom he says elsewhere, there are some remains even in our modern life—people, like my friend G. W. C., who see truth from good without learning it from books or pulpits, and who are supposed by those who do not understand them to be the victims of "enthusiastic spirits." He also says in this same passage, that the truths given to men by the interior way were preserved by the Lord for the use of their posterity, and became the external doctrines of the degenerate churches which succeeded.

"The men of the celestial church are such that they perceive all the goods and truths of heaven from the Lord *by influx into their interiors:* whence they see goods and truths inwardly in themselves, as implanted, and have no need to learn them by a posterior way, or to treasure them up in their memory."
—A. E. 739.

Now these "new truths" which so transcend the truths acquired by the external way, are not the rewards of learning and study, or of any scientific or rational processes of thought. They are not the products of self-derived intelligence, or of a large, cultured brain applied to abstruse subjects. Far from it. They come only to those whom Madam Guyon calls "annihilated souls." They belong to those who have passed through "great tribulation;" who have fought with "wild beasts," and been familiar with sorrows, humiliations, and despairs; who have trod the way of the cross, and have died to the selfhood and the world; and whose real nature is as invisible to their fellow-men, as the resurrected body of our Lord was to the Jews. The humble, the obscure, the ignorant, the miserable, the prodigals, the Magdalens, the self-rejected, will seek and find this divine illumination from within, far in advance of those who, enamored of themselves, their opinions, and their positions, exclude in a great measure that Omniscient Presence which alone is the Light of the World.

The opposition to the truths of regeneration as enunciated by Swedenborg, is not altogether due to the antagonism of the natural against the spiritual man, and that eternal warfare of the flesh against the spirit. It comes from men who are earnestly trying, I have no doubt, to keep the commandments, to perform heavenly uses, and to know and love the Lord in his second coming. Their opposition springs from the fear of the old ecclesiastical proprium, that its life is in danger, that its activities in which it takes such supreme delight may be taken away from it. People may outgrow the external church and all its sacraments and usages, or wear them indifferently as loose garments to be thrown aside and changed at pleasure! What! the Lord coming down to men individually, so that they will not need our guidance and instruction, and the grand paraphernalia of the external church be of little or no use but to children and to natural men not yet made spiritual! Away with such an idea! Our craft is in danger. "Great is Diana of the Ephesians!"

This ecclesiastical spirit is not peculiar to the clergy. The idolatry of the Church as an external institution, has long kept the light of heaven out of the minds of the laity. May all these dead things with their imaginary sanctities and fictitious values soon pass away, and make room for the descent of the Holy City from God out of heaven!

Yours fraternally,<br>W. H. H.

# LETTER XIII.

### THE SEED GROWING: THE PROPRIUM AND THE NEW LIFE.

MY DEAR FRIEND:—Your letter gave me great pleasure, for I now perceive that the little seed I have been continuously sowing in your mind for two or three years is beginning to grow, and will bring forth fruit, perhaps a hundred-fold.

When I last conversed with you, you were a genuine church-woman, belonging to what I call, with no disrespect, the Episcopalian clique of New-Church people. Harris was your *bête noir*. G. W. C. was the victim of enthusiastic spirits. I was strongly suspected. You would not subscribe to the *Independent*. You believed in church institutions, in a graded ministry, constituted authority, a beautiful liturgy, a calm and happy life according to the commandments, a choir with classic music, and in stained-glass windows. With all these, how could the heavenly doctrines fail to achieve the conquest of the world?

Well, I quietly mailed you, month after month, advance sheets of the Letters on Spiritual Subjects. The seed is growing. You now write me, that although you still think some of G. W. C.'s experiences are "fantastic," you are deeply indebted to us for a knowledge of the proprium which you never could have obtained from any other New-Church sources; and that our teachings have enabled you to realize the delusive subtleties and hidden depths of your own heart as you never did before. In consequence of this new light in your soul, you have entered upon a new state, you say, "a state of combat and of unrest," a state of torpor and indifference to spiritual things, in which your perceptions of truth are sadly obscured.

This state, my dear friend, however disagreeable and even melancholy it may be for a time, is a most hopeful and salutary state. It is merely the valley of the shadow of death, through which we must all pass on the way from the old to the new life. There must be a breaking up of old states of affection and thought, before we can leave the dead to bury their dead, and follow the Lord alone. There is no state of mind which seems to me so sad and hopeless, as that of very many excellent New-Church people who are satisfied with their spiritual condition, because they keep the commandments and are assiduous in the discharge of all their known duties. This is a purely Jewish or natural state of the religious life, which may exist in great perfection without a ray of spiritual enlightenment, or of influx from the celestial heavens. It is a fig-tree state, without a particle of the vine or the olive in it. It is the mere beginning, not the finality, of the New-Church life in the soul. When it is a fixed condition, and the party neither believes in nor desires any higher or more interior life upon earth, the mind and heart are permanently closed, and the "all things new" of the New Church are nothing but the things of the old dispensations repaired and varnished.

G. W. C. was looking the other day at a photograph of an exceedingly talented and distinguished minister. It was a calm, noble, peaceful, luminous countenance. "Behold," he said, "a splendid type of a civilization which is destined to become extinct. This is the old proprium exquisitely cultivated and refined, and thoroughly subjugated and accommodated to the uses and proprieties of civilized life. But not one particle of *this* flesh and blood, (the old proprium,) shall inherit the kingdom of heaven. This man's life will be razed down to its very roots, and all begin over again. Nothing but the new proprium goes to heaven, for heaven is the Lord; and the new proprium is not the old proprium glorified, but it is the Lord Himself *manifested in the life.*"

O, that the New Church would hear and comprehend the meaning of these words, and thus realize the supreme fact, that the Second Coming of the Lord is the genuine, organic manifestation of the life of Jesus Christ in the souls of his people! It is because this truth is brooding, like the Spirit of God, over the waters of the abyss in your own soul, that you are in "states of combat and unrest." The old principles which are satisfied with a good moral life, and some æsthetic improvements in the old order of things, are dissatisfied and unhappy at the approach of such radical and revolutionary ideas. What! give up *all* we have—actually *all*, and be nothing and have nothing—to follow Christ! To become as little children; to cease from man, "whose breath is in his nostrils"; to forget authorities and formulas; to leave churches, institutions, and all human help behind; to stand in the wilderness alone with the wild beasts; to realize the hell within us and around us, and our own utter helplessness; to hear the voice of the Lord, whispering in our inmost being, "Behold, I stand at the door and knock"; to open that mystic door of the human will in a spirit of utter humility and self-abandonment; and to feel the Divine breath moving from the centre of our subdued affections down through all our thoughts, down into the minutest ultimate activities of our sphere, subduing, rearranging, restoring all things a hundred-fold!—ah, my friend, THAT is the New Life.

In Him alone shall we find that life, who said and is forever saying unto us: "*Come unto me, all ye that labor and are heavy-laden, and I will give you rest.*"

Yours truly,

W. H. H.

# LETTER XIV.

*THE TERRORS OF THE NEW LIFE: SPIRITUAL TEMPTATIONS.*

MY DEAR FRIEND:—Have you never felt surprised at Swedenborg's statements, that there are temptations of three different discrete degrees, natural, spiritual, and celestial (A. C. 847)? that none can be tempted but those who are in celestial and spiritual good (A. C. 4299)? that our Lord's temptations by the angels were the deepest and hardest of all (A. C. 4295)? and that few in our times ever undergo anything like spiritual temptation, or even know what it is or what are its uses (A. C. 8965)?

It always seems to us that what we call our temptations are assaults upon our spiritual life. Is it possible that all the good people in Swedenborg's own day, the Catholic devotees, the Methodists, the Quietists, the Moravians, the Quakers, and others, who strenuously and painfully resisted the world, the flesh, and the devil, and kept the commandments amid great mental and bodily self-surrenders and tribulations—is it possible that these good souls were disturbed only by what Swedenborg calls natural anxieties, and knew nothing of the genuine struggle between good and evil, the result of which determines our final destiny? However that may be, one thing is certain, Swedenborg has taught some strange and deep things about temptation, never before known to the Christian world, and the most wonderful of which have perhaps never before been recognized or realized by his own most zealous and studious disciples. I have been indebted for my very imperfect knowledge of them, to the remarkable perceptions and experiences of my friend, G. W. C. You will first be very much astonished at what I am going to say; but you will very soon acknowledge it all as genuine truth.

G. W. C. was lately examining the photograph of a fine-looking, talented, and in every way excellent young New Churchman. He was one of those who had enjoyed the best ecclesiastical culture, and had kept the commandments from his youth up. He was bright, joyous, and sweet-tempered, loving everybody and deserving to be loved by all. He was full of worldly desires and ambitions, but they were all regulated by the strictest principles of honor, propriety, and justice. He was in fact a model young man, to whom parents, teachers, and pastors might point with pride and pleasure, as the perfect fruit of the best doctrinal and moral training. All this G. W. C. recognized in his psychometrical analysis; and then added, "but he has never had his interior hells opened in the least, and he has no knowledge whatever of the proprium, nor the faintest conception of the new life."

Now this young man had no doubt often resisted the infestations of evil spirits persuading him to break the commandments of God, and perhaps had often praised the Lord for protecting him in what he regarded as great and terrible temptations. And yet he has not the slightest idea of the meaning of spiritual temptations—from which he has been mercifully withheld, because his religious development has not advanced a step beyond the best models of Old-church or even of Jewish culture. He is the young man whom Jesus looked upon and loved on account of his orderly and beautiful external life. But he has no desire to be "perfect" in the sense in which Jesus used that word. He would be "exceedingly sorrowful" if he were required to give up his "great possessions"—to lay down the life of the proprium, and to follow the Lord alone through all the terrors and sufferings of regeneration.

It is perhaps necessary for the present stability and progress of society, that this man, and many like him, should be held in the external and useful activities of the suppressed proprium. But he cannot enter the kingdom of heaven, until, either here or in the world of spirits, he has put off all the external states of affection and thought which have engendered his present character and status; until he has been vastated of all his apparent goods and truths, and by infestations and genuine spiritual temptations has been brought in the inmost sphere of his affections to that duel to the death between good and evil, which terminates in the triumph of one or the other.

Now, my dear friend, in my opinion, you are as much like this estimable young gentleman as a woman can ever be said to be like a man. But your last letter assures me that you are advancing toward interior states, which would probably be premature and disastrous to him. I will quote a few paragraphs from that letter, which called forth an extraordinary declaration from G. W. C.

"I do fully see that there is nothing good, or true, or living in myself, and that all of life, or goodness, or truth is in the Lord. It is true, as you suggest, that this may be merely an intellectual apprehension, and not from the will. Yet it does not seem that despair would arise from any further revelation of my helplessness, for I know it is utter, and I look for no strength—nor of any evil, for I know as Swedenborg says 'from living experience' that there is no good in this selfhood of mine. I have had illusion after illusion destroyed by the bitterest suffering, until I know that even what seems noblest is a subtile form of self-love.

"I perceive plainly the immense power that the desire of being well thought of, the love of praise and fear of disapproval, have had over me; and these motives are still perhaps as strong; but I am not now blind to their worthlessness, or to the infinite distance between 'a living soul' and a character which inwardly is self-love and outwardly respectable.

"Instead of criticising your last letter, I would rather ask a question. How can one overcome or rather be freed from what Swedenborg calls 'infestations'—moods of darkness, evil desires, false thoughts, hideous fantasies, profane suggestions, which you do not feel tempted by, for you utterly abhor them, and yet you are to a degree overpowered by their oppression and presence?

"I do not feel that they could destroy the life of my soul, for that is solely from the Lord, and cannot be even assailed by them; but such states are very painful."

Alas! my dear friend, the states which next await you will be far more painful and even intolerable. G. W. C., on reading the above extracts from your letter, said to this effect: "She is still merely in external temptations. All these things —evil desires, profane suggestions, hideous fantasies, etc., are still objective to her, things outside of her, with which she thinks she has no vital connection, and which she seemingly resists, condemns, and abhors. But as her external states recede and she comes consciously into her own internal life, the case will be reversed. She will feel the evil desires, profane suggestions, false thoughts, etc., etc., as subjective things, something inside of her, yea, her very self—her very life and love, to which she clings with the tenacity of self-preservation, and feels that she would utterly perish without them."

When a man is in this state, he is taken possession of by evil spirits who are used by the Lord to reveal to him the hells that are within him. But he feels the hell to be his own life. He is alive and boiling over with all infernal passions and desires. Truth has apparently no power: he takes no interest in it: he may even deny it utterly. The Lord is far off—indeed, to all appearance, totally absent; and he has no feeling toward Him but disgust or hatred. Conscience seems extinguished; prayer is useless; and there is no trace of spiritual life about him, but a vague feeling that somehow or other it is necessary to keep the commandments. It is a wonder to him that he does not rush headlong into the commission of all sorts of evils; and yet he is restrained, for the Lord is then incredibly near him. None are admitted into these tribulations but those who have interior states of celestial and spiritual good, which are brought forth into view and ultimated only by this terrible struggle between the old and the new proprium, a last struggle not only for dominion but for life. Nor is a man released from these struggles until he thoroughly distrusts and abhors himself, and utterly despairs of salvation. In no other way, Swedenborg repeatedly declares, can the will-principle of the old proprium be thoroughly broken, and man reduced into those states of genuine humiliation, which are necessary to the new birth. Madam Guyon preceded Swedenborg in his knowledge of these things.

This state of vastation and temptation is meant by our Lord, when He says: *"Can the children of the bridechamber mourn so long as the bridegroom is with them? But the days will come when the bridegroom shall be taken from them, and then shall they fast."*—MATT. ix. 15. And the uses of this state are implied in the spiritual sense of the next two verses, which seem to have no connection in the letter with what has preceded. The use is, to enable us to divest ourselves utterly of our old garments, and to throw away the old bottles, so that we may receive new garments and new bottles for the entirely new wine of the spiritual life.

Now, my dear friend, all this is made clear by Swedenborg. You have, no doubt, read hundreds of passages in his writings which would have prepared you for their comprehension; but they made no permanent impression upon your mind. If you would know how feeble are the greatest temptations of the man of the Old Church in comparison with those that await the man of the New Church, study the following paragraphs:

"The nature of temptation is known to few, if any, because so few in the present day undergo temptations; and *those that do so, know no other than that there is something inherent in themselves that suffers.* On such occasions wicked spirits excite the remembrance of all the falsities and evils which a man has thought or done from infancy, and this in an indescribably cunning and malicious manner. The angels, however, who are attendant upon man, bring forth his goods and truths and thereby defend him; but opposition being felt and recognized by man, occasions remorse and the pangs of conscience.

"Temptation is of two kinds, one as to the understanding, and the other as to the will. When man is tempted as to the things of the understanding, then wicked spirits excite the evil actions of which he has been guilty, here signified by the 'unclean beasts,' and thus accuse and condemn him; and at the same time they call forth his good actions, represented by 'clean beasts,' which they pervert by a thousand devices; and also whatever has been the subject of his thoughts, denoted by the 'fowl'; and all that is here typified by 'every thing which creepeth upon the ground.'

"This temptation is slight, and is perceived only by the

recollection of these things and by a certain anxiety thence proceeding—[all this, we may interpolate, being familiar to the spiritual experiences of the old church]; but when man is tempted as to the things of the will, then what he has done and thought is not so much excited, but evil genii (for by that name may evil spirits of this kind be called) *inflame him with such of their own desires and filthy lusts as he is tainted with*, and thus carry on the combat by man's own cupidity. This they effect in so malicious and clandestine a manner, that it is impossible to suppose them its agents; for *they infuse themselves into the life of his impure affections*, and in the same instant turn and bend the affection for good and truth into the love of evil and the false, so that *man cannot possibly know but that it is done of himself*, and thus flows in of its own accord. This temptation, of which more will be said hereafter, is *most grievous, and is perceived as internal agony and tormenting fire*. Multiplied experience [mark this!] has assured me of the correctness of this description, and has also informed me of the period when this influx or inundation from the evil spirits or genii takes place, as well as of its origin, nature, or mode of operation."—A. C. 751.

These interior temptations, in which a man is made subjectively conscious of the hell of the proprium, can only come to him after he has been baptized into the truth and had the heavens opened to him; after he has felt the influx of the dove of peace and heard the divine voice of approval within him. These are preparations for the great combat which is impending. For after these things had happened to our Lord, it is added: "*And immediately the spirit driveth him into the wilderness, and he was there in the wilderness forty days, tempted of Satan; and he was with the wild beasts.*" And it is only by a study of the Psalms from the standpoint of a knowledge of spiritual temptations, that we can get any clear conception of the stupendous meanings involved in the wailings, humiliations, agonies, and despairs, which characterize those mystical utterances of the Lord.

The temptations of the man of the Old Church, and our own so far as we are still only in the life of that church (as almost all of us are), are purely objective; and their uses are, to dissipate the sensuous blindness of the natural man, to make us know our wretched and lost condition, to distinguish between good and evil, between the false and the true, and to induce us to compel ourselves to a life of obedience from the love of truth. It is a fight against forces and persons outside of ourselves, and our resistance and conquest has a tendency to beget the pride of self-merit and the complacency of self-righteousness, notwithstanding all intellectual disclaimers to the contrary. It is a case of suppressed proprium. It is the government of truth, not of love; a life regulated by the cognitions of the intellect, and not by the spontaneous evolutions of a heavenly will.

This spontaneous evolution of a heavenly will—the true life awaiting the New Church—can only be attained by the total subjugation and separation of the old will-principle from the man. It is a purely subjective work—requiring no ecclesiastical machinery, but is effected immediately by the Lord alone. The man is made conscious of the hell in which he lives, of the hell which he is, not by mere cognitions of truths, but by actual, organic perceptions of states. He suffers the spheres of evil spirits and the pains of hell, until he abhors and loathes himself, and sinks into absolute humiliation and despair. When the contest is over, and the old selfhood is separated and the new proprium is born, the man is entirely a new creature, something entirely different from his old self. He is "meek and lowly of heart," appropriating neither good nor evil to himself, having no will not coincident with the Lord's will, taking no thought for the morrow, and desiring no life but that into which the Lord shall lead him.

This man is now capable of manifesting in his life the traits which Swedenborg says are characteristic of the heavenly nature.

"In heaven they are the greatest who are the least: they are the wisest who believe and perceive themselves to be least wise: they are the happiest who desire others to be most happy, and themselves least so. Heaven consists in desiring to be beneath all, as hell consists in desiring to be above all: consequently, in the glory of heaven there is nothing at all of the glory of this world."—A. C. 2654.

When this "tabernacle of God"—this New Church celestial, is erected in the midst of the temple in the holy city, and fully established upon earth, it will be a fixed gateway between the Divine and nature. Then our Lord descending through the new proprium, and working from centres to circumferences, will effect changes in the earths, the heavens, and the hells, of which we have hitherto had scarcely the faintest conception.

For this final and universal coming of the Lord, let us all pray, "*Even so come, Lord Jesus.*"

Yours truly,<br>W. H. H.

# LETTER XV.

### THE CELESTIAL MAN AGAIN.

MY DEAR SIR:—Your letter gives me great pleasure. You are young in the New Church, and yet you appreciate and enjoy enunciations upon spiritual subjects which are considered by many as strong meat for men and not milk for babes. The reason is, that you are in states of more or less clear perception of truth. I have met, to my astonishment, people who have never known anything about Swedenborg, who can see and believe the truths I have presented more readily than many of those who have been long versed in the doctrines of the Church. And of professed Newchurchmen, "not many wise men after the flesh, not many mighty, not many noble," have accepted these things, but the obscure, the lowly, the penitent, the babes and sucklings, the women who "keep silence with all subjection," etc.; all of which proves that they are truths of the Lord's celestial kingdom.

You ask me whether the celestial man will resist impositions, go to law, defend his rights of person and property, etc. So far as a man is in natural, rational, or spiritual states, he does these things, working of himself, or as of himself, from standpoints of interest, reason, duty, and conscience. He is permitted to do so, he is justified in doing so, by the laws of moral and civil right and justice. But the celestial man has passed through these states and "remembers them no more." He does not act from a sense of right, justice, and reason, or from duty and conscience, but from the standpoints of love alone. He has ceased to resist and to combat. The Lord's life is so organically established in him, that he lives exactly as the Lord would live, if He were re-incarnated in his body and under his conditions. He may withdraw himself, he may conceal himself, he may answer them nothing; but he will endure all things, forgive all things; and he will never, never act from a regard to his own rights and interests, but always with a view of doing the utmost good to the neighbor.

Some might suppose that such a character is impossible under the conditions of this world, and that he would be trodden under foot of men. This is not so. The very nature of this celestial man has a tendency to preserve him from the enmity and the infestations of his fellows. He always gives the soft answer that turneth away wrath. He never makes himself obnoxious by his pretensions. He infringes upon no one's rights, he hurts no one's feelings, he stands in no one's way. His sweet, gentle, unobtrusive sphere calls forth the remains of good and truth in all who come into contact with him. The hells interiorly flee at his coming, and he stands amid the evil forms of society like a child among wicked men, who instinctively soften their words and restrain their conduct in his presence.

Moreover the man who has spared himself no sacrifice or suffering in getting rid of the old proprium, finds himself walking more and more securely within the personal, protective atmospheres of the Lord. After all said and done by infidels, agnostics, and lukewarm Christians, the Lord *does* govern this world by his special providences down to the minutest particulars of every man's life. The celestial man believes this, knows it, feels it, and acts accordingly. He fears no evil, he takes no thought for the morrow. He says always to himself, "Except the Lord build the house, they labor in vain that build it." And the consequence is, that he is continually under the direct leading of the Lord, moving in the current of spontaneous obedience to divine law, his ways being protected by invisible cherubim, and made smooth and happy by unobserved and unrecorded miracles.

"*Because thou hast made the Lord, my refuge, the most High, thy habitation:*

"*There shall no evil befall thee, neither shall any plague come nigh thy dwelling;*

"*For He shall give his angels charge over thee, to keep thee in all thy ways.*

"*They shall bear thee up in their hands, lest thou dash thy foot against a stone.*

"*Thou shalt tread upon the lion and the adder; the young lion and the dragon shalt thou trample under feet.*

"*Because he hath set his love upon me, therefore will I deliver him: I will set him on high, because he hath known my name.*"—PSALMS xci. 9–14.

It is entirely useless to lay down rules for the government of the celestial man. He is a law unto himself, because the law of the Lord is written upon his heart, and he knows of the doctrine because he does the will of his Maker. Nor can natural and spiritual men become celestial men by compelling themselves to obey the laws of the celestial life. This was the supreme mistake of the Quakers. A man should not strive to be anything, or to attain to any particular degree. The ambition to be good must give way to the simple and earnest desire to be the Lord's. He alone knows our organic forms, our uses, our destinies. Let us shun all evils as sins against Him. Let us do whatever our hands may find to do, as the exact thing provided and sent by Him for us to do. Then whatever organic openings of the interior may take place in us, will be made in an orderly and heavenly manner by the Lord alone; and He will introduce us into the degree and states of life, in which we can render the greatest service to the neighbor.

Yours truly,<br>W. H. H.

# LETTER XVI.

*THE DESCENT OF THE LORD THROUGH THE CONJUGIAL SPHERE.*

MY DEAR FRIEND:—I am glad that you have been so deeply impressed with our views of the *organic nature* of the Second Coming of the Lord. Spiritual illumination through Swedenborg is but one element of his coming. Divine Truth is substance and form, and in this new age it brings the personal atmospheres of the Divine Man. The Lord is entering the Body of Humanity by the opening of all the discrete degrees of the mind; and He comes to abide, and to reduce the natural plane into perfect correspondence with the heavens.

Our LORD descended and manifested Himself to men in ancient times through the persons of angels infilled with his glory. He descended and took representative but organic foothold in the world through the lives of Abraham, Isaac, Jacob, and Joseph, a wonderful manifestation but little studied or comprehended by the church. He descended representatively through the ritual, laws, and history of the Jewish people. He gave those ultimates fixity and perpetuity in the literal sense of the written Word. He descended into the physical and atomic ultimates of nature and the natural plane of the human mind, by assuming the external form and limitations of humanity. By opening the spiritual degree of the mind of Swedenborg, He has descended as the spiritual sense of the Word, or the Divine Truth. His last and perfect manifestation, the crown of all the rest, will be as the Divine Love. It will be effected by the continuous opening of the celestial degree, and He will come as the Bridegroom, entering into the conjugial principle, and planting Himself in the married things of the mind, and thence operating to bring all essences and forms, all persons and things into those marriage relations, which will constitute the life of the New Church, and the sabbath of the world.

What stupendous processes, what amazing phenomena, what organic and radical revolutions, are involved in this Divine movement from primates to ultimates! By how many names will it be called, how many totally different appearances will it put on, how many mistakes will be made, what errors, fantasies, imperfect developments, and false claims will arise, what domestic and social and national commotions, etc., etc.! All this will be in accordance with organic law, because the divine influx must enter into the existing forms of the human mind, and its manifestations *must* be according to the states and receptivities of the forms into which it flows.

The greatest, profoundest, and most radical revolutions will of course occur in the relations between man and woman. A friend once sneeringly said to me, that there was always a woman at the bottom of all the spiritualism in the New Church. How could it be otherwise? Every man is in reality a woman-man and every woman is a man-woman ; and our search for our spiritual counterparts is only the spontaneous, inevitable, irrepressible effort of our souls to understand themselves, or to realize our own being. Our reaching out after that perfect ideal marriage which is synonymous with love, peace, joy, heaven, is caused by the divine movement **or** *conatus* that flows forth for the creation and sustentation of the life, order, beauty, and glory of the universe.

The heavenly marriage, which is heaven in us, is from the divine good that is *in* the Lord and the divine truth which is *from* Him. Thence proceed first of all conjugial love and the love of children; and he who is in conjugial love is in all the other loves, and in all the delights and uses of heaven. Therefore the organic pathway of the Lord, in his descent from primates to ultimates, must be through the conjugial principle in whatever forms it has been planted in the human mind. Given a single conjugial pair on earth, who are truly regenerate and in the heavenly marriage, whose propriums have not been merely suppressed and concealed, but actually subjugated and removed, who are in the new life and in a state of conjugial union or unitized sex; and the Lord has found an open door by which He can enter, and a fulcrum or centre from which He can operate on every human being in the world, and even upon the atomic elements of nature. A few hundred such *organic bases* would aid more powerfully in the descent of the New Jerusalem out of heaven, than all the churches in Christendom, even though they preached Swedenborg from every pulpit.

What special phenomena will be produced by the descent of the Lord into the conjugial principle, can only be surmised from general truths and their bearings. The phenomena must be unfolded or evolved, a process of which we only see the faint beginnings, before they can be studied or rationally comprehended. We know that the phenomena will be infinitely varied, and that they will be of two great classes, the good and the evil; for the Lord's life received and appropriated according to his divine will, makes all the phenomena of heaven ; and his life received and perverted to selfish ends, makes all the phenomena of hell. And so will it be when, by the opening of the interiors, the heavens and hells within us are unfolded upon the earth.

There will be a gradual but ever-increasing development of the regenerate life in the church, a marriage of the spiritual truths of the Word already revealed to us, and the celestial goods which are now descending from heaven. More and more conjugial marriages will take place, and the conjugial love will become more and more potent in the practical affairs of life. Man and woman will live together and *work* together more and more as one person.

The love and care of children will grow more and more ardent and delightful; and as a consequence all domestic and social virtues will increase, and the life of man be more and more dominated by the love of use, and brightened with the wisdom and sweetened with the charities of heaven. There will be openings of the interior senses, temptations and vastations such as have never been experienced before, consciousness of conjugial union, beginnings of internal respiration, great illuminations of the rational principle, states of perception whence come heavenly wisdom and peace, and various communications with spirits and angels, not as ends or things to be desired of themselves, but as inevitable, organic accompaniments and preparations attending those tremendous radical changes of state which will be induced in the most gradual and orderly manner upon the whole human race.

On the other hand, and by the operation of the same laws upon the evil, there will be a fearful increase of sensuality in all its forms, a growth of adulterous and bestial passion, destruction of unborn children, neglect of marital and parental duties, and diabolical efforts made for the freedom of divorce, the abolition of marriage, and the destruction of all religion. This class also will have its spiritual manifestations, its play of sexual affinities simulating conjugial love, its assumptions, assertions, and aggressions, and its organized fantasies which it will call philosophic wisdom, all tending however to the deification of self and nature.

There would be chaos upon earth if this opening of the interiors were to occur suddenly and extensively throughout the race. For the proprium of the natural man is born into and lives in the hells of adultery, drunkenness, and gambling, with all their attendant fantasies and insanities. Our closed conditions simply conceal our real natures from ourselves and others. The angels have the same essential nature in themselves, but they live consciously in the new proprium, the new life derived from the Lord, which perpetually withholds them, with their own consent, from their inherent life. Such will be the case with regenerate men on earth in the coming New Church. Such, however, are the dangers and difficulties of the opening, that it will be effected at first by a little here and a little there, and by innumerable preparations, warnings, and instructions, to prevent delusions, self-exaltations, and profanations.

What is the cause of this terrible danger in having our spiritual senses and perceptions opened? It lies in the fact that our whole interior life is cast in the mold of all the accumulated evils and falsities of past generations. The proprium enters into everything and bends it to its own gratification and advantage. It wants to be fed constantly on sugar-plums, and resists everything which exposes its character and threatens its subjugation as the consummation of the evil and the false. Actuated by proprium and deceived by cunning spirits who assume the most heavenly appearances of goodness and truth, every man and every woman would feel themselves mismated, and their search for conjugial partners would terminate in an unbridled lust of varieties. Those who are early let into these new experiences, will have great temptation to imagine that they are favored instruments of heaven, far advanced in spiritual purification, and to assume oracular and authoritative tones to those who are less receptive of divine influx. The possibilities of fantasy and delusion are here infinite.

It is a possible thing for a man of really innocent and celestial character, especially if he be in the persuasive faith of the Old Church, to become obsessed by wicked and adulterous spirits, who assume the celestial so as to infuse into him all the delightful sensations of the conjugial sphere, even conveying a fixed impression that the Lord Himself is present directing the phenomena. If not expelled, such spirits will lead the man with the utmost subtlety into spiritual adulteries, and finally into the lust of varieties, and so ultimate their hells upon earth. Such a state is the more dreadful, because the man *cannot be made to see his real condition;* for his will-principle is obsessed, and he is compelled to think only that is true which corresponds to it. His proprium will utterly refuse to surrender its gratifications, but will justify them in the subtlest and most cunning manner, calling Swedenborg and the Word itself to its support.

The impending progressive opening of the interiors, which is inevitable and necessary, no matter how dangerous and destructive it may be, will be exceedingly dangerous to those who are *confirmed* in the interior evils and falsities of the Old Church, in which indeed a great many of our own people are involved far more deeply than they imagine. The divine mercy will no doubt hold this class fast in closed conditions, until the genuine New Jerusalem has been pretty well established upon the earth through other centres, so that they will come last into the light of the new life, without having their will-principle broken or their free agency infringed upon. The openings will be far less dangerous to the Gentiles, and to that unbelieving gentile Christendom which lies all about us; for in states of ignorance or denial the truths which are not accepted cannot be profaned. They will be least dangerous to those who are armed with the knowledges of spiritual things to be derived from Swedenborg; and they will not be dangerous at all to those Newchurchmen who are consciously in the body of the Lord, who abstain from evils as sins against Him, who cultivate the conjugial love as the centre of divine influx into the soul, and who look to the Divine Humanity, and not to angels, spirits, or men, for constant guidance and support.

Such, my dear sir, are some of the most general truths concerning the descent of the Lord through the conjugial sphere into the spiritual truths of the Word, and thence into the ultimates of the natural plane, for the establishment of his New Church upon earth, in which his will shall be universally and organically done even as it is in heaven.

There is but one sure ground of right and safety in the tremendous difficulties into which the opening of the interiors will plunge us; and that is this: the external institution of marriage between one man and one woman must be preserved in all its legal and social vitality, at all hazards, under all circumstances, and at all temporal and spiritual sacrifices, until death shall separate the parties. From the celestial standpoint no ground of divorce is admissible, not even adultery.* That is a spiritual permission according to the law of truth; but the law of love demands something different. The celestial man bears every wrong, seeking no redress; he loves without demanding to be loved in return; he forgives totally, infinitely, and forever; and, bearing the sorrows of separation in his own bosom, he clings with the utmost tenacity to the ultimate forms of union.

The reason of this conduct on the part of the celestial man, (and remember that the Lord's New Church is to be a celestial man,) is this: he does not only regard the monogamical marriage from the spiritual standpoint as an ideal representative of goodness and truth, and of the union of the Lord with his church, but he also realizes in all the sensories of his body, that it is the *central organic basis* upon which the heavens rest and into which they flow; an objective creation as vital and as necessary as the sun, perpetually kept in existence by the influx of the Divine life; an ultimate correspondential form, more potent than all the laws and rituals of the Jewish church, on the stability and purity of which the peace, order, and happiness of the heavens and the earth depend.

This transcendent view of the matter is involved in the interior senses of those wonderful words of our Lord found in Matt. xix. 4-6:

---

* The reader must not understand from this, that the author means to teach that the Lord's permission (Matt. v. 32—"saving for the cause," etc.) is now revoked. It is still granted to such as are not in a state to accept or see what he regards as the highest or celestial truth on this subject.

"*Have ye not read, that He who made them at the beginning, made them male and female,*

"*And said: For this cause shall a man leave father and mother, and shall cleave to his wife; and they twain shall be one flesh?*

"*Therefore they are no more twain, but one flesh. What therefore God hath joined together, let no man put asunder.*"

Marriage is not institutionally sacred like baptism and the holy supper, on account of its spiritual correspondence or its representative character; but it is *organically sacred* from the beginning of the creation, being the first and supreme avenue by which the Divine life enters into the race. Therefore the religious life of the world, or the interior states of mankind as to goodness and truth, depends upon the condition of the marriage relation. Its external forms are like the forms of the letter of the Word, being the ultimate basis and containant into which all interior and superior things flow, and in which their fixity, security, and perpetuity are maintained.

No good spirit or angel will therefore ever flow into a man to dissatisfy him with his married state, or to induce acquiescence in the affections and thoughts of the old proprium on the subject. On the contrary they will always inculcate submission and resignation, however lamentable the state of the married partners may be. They will teach and help both male and female to bear their crosses with faith and hope. So long as the external forms are maintained, the angels can flow in and assist in the great work of regeneration, by combating the evil spirits who assault us. But when the external bonds are sundered, both parties are in danger of falling deeper into the adulterous hells of the proprium, farther and farther from the reach of heavenly influences. "The blood of the martyrs is the seed of the church." The martyrs of the early New Church will be those who withstand the subtlest allurements of the proprium, and refuse to build their castle of spiritual happiness on any other foundation than the resolutely fulfilled obligations of external duty and honor.

Yours fraternally,
W. H. H.

# LETTER XVII.

*DIVORCE, FROM THE STAND-POINT OF THE CELESTIAL CHURCH.*

MY DEAR MADAM:—Your letter in relation to divorce, was written (unconsciously perhaps to yourself) from the sphere of that great modern movement (including woman's rights, socialism, and a thousand other things), which would emancipate us from all irrational or disagreeable usages of church and state, and give us the largest amount of individual liberty. It was the voice of woman *separate from man*, asserting her claim to the means of separate individual happiness and development. Whilst there is a great deal of good in this movement—the necessary destructions which prepare the way for a new order of things—there is also a great deal of evil.

I will answer your questions seriatim.

"Has God joined together those who ignorantly marry for worldly reasons, or for baser motives?"

Certainly. God has *joined* them together, because they have voluntarily entered into the forms of his external law of marriage, and assumed its responsibilities "for better or worse." Junction, however, or adjunction, is not *conjunction;* and the external bond of marriage is the organic basis or containant in which two souls merely *adjoined* at first, may become by spiritual processes more and more *conjoined* to eternity. Our personal feelings and interests which all arise from the proprium, have nothing to do either before or after marriage with the sanctity and perpetuity of its external forms which God has established as the orderly organic basis for the perpetuation of the race, the preservation of society, and the regeneration of the individual.

"If the woman so married grows to desire a purer and higher life, does not companionship with one whose desires and life grow continually baser, tend to drag her spiritually downward?"

No: it does not. It simply opens a field, or presents opportunities, for her higher spiritual development. Under such conditions she is placed, within the protective influences of God's external law, in a position to combat and conquer the deepest hells. During this terrible ordeal of self-sacrifice and martyrdom, she not only develops the celestial life in herself, but renders the salvation of the recreant husband more and more probable and possible, and stands as a mighty barrier against the influx of the adulterous hells into general society. I hold in my memory two cases of extraordinary character, and I have no doubt there are thousands of others in the sacred but unrecorded history of wifely heroisms. One husband was the most brutal drunkard I have almost ever known; the other, an adulterer of the worst grade and under peculiarly aggravating circumstances. Not one woman in a thousand would have endured for a month, what these two heavenly women, wives of these men, endured for nearly twenty years. With infinite patience, perseverance, forbearance, and forgiveness, they discharged their own personal, social, and religious duties, until both of these men were permanently reformed, and became good, faithful, and affectionate husbands.

The fallacy which underlies all these pleas or apologies for divorce, is this: they inculcate the idea that by the mere *change of surroundings* we may *change our own spiritual states.* This is an appearance and not a reality. Change of surroundings can only *suppress* for a time the manifestation of our true spiritual condition. Our spiritual states are only really changed for the better, *by the unfolding of the Lord within us from centres to circumferences.* O, the world of meaning which is involved in that idea! External surroundings which enable us to manifest the humility, patience, forgiveness, and self-annihilation of our Lord, are not to be deprecated and abandoned, as abhorrent and painful, but to be clung to with the utmost tenacity. This doctrine is given to the saints and martyrs who *ought* to constitute the entire population of the Christian Church.

You then suppose an extreme case of wrong and suffering, inheritance of terrible diseases, demoralization and corruption of children, etc., etc. Surely these are good reasons for divorce? No: cries the voice of celestial love through the trumpet of spiritual truth. No: these cases and conditions are all met by reference to the *laws of separation* and living apart without divorce, each case standing on its individual merits, and the mode, time, and extent of separation being determined and modified by all the circumstances of the case. Thus *separation*, temporary or permanent, partial or complete, may be made to satisfy all the demands of wounded honor or sensitive duty, without resorting to the extreme measure of shattering the organic vessel, external marriage, into which the conjugial life of the heavens flows.

"I am strongly inclined," you say, "to believe that as we repudiate a false Church, so must we repudiate false personal relations."

The laws of external marriage, even in their personal relations, are never false, because God has ordained them. Parties, through ignorance or otherwise, may transgress, override, or repudiate the law, in which event *they become false to the law,* and incur its penalties. The law, however, always remains true to them; and all, at any time, after the most flagrant transgressions, may claim its spiritual protection by a return to a life of obedience to its requirements.

We are permitted, in the exercise of our own rationality, to judge as to the truth or falsity of the claims of a church; for Christ ordained no form for an external church, and we are at liberty to accept or repudiate any forms claiming to be churches. We have no such rational option given us in relation to the institution of external marriage, because it is as organic, sacred, and eternal as the heavens which rest upon it and flow through it.

Hear what our Lord says:

*"From the beginning of the creation, God made them male and female.*

*"For this cause shall a man leave father and mother, and cleave to his wife;*

*"And they twain shall be one flesh: so that they are no more twain but one flesh.*

*"What therefore God hath joined together, let no man put asunder."*—MARK x. 6-9.

Hear also what Paul says:

*"Unto the married, I command, yet not I, but the Lord: Let not the wife depart from her husband:*

*"But and if she depart, let her remain unmarried, or be reconciled to her husband, and let not the husband put away his wife."*—1 COR. vii. 10, 11.

We must not judge of the value of the external bonds of

marriage, from the poor results obtained at present among men. Those bonds are holy and indissoluble on account of their divine possibilities—on account of the end in view in the Divine Mind. They make it possible for a male to be transformed into a husband; for a female to be transformed into a wife; and for two souls to become one blended form of wisdom and love from centre to circumference. The stupendous process may go on, and ought to go on, from the beginning even to perfect unitization of sex, when both make one angel in the image of God. When it is accomplished, it is folly to suppose that two such souls could ever be sundered by man or devil. It is only *in the beginning and during the process* that separation is possible; and to prevent it under all conditions, the law is given, "What God hath joined together, let no man put asunder."

But with earnestness of feeling and apparent cogency of reason you go still further. "Can the conjugial life of God flow into an inverted form of conjugial love? The Lord granted divorce for adultery, because that act, I suppose, broke the actual spiritual bond, and left no form into which the true conjugial life could flow; and a mere sham relation could be no foundation for spiritual substance."

Now, the conjugial life of God flows always into the external forms of marriage, which must be conceived of separately from the parties who have entered into those forms. The forms of the Holy Supper are not perverted and rendered useless, because individuals partake of it unworthily, and eat and drink damnation to themselves. So a man may enter into the external relations of marriage, and fail to accept its organic opportunities of spiritual development; but nothing he can do can pervert or destroy the institution which is something outside of himself, and in which his married partner may go on growing in the grace and power of conjugial love without an iota of his co-operation, and, indeed, it may be for another husband. This is plainly taught by Swedenborg.

"Love truly conjugial may exist with *one* of the married partners and not at the same time with the other. One may from the heart devote himself to chaste marriage, while the other knows not what the chaste marriage is: one may love the things of the church whilst the other loves the things of the world alone: as to their minds, one may be in *heaven* and the other in *hell:* hence there may be conjugial love with one and not with the other."—C. L. 226.

Now, my dear friend, you must be mistaken in supposing that our Lord permitted divorce because adultery on one side destroys the internal bonds of marriage, so that the spiritual life of the other party is imperiled if she maintain the external relation. Do you not think the Lord would have *commanded divorce for adultery in the most imperative manner*, if the suffering and antagonism induced were really and of necessity destructive to the spiritual life of the innocent party? Moses allowed the Jews to put away their wives for many reasons, of which adultery was one, on account of the hardness of their hearts. Our Lord limits the cause for divorce to adultery alone; but it still remained a *permission* and not a *command*. When He says: "Whosoever shall marry her that is divorced committeth adultery," does it not imply that a divorced woman is still, interiorly speaking, indissolubly connected with her first husband?

"What is the use," you say, "of maintaining an external relation, when all the internal affections and thoughts are entirely alienated?"

Swedenborg fully answers this question also.

"In case of matrimony in which the internal affections *do not conjoin*, there are external affections which *assume a semblance of the internal*, and tend to consociate."—C. L. 277.

"*Assumed conjugial semblances* in the case of a spiritual man conjoined to a natural, are founded in justice and judgment. The reason of this is, that the spiritual man (or spiritual woman) acts in all things from justice and judgment. Therefore he does not regard *these assumed semblances as alienated from their internal affections, but as connected with them;* for he is in earnest, and respects *amendment as an end.*"—C. L. 280.

All this plainly means, that so long as utterly uncongenial married partners respect and maintain the external bonds of marriage, and assume an outward semblance of unity and duty, they are subject to spiritual influxes which may lead to amendment, reconciliation, and even final and perfect union. Only within the external bonds of marriage is there any hope, or safety, or promise of the conjugial life. Nor does a man break these bonds by adultery or any other wicked conduct. He may break his marriage vows, but the external invisible bonds of marriage hold him to his wife until they are sundered by death or legal enactment. The former is God's method, the latter is man's. Within their protective limits there is always a hope that the believing wife may save and sanctify the unbelieving husband, and *vice versâ*. (1 COR. vii. 14-16.)

Even well-informed New-Church people seem often not to have grasped the idea of the genuine and rational *uses* of the institution of marriage. They demand that it shall be, *in the beginning and all the way through*, what it was only expected or designed to be in the end—a perfect thing, its internal and external life and forms being always in beautiful and heavenly correspondence. They forget that it is a means to an end—an organic vessel for the insemination, growth, and perfection of the conjugial principle, which leads to the conjugial love, and that to the conjugial marriage which has seldom or perhaps never been fully attained upon earth. The imagination pictures her magnificent ideal, which is the reality of the future, but the soul is unhappy and desperate if it cannot realize it now and at once, and chafes under the slow and laborious process of converting stagnant marshes into orchards and gardens, and wild beasts into natural men, and natural men into husbands of the angelic type. Admitting that all marriages are imperfect, and most of them miserable in one way or other, yet the institution of marriage, holding within its golden bonds the most chaotic materials, has ever been the greatest conservator, civilizer, and spiritualizer of men and nations. When perfected, marriage will be heaven, with the Lord as its life.

The conjugial principle is implanted in every man from birth among the celestial remains of infancy. It is manifested first *in time*, through all the gross and unreceptive media of the natural mind, as *the love of the sex*. When some woman, mirroring her little finite share of the divine perfections, fires the imagination and heart of a man, the conjugial principle is awakened or vivified in him and comes downward and forward, and manifests itself as the wonderful and mysterious passion of love. The conjugial principle, says Swedenborg, is *the desire for marriage with one woman only*. The conjugial love is thus implanted in the mind, and the vague love of the sex becomes the chaste love of one of the sex. This conjugial love grows stronger and stronger between the parties, through mutual joys and sorrows, sufferings and trials, forbearances and forgivenesses. Under these influences, the conjugial marriage, keeping step always with the progress of spiritual regeneration, becomes possible. Beginning feebly and faintly on earth, it is perfected in heaven, where Swedenborg says of it, in a free translation:

"There exist in the heavens conjugial pairs who are in such a state of conjugial love, that the two may be one flesh, and also are actually so whenever they will it; and then they appear as a single man," (unus homo).—A. E. 1004.

This is a state which my friend G. W. C. calls unitization of sex, and which Swedenborg calls conjugial unition. This perfected state and all the intermediate states rest upon the external institution of marriage as their proper organic ultimate basis and containant. Within the protective limits of that ultimate, men and women are open, therefore, under proper conditions, to influxes from all the heavens. Outside of those limits we are remanded again to the sphere of animal life and the mere love of the sex. Divorce must therefore under all circumstances be a retrograde movement of the spiritual life. A second marriage does not restore the golden opportunities of the first, and open the heavens again; for so long as the first partner lives, there will be the faint odor of an adulterous taint about it, which must repel the sensitive life of the celestial sphere. This is for those who can receive it.

When our Lord gives the permission of divorce on account of adultery, He is conversing about the laws of Moses, and is speaking from the stand-point of spiritual truth. It is the office of truth to judge, and if necessary, to condemn; and divorce is the work of condemnation, for it rejects, casts off, and cuts loose from all hope. When, however, He forgives the adulteress, He speaks from the celestial sphere, and soon afterward says: "Ye judge after the flesh: I judge no man." The celestial never judges or condemns. Being joined with its corresponding truth, its life is the life of forgiveness and up-building salvation. It is in the sabbath state, is utterly dead to self, surrenders everything to the welfare of others, and is ready always to assume the evils of others, like our Lord, and to suffer with them and for them, actually preferring to live in hell *with the Lord*, if thereby it could mitigate one pang of human misery. And in many of our domestic hells, opening into the hells of the spiritual world, there are men and women of the celestial type, bearing the evils of others and looking to the Lord alone for strength and victory.

In the New Church celestial now being ushered into the world, there will be no divorces, or second marriages, or domestic infelicities. The men will be wise, the women beautiful, the children perfect. Riches, power, distinction, pleasure will weigh with them no more than the dust in the balance. From the least to the greatest of them they shall know the Lord. This great and notable day of the Lord, which theologians put so far off that few people think of its coming, is close at hand. To those who are disheartened and appalled at the apparent state of the church, who doubt whether the great Red Sea of human passion can be stayed in its course, and who tremble lest the Egyptians of sensualistic science shall overwhelm the religious life of the race, we say:

"*Fear ye not: stand still, and see the salvation of the Lord, which He will show you to-day: for the Egyptians whom ye* have seen to-day, ye shall see them no more again forever."— EXODUS xiv. 13.

Now what is the ground of the opposition which men and women, even in the New Church, will raise to the principles laid down in this letter? Is it from a more comprehensive survey of New-Church truth? from a clearer perception of the meaning of the Word? from a deeper love for the neighbor? from a profounder yearning after the new life? from a more thorough annihilation of self? from a more perfect following after the Lord? Or is it not the voice of the old proprium, with its wounded sensibilities, disappointed hopes, outraged feelings, trampled rights, and selfish interests, crying out for liberty and satisfaction, and a new state, in which its own desires can be gratified, and its own individual development be permanently secured? The natural man rejects the celestial truths now enunciated, because he does not wish to know them, nor to be brought into judgment by them; and because he *measures all good* by the exaltations and gratifications of his own proprium.

For the unhappy men and women so cruelly mated, whose cause you have so eloquently pleaded, there is one source of consolation, and the only true source never to be taken from them. It is this:

"*Come unto me, all ye that labor and are heavy laden, and I will give you rest.*

"*Take my yoke upon you, and learn of me: for I am meek and lowly in heart: and ye shall find rest unto your souls.*

"*For my yoke is easy, and my burden is light.*"—MATT. xi. 28–30.

Praying that we may all be found among the "meek and lowly in heart," I remain,

Yours truly,     W. H. H.

## LETTER XVIII.

*OBJECTIONS ANSWERED.*

DEAR FRIEND:—When I wrote the letter entitled "Divorce, from the Stand-point of the Celestial Church," my friend G. W. C. remarked: "The feminine mind of the New Church, with its intuitive perception of truth, will accept your views more or less fully according to the states of the individual. The average masculine mind of the Church will hold them at arm's length, criticise them severely, pile objection upon objection, and be satisfied with difficulty." His prediction has been verified.

My lady correspondents have encouraged my heart and strengthened my hands in the contest of interior truth against exterior appearances, as Aaron and Hur held up the hands of Moses in the wilderness. One of these calls the truths I have presented "pure water from the river of life," and declares she has no words to express her realization of their "holy depth and usefulness." Another rejoices in these timely utterances, and especially that the *N. J. Messenger* gave them, in their fundamental points, such earnest and emphatic approval. A third, indorsing all I wrote, thanks me in the most eloquent terms for the article as the genuine antidote to the poison of the Woman's Rights idea. Those who have suffered most from unhappy marriages, are the warmest in their approbation of my position. Even a divorced lady, great and innocent sufferer as she is, perceives the radiance of celestial truth in the article, and declares: "If I had read that article a year ago, I would have weighed the matter another fifteen years before I would have applied for a divorce."

Now for some of the objections from the masculine side, which you have presented.

Your first position is, that the celestial man has nothing to do with the matter and nothing to say on the subject. Being organically builded into the heavenly marriage, where divorce is not only impossible but inconceivable, the celestial man, you think, will remand all questions of violated laws as to the sexual relations, to the spiritual and natural men, who are in states of humanity less mature and developed than his own. This would be true if the celestial man whom *we* are thinking and writing about, were an angel of the third or celestial heaven, existing in a discrete degree above and within our natural sphere, and communicating with us only by influx and correspondence. That is not the celestial man we are practically interested in at present. We do not expect the celestial angels to descend and make their abode among men, and govern our affairs from their own stand-points; nor do we expect living human beings to be elevated above their own discrete degree, and live with the celestial angels. These things are simply impossible.

The three interior degrees of the mind, however, which are properly called celestial, spiritual, and rational, co-exist in the natural plane of our life, not in *discrete* but in *simultaneous* order. They are respectively opened and vivified according as men become, by faith and obedience, receptive of the life flowing from the heavens above them. The celestial-natural man of simultaneous order, does not propose to transform the earth into a third heaven, but is a medium through whom the celestial life of that heaven can flow down, transforming and becoming transformed, according to the states, exigencies, and evolutions of the natural degree.

The celestial life, not as it is in the third heaven, but as it becomes in the inmost degree of the natural mind when that degree is opened to the Lord, will be the vital principle of the church of the future—of that New Jerusalem which descends from God out of heaven. When conjoined organically with its corresponding spiritual life, or life from the Lord's spiritual kingdom and from the spiritual sense of the Word, the two will constitute the church, which, as Swedenborg says, is always the heart and lungs of the world. The perception of the celestial-natural man and the illumination of the spiritual-natural man, will always harmonize and correspond, just in proportion as the marriage of good and truth is effected in the spirit, and the union of charity and faith is established in the life. This church will be the supreme, central, impregnating, and vivifying power in the natural sphere—however feeble, immature, and unorganized it seems at present. Its opinions and conduct upon all questions, private, sexual, social, civil, and ecclesiastical, will be matters of supreme interest to mankind; and its perceptions in relation to marriage and divorce are, at the present juncture of human affairs, of special importance.

How far you seem from understanding or at least accepting the genuine New-Church idea of marriage, is evident from a single sentence in which you affirm that the legalized monogamical marriage of Christendom, is a mere permission of Divine Providence, like polygamy and concubinage, a mere accommodation to a little more advanced state of human development than is implied in the prevalence of the latter vices. You repudiate the idea so strongly presented by Swedenborg, that "the institution of monogamical marriage is founded upon the Word of the Lord," and that there is "a divine law inscribed upon marriages," which makes the preservation of their external forms imperative amid the most extreme internal dissimilitudes—nothing whatever but adultery being allowed as an excuse for dissolving the covenant before death. "Assumed external conjugial semblances," as expedients to preserve the marriage bond intact, are spoken of by Swedenborg as eminently right, just, and proper; because the external institution of marriage has something vital, sacred, and transcendently useful in it, irrespective of the similarities or dissimilarities of the parties entering into it (see C. L., especially 276–92).

It is easy to discover the source of your error. You have followed the line of the order of influx, instead of the line of the order of creation. Influx is from within outward and from above downward; creation moves oppositely, from exteriors to interiors, from lower forms to higher forms. Your conception of marriage begins where its uses are really perfected, and you therefore overlook its spiritual uses in its early stages. The external institution of marriage is the ultimate form, representative and correspondent of the heavenly marriage of goodness and truth. Hence its holiness and usefulness. The angelic pairs rest upon it and have power, *with us and for us*, through it. But man is not born into the heavenly marriage. He is born sensuo-corporeal, with only an animal's love of the sex. Within the bonds of the one indissoluble marriage, the man is transformed into a husband and the woman into a wife. From sensual we become rational, spiritual, celestial, growing upward and inward, through means appointed and vivified by the Lord; and these means are preëminently the Word, the church, and the institution of external monogamical marriage. These lead finally to that perfect form of spiritual unition—to God's marriage which no man can sunder; but that is only attainable by processes on the natural plane, which transform a man into a husband and a woman into a wife. It is for these magnificent truths, practically repudiated or ignored in your letter, that Swedenborg's teachings on this subject are so immeasurably in advance of all others.

The permissions by Divine Providence, of polygamy, concubinage, etc., etc., will be no doubt continued so long as they may be necessary in evil, false, and immature states of human society. The natural man will be permitted "to defend the chastity and honor of woman" in his own imperious way, even with bowie-knife and revolver; and the violence of his proprium may be very useful in repressing the influx of adulterous hells, or in restraining their manifestation, as duelling is said to be useful in suppressing the ill manners of a sensual and external people. But the institution of marriage is not a divine permission, but *a direct provision of the Divine Providence* for the protection, conservation, purification, and regeneration of human society. It is sacred like the letter of the Word, notwithstanding all contrary appearances, and however evilly and falsely it may be turned and perverted; and like the letter of the Word, it is a recipient vessel for all the potentialities of spiritual and celestial life.

How little, my dear friend, do you comprehend the character of the celestial man, or the descent of the celestial church! The celestial man has no *rights* to defend, having no proprium but the new proprium, which is a finited expression of the Lord's love. If you smite him on one cheek, he will turn the other to be smitten. If you take away his cloak, he will give you his coat also. The celestial man has no *du-*

*ties* to perform, and no conscience to worry him about their performance. The natural man contends for his rights; the spiritual man is dutiful, and compels himself to obey the divine law. The celestial man is altogether free and spontaneous. He *lives* out the divine truth joyously and easily, because the divine love has displaced the selfhood in his soul. He has lost his life—and found it. He bears everything, hopes everything, forgives everything. He rejoices in tribulations, self-sacrifices, and sufferings, if they bear the heavenly fruit of good to the neighbor. Such a man or woman, initiated organically into the Lord's celestial-natural church, will not only cling to the bonds of marriage under all circumstances until death; but will descend into the hells of the unconjugial partner, bearing the atmospheres of the Lord with him; will contend with the wild beasts as He did; and will be no more contaminated by his horrible surroundings, than He was when He "poured out his soul unto death" and was "numbered with the transgressors"—when He "bare the sins of many," and made intercession for sinners.

This extraordinary phase of humanity, the celestial-natural man, is now being developed upon the earth. He is coming without the leave, indeed without the knowledge, of scorners and sceptics; and his coming means the presence of the Lord in ultimates with angelic states of life, as gifts for his children. Through men and women of this type, our Lord will assume the hells in the Body of Humanity as He once assumed them in his own natural form; will deliver us from the old Babylon which has made us all drunk with the wine of her fornications; and, occupying the gateway between the spiritual and the natural worlds, will redeem the hells, and reorganize governments, churches, institutions, and even the physical constitution of man. Yes—He is coming! The great "rose dawn" of the Celestial Church is visible above the eastern hills. Let every one of us prepare a way for the Lord in our own hearts, and make straight his paths: "for He cometh, for He cometh, to judge the earth."

In order to make the case a little clearer to your mind, I will give you some extracts from a letter of a New-Church minister, full of original, striking, and interesting thoughts, and presenting objections to G. W. C.'s perceptions on the subject of Divorce, which are worthy of profound consideration.

"The first advent of the Lord was not his real coming: it was only prophetic and representative of it. At his first coming, 'everything the Lord did in the world was representative, and everything He said was significative.' (A. E. 405.) At his second coming, He comes to abide as a permanently visible God upon the earth, more really present than at his first coming. In truth, heaven is coming down to earth—*heaven*—because the Lord comes. Of course this is an apparent truth: the reality is rather that earth is raised to heaven, or in other words, the church by regeneration and the opening of its interiors, is raised to a heavenly state, so that earth and heaven are made one. The New Jerusalem *comes down*. The heavenly state is no longer confined to heaven, but is extended and transferred to earth. In other words, all the phenomena which we are accustomed to conceive of as taking place in heaven, are to take place on earth."

This is a clear statement of what is really meant by the coming of the Lord with his holy angels—the descent of the divine life into the Body of Humanity, which He will infill, according to reception, with the heavenly states of love and wisdom which the angels enjoy. But it is necessary to guard the mind against the idea that heaven and earth are to be upon the same plane, which the writer does not intend to teach. They will remain forever discrete, but they will be brought into perfect correspondence, so that what takes place in heaven spiritually, will take place upon earth naturally, the evil influence of the hells having been totally eliminated. The earth will remain forever the seed-field of creation, propagation, and evolution. Therefore the things which take place upon earth and the laws which govern them, will be different from those which take place in heaven; but still they will be perfectly correspondent.

"There is a certain work," he continues, "which in the past has been necessarily performed in the world of spirits. This work will, in the present dispensation, be performed on earth; for if the Lord and heaven come down to earth, much more will the world of spirits and its work come down to earth. The final preparation of the soul for heaven, which has hitherto been conceived of as taking place after death, will now take place before death. This is a better place for it than the world of spirits. Swedenborg says that some go immediately to heaven after death. In the present dispensation they will not wait so long as that. They will go to heaven before death. This is the very idea of the second coming of the Lord, and of the New Jerusalem coming down."

Do you not see that this writer is leading us cautiously and logically to a powerful argument in favor of divorce and its almost indefinite extension? He is one of the very few New-Church ministers who have discovered the tremendous truth, that the general judgment predicted by the Lord and the Word has not come but is coming; that Swedenborg's last judgment was only a small, partial, and trifling affair in comparison; only a judgment upon the *last* church (for every church has had its judgment), or rather upon that portion of it that went neither to heaven nor hell, but remained in mixed states, hanging in the world of spirits like a great cloud between heaven and earth. That judgment let the light of spiritual truth through into the world, as a messenger to prepare the way of the Lord. This writer perceives that the real, final, universal judgment is to be produced by the personal descent of the Lord from centres to circumferences. The work in the world of spirits (the unfolding of interior states by casting off externals) will really be done upon earth.

"In the world of spirits, we are taught, the external bonds of marriage are loosened; and disregarding all previous relations of that kind, those come together who are or can be, conjugially united. This loosening of external bonds does not tend to the disintegration of society, as it would have done under a former dispensation, because the New Jerusalem or heaven has come down to the earth. The external bonds of marriage are not to be destroyed, but they are to be 'loosened' so that there can be adjustments from spiritual motives, and men and women shall not be held together by a mere blind law, which recognizes no distinction. The latter has been necessary; but it is not to be necessary when the Lord comes. External divorces may therefore be allowed, that internal marriages may take place. Yet these divorces will be more frequent at first than afterward, because marriages in the new dispensation will not be so ignorantly contracted as before."

This writer assumes our own position, that the personal atmosphere of the Lord is entering the Body of Humanity; that the judgment impends; that our interiors will be opened so that the inner life will proclaim itself in ultimates; that old states and conditions are to be unsettled and broken up, and a general readjustment and reconstruction are to be effected. Now if church and state, with all their varied institutional forms, are to be dissolved and rebuilded, why should not all the evil and false marriages in the world be subjected to the same process? Why should not the opportunities of divorce be vastly enlarged and extended? Indeed, how can the necessary disintegrations and readjustments take place, unless the bonds of marriage are greatly "loosened"? This apparently logical inference is drawn from a one-sided or partial view of the subject.

This writer thinks there will be no danger to society from the extended facilities of divorce, because heaven is coming, and in heaven all live in mutual love; and when external bonds there are removed, the parties are only drawn more closely together. But the very paragraph he quotes (A. C. 5002) also says, that when external bonds are removed with the wicked, they break forth into all extremes of hatred and violence. Our friend ignores the fact that the opening of the interiors brings the hells as well as the heavens down to earth. It all seems plain sailing, and lovely and beautiful and just, when heavenly souls are unchained from devilish partners, and allowed to seek their own conjugial mates. But who does not see that when the bonds of marriage are loosened and divorce made easy, the flood-gates of hell are opened also; and that the in-flowing adulterous passions and lust of varieties would precipitate mankind into contentions, miseries, sufferings, and crimes indescribable?

This terrible state of things is no doubt coming, and is a hideous part of the general judgment—the lake of fire into which the old proprium plunges itself when let loose to work "its own sweet will." But it is not to be expected that New-churchmen shall aid in this vastating and devastating process. Will they not rather raise a standard against it? Will they not plant themselves on the rock of ultimate truth at any price of self-denial and individual suffering? Will they not cling to the letter of the Word and to the external institution of marriage, as *fixed*, organic forms instinct with spiritual power, capable and alone capable of protecting and preserving us from the overwhelming influx of the hells?

"Because the external bonds of marriage," says my friend G. W. C., "are loosened in the world of spirits, it does not follow that they will be loosened upon earth, when the earth comes to put on the state of the world of spirits by entering into judgment. In the world of spirits externals are not fixed, but simply reflect the changing internals of the spirit. On the earth *externals are fixed*, and cannot change according to the changes of man's internal states; and so will it ever be, so long as the difference between materiality and substantiality exists."

The sun of the natural world is a fixed, organic form, into which the spiritual forces of the sun of heaven enter, and there become the creative forces of nature. The letter of the Word is a fixed organic form, into which the celestial and spiritual goods and truths of the Lord through the heavens enter, and thence become the forces of the regenerating life. Just so the external institution of marriage between one man and one woman is a fixed organic form, into which the divine life flows, and manifests itself as conjugial love, mutual love, charity, and all the virtues and graces of a truly human existence. The external bonds of marriage are betrothals, nuptials, cohabitation, and living together, instituted by mutual consent, sanctioned by the church, and legalized by the civil power, so that the parties are regarded, both spiritually and naturally, as one in thought, feeling, and interest. The enormous importance, value, and power of this institution upon which the order of the heavens is based, may be further comprehended from these very suggestive remarks of G. W. C.

"Marriage is not based on the civil law and its requirements. External marriage is based on the commandment of God (in order that a human society, capable of progress, should exist), and it is entered upon by consent of parties. How many parties enter directly or indirectly into the contract, it would be difficult to show. From the stand-point of the good of society alone, we see that the whole external community, and, indeed, the whole world of associated man, has a vital interest in it. Vast ramifications of its sphere run also through the spirit-world, and the life-principle of many persons in the world of spirits and in the heavens, is always deeply involved with each and every external marriage *as the basis and containant of a higher life to them in the interior.* Can a contract be fairly broken without the consent of all these *visible* and *invisible* parties in interest?"

The celestial man can never go back on his assertions (and remember, that to assert is not to dictate), for what he calls truth is seen from the state of good he is in. The celestial man perceives that the external institution of marriage is a fixed, sacred, and eternal ultimate of divine power for the regeneration of the individual and the race. Recognizing the infinite loving accommodations of our Lord to all degrees and states of life, He still clearly perceives that all the spiritual changes, adjustments, and readjustments, necessary for the new life, can be better effected WITHIN the bonds of marriage than

OUTSIDE of them. The miseries of ill-assorted marriages are not so great as those which will inevitably follow the slightest loosening of the bonds of marriage. The time will come when all the living will have been delivered from their prison-houses, and all the new-born will be ushered into life, dowered with the certainty of a blissful married state.

Yours fraternally,
W. H. H.

# LETTER XIX.

*THE CELESTIAL FORGIVE ALL THINGS, EVEN ADULTERY.*

MY DEAR FRIEND:—You are apprehensive that my statement, that the celestial admit no causes of divorce, not even adultery, may be considered antagonistic to the teachings of Swedenborg and the Word. You think so because you have momentarily forgotten the doctrine of discrete degrees, and the fact that what is enjoined or permitted upon a lower plane, as "an eye for an eye, and a tooth for a tooth," may be absolutely prohibited on a higher plane—"*but I say unto you.*" (Matt. v. 32–48.)

Moses, who represented divine spiritual truth, permitted the natural and sensual Jews to divorce their wives for causes which interior men absolutely repudiate. Swedenborg, in accommodation to the usages of his day, permits concubinage and separations to the unregenerate natural man (see C. L.), which the spiritual man instinctively and with horror refuses to accept as laws of permission applicable to his own spiritual state. The Jews were permitted to put away their wives on account of "the hardness of their hearts," because the celestial degree was closed in them; and our Lord who always stoops and writes with his finger on the ground, or accommodates Himself to our lowest natural states, gave permissions within the limits of which it was still possible for something of spiritual life to be preserved.

But He expressly declares that "*from the beginning it was not so*"—that man and woman were made to be one in spirit and in body—one and inseparable. In the celestial-degree separations are therefore impossible. In the spiritual degree and the spiritual church He was about to establish ("I say unto you"), only one cause of divorce was admissible; and that was not adultery, as is commonly supposed, but prostitution. The Word employs two different expressions on this subject (Matt. v. 32, and xix. 9). The Greek word πορνεία (*porneia*) translated fornication, has a far deeper and stronger signification. It means prostitution, the life of the harlot, the confirmed and fixed state of the sensual reprobate. It is true that heaven is closed to any one who commits adultery; but it may be opened again by earnest prayer and repentance. The spiritual man has no right to separate himself totally and forever from his wife, until from an adulteress she becomes a prostitute. The celestial man occupies a still higher plane, as we will presently see.

Our Lord recognizes, indeed teaches, the discrete degrees of doctrine upon this subject. When the Jews, appalled by the apparent strictness of his limitations, say to Him: If such be the case, "it is not good to marry:" He replies,

"*All men cannot receive this saying, save they to whom it is given.*"

He then goes on to mention three discrete classes of eunuchs, who are, according to Swedenborg (A. C. 394), the subjects of the heavenly marriage, and represent the celestial, spiritual, and natural degrees of that marriage; concluding with these words: "He that is able to receive it, let him receive it."

Matthew is the only evangelist who alludes to any cause as sanctioning divorce. Mark (x. 11) and Luke (xvi. 18) say, without any excepting clause, that he who puts away his wife and marries another, commits adultery. John, writing from the celestial sphere, has no hint of divorce, but teaches the unconditional and perpetual forgiveness of the sinner. The story of the woman taken in adultery, is not to be found in the oldest copies we have of the New Testament; and it was long repudiated by the men of the spiritual church, no doubt because it contained a doctrine which they were not prepared to accept or even to understand. Its spiritual sense, as revealed by Swedenborg, establishes its claim to divine inspiration; and the fact that the incident is narrated just after Jesus descends from the Mount of Olives "early in the morning" into the temple, and sits down to teach the people, shows to those acquainted with the science of correspondences, that its heavenly light came down from the celestial through the spiritual into the natural sphere of life for our instruction.

The celestial (divine good) judges all to heaven; the spiritual (divine truth, or the laws of order) condemns all to hell. A. C. 2258. It is only by the union of the two, that justice is tempered with mercy. The process of divorce implies accusation, judgment, and punishment. The celestial man cannot possibly engage in such work. It is repugnant to his organic nature to accuse, condemn, or punish. This is the proper work of spiritual truth. While, therefore, divorce on sufficient grounds is permitted to the natural and even to the spiritual man, the celestial man utterly refuses to avail himself of any such permissions. He may withdraw himself, but he refuses to recognize the dissolution of the external marriage bond during the life of the offending party, not only because he cannot accuse, condemn, or punish, but because his love reaches forth indefinitely, and can never despair of the final reformation and salvation of the sinner whom he would always willingly die to save; for "the life of the celestial man," as G. W. C. says, "is Christ's life in limitations."

How little we really know of the celestial man, notwithstanding Swedenborg's unfoldings! Few of us will recognize him when we see him. He will come to his own, and his own will receive him not. In the eyes of the natural and spiritual man, he will do all sorts of foolish things, perhaps, and entertain all sorts of questionable opinions; and they will pronounce him a crank or a spiritualist or a victim of enthusiastic spirits. He will care nothing whatever for their opinions of him, and will take their exact measure, not from what they say of themselves, but from what his own perceptions tell him they are. A patient, quiet, unpretentious, happy kind of a fellow, never combating, never disputing; whom it is impossible to insult; always in the rear, or at the sides, or somewhere out of sight, loving his neighbor more than himself without professing to love him even as much. He ignores church matters and authorities so absolutely, that most people would think he was no Christian at all. We may even think him a fool, but he has immeasurable stores of wisdom, vastly transcending our spiritual treasures, especially on the subject of marriage, which he either cannot or will not communicate to us. Look out for this man of the antediluvian type, for he is about to be unfolded into the world. Will he not perish for want of a suitable environment?

Yours truly,

W. H. H.

# LETTER XX.

*SWEDENBORG'S VIEW OF EXTERNAL AND INTERNAL.*

MY DEAR SIR:—As you believe the writings of Swedenborg are divine, and as I accord them an authority second only to that of the Word, it must be a matter of great interest to us to know what they really do teach. As we differ on some important points, we may both be benefited and possibly brought nearer together by comparing opinions in an amicable manner.

In the first place, it would be well for you—who seem to think that there is no orderly state of the human spirit in this world, but that of *a closed and fixed natural condition entirely instructed from without*—to consider profoundly the following extract from Swedenborg, which gives the key to the spiritual states of Guyon and Fenelon, and of a great many people at the present time, concerning those at this day who are, as it were, a remnant of the Ancient Church:—

"There are still some who retain and preserve much of the Ancient Church, and who are especially distinguished by that feature of it by which *they perceive whether anything is good*. For this reason, also, they are rejected of others, *who suppose that they are to be classed with enthusiasts;* when yet this was a peculiarity of the Ancient Church, that they had *a perception of what was good, and thence of what they should do*, acknowledging the operation of spirits, but recognizing in themselves that only of the Lord's spirit, and rejecting others."—S. D. 1987.

There is no difference of opinion between us, although you seem to think so, in relation to the importance and uses of external truth, the external church, the external Word, and external instruction of all kinds. Man is now born in utter ignorance (though he might be born into all knowledges, A. C. 1902); and he must be initiated into truths by instruction, so that from natural he may become spiritual, and from spiritual celestial. Even the progress of our Lord in the union of the human essence with the Divine, was effected according to this instruction by continual revelations. (A. C. 2500.) We only differ as to the stand-points from which we view these things. Looking from an exterior sensual stand-point, you view them as objects of thought. Looking from an interior natural stand-point, I see them subjectively, or as correspondences which reveal to me the causes which produce them. (A. C. 10,204.) You are perfectly right as far as you go. Not going as far as I go legitimately and logically, I seem to you to go wrong.

I plant myself firmly upon such general truths as the following announced by Swedenborg:

There is nothing in externals but what is produced from the interior, and thus successively from the inmost.—A. C. 994-5.

The things which appear in externals flow in from the interior, and solely from the Lord.—A. C. 1954.

Thoughts and ideas exist by virtue of influx from within and not from without.—A. C. 3220.

The internal clothes itself with such things in the external as may enable it, in that inferior sphere, to produce effect.— A. C. 6275.

The life of the external man is sensual and exterior, or it is natural and interior, according as his truths are from external objects or from the causes of them.—A. C. 10,254.

Your fundamental error, it seems to me, is that you take the condition of man in his lowest external state as the normal type and standard which regulates God's government toward him, regardless of what he has been in the past or what he may be in the future. You seem to forget that he is now in an abnormal, disorderly state, from which the Second Coming of the Lord is to rescue him. The loss of perception, the development of conscience, the ultimation of the Word in several forms, the establishment of external worship (A. C. 4493), and the necessity for external instruction, are all signs and proofs of the decadence of the spiritual life, and of a fall from interior and superior to exterior and inferior conditions.

You do not seem to realize the stupendous fact that the New Church is to be a celestial Church, and the life of genuine Newchurchmen is to be a celestial life. You do not rise in your philosophy or theology above the conception of a life of obedience in the external man. You forget that the marriage of good and truth, the heavenly marriage, does not take place between good and truth of one and the same degree, but between the inferior of the one and the superior of the other. (A. C. 3952.) Thus the natural truths of the Word are married to the spiritual goods of a superior degree, and this produced the spirituality of the first Christian Church. So the spiritual truth of the New Church in us, must be married to the celestial goods of the degree above, and that will ultimate the celestial life in the world.

Study the laws and phenomena of the celestial life as unfolded in Swedenborg, if you would understand and even foresee the forms in which the heart of the Lord's New Church will finally be manifested in the world. You will then perceive that there are two sources of revelation and instruction; one that takes a comparatively external way through the understanding, necessitated by the fall of man; and the other, a far higher, holier, more interior, and productive way, through the regenerated will. You will see that after man is initiated into truths according to your own conceptions, if those truths are really conjoined to good, he rises into a discretely higher state, when not only the former truths become clearer and clearer to him, but innumerable other truths never known or revealed to him before, are imparted to him; until "the light of truth from good increases immensely, and becomes a continuous lucidity—for he is then in the light of heaven, which is from the Lord." (A. C. 3833.)

Read also the following memorable paragraph from Swedenborg, and see in it the state which not only once existed generally in the world, but which has occasionally cropped out in all ages and churches, and which is the sure heritage of the men of the New Church in whom spiritual truths shall be conjoined to celestial goods.

"The men of the celestial church are such that they perceive all the goods and truths of heaven from the Lord by influx into their interiors: whence they see goods and truths inwardly in themselves as implanted, and have no need to learn them by a posterior way, or to treasure them up in their memory."—A. E. 739.

Now it possibly seems to you that such people are possessed by enthusiastic spirits, and receive their revelations and instructions outside of the Word and the church. But it is not so. The Word which created all things, is something infinitely greater than that little portion of it which we see in the literal sense and in the writings of Swedenborg; for it is the infinite Divine Wisdom—the Divine Truth, omnipresent, omniscient, omnipotent. When we are in the Lord and the Lord in us, we are in the Word, in heaven, in the church. If we abide in the Vine, we shall bring forth much fruit, but not otherwise; for without Him we can do nothing.

You are afraid that if our regeneration were so close an image of the Lord's glorification as I represent it to be, "we would all be the Lord," and the Doctrines would be charged with Pantheism. Have you no clear conception of the meaning of the life which is "hid with Christ in God"—or of our Lord's own words, "He that eateth my flesh and drinketh my blood, dwelleth in me and I in him"? Does not Swedenborg say that when the externals of an angel are quiescent, he knows no otherwise than that he is the Lord Himself? Does he not say that the new proprium is a new life given us to feel as if it were our own, but that it is really the Lord in us, while we ourselves in our own proprium are filthy masses of excrement? Why is it that Newchurchmen have never yet, in their writings, sermons, or journals, fully accepted Swedenborg's doctrine of the new proprium, and pushed it to its only logical issue—the perfect sanctification of the soul and the redemption of the body from the power of all sin? or, in other words, the Lord's life in us, and not our own?

You are clearly wrong, I think, in affirming that there is no source of knowledge but external instruction through the Word and the Writings. That may be true of the child, but it is not so of the adult who, in the course of his regenerating life, has had the spiritual or celestial degree opened in him. Such a man is *in* the celestial and spiritual senses of the Word without knowing it; and he may be illumined from within by the light of heaven flowing through a regenerated will into his understanding. There is no other way of accounting for the tremendous spiritual, rational, and scientific progress of the last hundred years, which has *not* been made by the formation of vessels of reception by instruction in the Writings. The interior Word is descending everywhere through the opening of the celestial degree, and producing innumerable approximations to divine truth in the minds of men, without the slightest aid from the writings of Swedenborg, or from those who seize upon them to build up an external church without the least authority from the Lord for doing so.

You say that the external heaven and earth of the human proprium is to flee away, just as the external heaven and earth of the spiritual world fled away at the Last Judgment, viz.: by instruction in divine truth by divinely appointed means. Such is not Swedenborg's account of the matter. Influx for judgment and for instruction are two different processes. Read his account of the causes of the breaking up of the external heavens and earth, whether they exist in the spiritual or the natural world.

"The Lord, when the judgment was at hand, *caused the heavens to draw near over the world of spirits, and by this approach of the heavens* such a change of state in the interiors of the minds of those who were below was effected, that they saw nothing but terrors before their eyes."—A. R. 342.

"Winds exist [in the spiritual world] from a *strong and powerful influx of the Divine through the heavens* into the lower parts of the spiritual world; and when the influx comes, it fills truths and goods, that is, *it fills those who are in truths and goods with the Divine* as to their soul and spirit; but those whose interiors consist merely of falsities and evils, and their exteriors of truths mixed with falsities and of good mixed with evils, cannot sustain such influx from the Divine; consequently they betake themselves to their own falsities and evils which they love, and reject the truths and goods which they do not love, except for the sake of self and of the appearance."—A. E. 419.

"When the Divine proceeding from the Lord *flows in intensely*, the apparent goods with the evil are dissipated, since they are not goods in themselves but evils, and evils cannot sustain the influx of the Divine. Hence it comes to pass that *the externals of such are shut, and these being shut, the interiors are opened*, in which there are nothing but evils and falsities thence derived; whence they come into grief, anguish, and torment, and in consequence thereof cast themselves down into the hells where similar evils and falsities have place."—A. E. 419.

From these paragraphs you see that the organic spiritual causes of the Last Judgment were not "instructions according to divinely appointed means," but a more intense influx of the Divine through the heavens into the world of spirits, the descent of the Lord, the approach of the heavens above the world of spirits nearer to it, and the opening of the interiors of the people in that world; so that the good became better and were elevated into heavenly places, and the evil became worse and precipitated themselves into infernal consociation.

I believe that the causes thus inaugurated in the spiritual world are still operative, and that judgment and the coming of the Lord are continuous events—keys to the history of the last hundred years, and to the still more astonishing history which is impending. You do not believe it, mainly because

Swedenborg has not said so. Swedenborg was no prophet, and did not undertake to unveil the future. What was the future to him has now unfolded itself, and it can only be explained by the sublime principles and truths revealed in the writings of the herald of the New Church. You refuse to see anything outside of Swedenborg. I accept all phenomena, all authenticated facts, including all the evil effects of the Lord's coming to the evil, not excepting Spiritualism of which I am not "foolishly afraid," and study and explain them by the light of the heavenly doctrines. When you have attained to the same degree of rationality, you will discover that I am not a spiritist nor a victim of enthusiastic spirits. In the meantime, let us allow the largest liberty of opinion to each and all, and still, like John's little children, let us "love one another."

Yours fraternally,

W. H. H.

# LETTER XXI.

*THE PHILOSOPHY OF CREATION: NATURE ABSOLUTELY DEAD.*

MY DEAR FRIEND:—You ask me what I mean by my statement, that all external phenomena are caused by the influx of the heavens and the hells into the natural plane of the human mind.

This is an infinite subject of which Swedenborg says many volumes might be written, and every attempt of ours to conceive it or understand it must be feeble and obscure, because we think from time and space of phenomena whose real causes are independent of time and space. Still, with the mighty help of Swedenborg we may make some valuable approximations to the truth.

The natural plane of the human mind with its three continuous degrees, exterior-rational, scientific, and sensual, is the basis or ultimate upon which the entire spiritual world rests, and into which and through which the heavens and the hells perpetually flow. Swedenborg says that man in this degree of his life, is "the gateway between the Divine and nature." All within and above him is spiritual, all outside of and below him is natural. All the former things are substantial, all the latter things are material. All the former are living and never die: all the latter are dead and never live.

It is a fixed point of Swedenborg's philosophy, that what we call nature is absolutely dead. The sun is dead, and all things derived from it are dead. The forms of matter have no properties, no affinities, no motions, no transformations, due to any causes below the natural plane of the human mind. There are nothing but effects below that plane : all the causes lie in it or above it. Everything in nature owes its cause and all its phenomena to somewhat in the spiritual world. (A. C. 8211.) Material forms are discreted from pre-existent spiritual forms or substances, and have no life or power of motion or change in themselves. "The substantial," says Swedenborg, "is the primitive element of the material." This extreme and true position of Swedenborg must be maintained clearly in the mind, or we open the flood-gates of Naturalism, and fall into confusion and darkness.

"Were what is spiritual separated from what is natural, that which is natural would be annihilated. All things derive their origin in this manner. Everything, both in general and in particular, is from the Lord. From Him is the celestial principle; by the celestial from Him exists the spiritual principle; by the spiritual, the natural; and by the natural, the corporeal and sensual; and as each thus exists from the Lord, so also does it subsist, for subsistence is perpetual existence."—A. C. 775.

"Whatsoever exists in the natural world derives its birth and cause from those things which exist in the spiritual world, since universal nature is nothing else but a theatre representative of the Lord's kingdom. Hence come correspondences. The variations of light and shade, also of heat and cold in the earths, are indeed from the sun, viz., from the difference of its altitudes every year and every day in the various regions of the earth; but these causes which are proximate and in the natural world, were created according to those things in the spiritual world, as by their prior causes efficient of the posterior causes which exist in the natural world; for there is nothing at all given in the natural world, which does not derive its cause and birth from the spiritual."—A. C. 8211.

We thus see that all proximate causes in the natural world are simply effects of prior spiritual causes. It is from the stand-point of these truths, my dear sir, that I made and reiterate the statement, that sidereal motions, planetary movements, geological changes, storms of wind and water, chemical affinities and transformations, vegetable and animal forms and forces, and I may add, all diseases and accidents, all the phenomena of evolution, and all the developments of history, language, art, science, religions, are caused, directed, and modified by the influx of the creative life through the heavens and the hells into the natural plane of the human mind. If I have been able to comprehend it at all, this is a fundamental point of Swedenborg's philosophy of creation. Hear him again:

"Man is created according to the forms of the three heavens, and thus there is impressed on him the image of heaven; so that man is, in the least form, a little heaven, and thence comes his correspondence with the heavens. Hence, also it is, that *through man alone* there is a descent from the heavens into the world, and an ascent from the world into the heavens."—A. C. 4041-2.

Such evidence might be indefinitely extended; but it seems to me unnecessary. Your only real difficulty appears to be, that sidereal motions, geological changes, etc., etc., existed before the creation of the finite human mind. But how about the Divine Mind, which is only the infinitely human mind from which all substances and materials receive their conatus and impetus toward the human form? In Him all human forms, forces, and revolutions exist in an eternal Now and Here. Could not the Divine Mind have moulded the physical universe for the ultimation of man, by creative influx through the substantial spiritual forms of the race, before they received conscious natural existence by fixation upon the natural plane? These ideas may be too high and too deep for us to grasp; but the truth lies somewhere there in the spiritual sphere, and not at all in the natural sphere where the evolutionists teach that a primordial substance appeared of itself, and spontaneously developed and evolved, without spiritual or divine influx, into the splendid cosmos we see around us.

But you may say: If the phenomena preparatory to the creation of man were evolved through the Divine Natural Humanity, the effects in ultimates should betray no indications of imperfection or disorder: how then about the hideous monsters of our primeval eras, the desperate struggle for existence, the survival of the fittest, etc.? We are greatly mistaken when we reason from the creation of our single world, as if it was the first and only one created, and stood all alone by itself for analysis. The problem, instead of being so simple, is infinitely complex. The natural plane, and indeed all the planes of the human mind, extend throughout the created universe; and every world receives influx from all the others. We belong to the cuticle of the Grand Man. We have infinite consociations with other spheres, external and internal, of which we know nothing. The geological and embryonic phenomena of our earth, may have been caused by influxes from remote spheres of the spiritual universe.

Leaving the past behind us, of which we know so little, and

taking all things just as they now stand, we can surely comprehend, without any great effort, the idea, that the grand complex of all the phenomena of nature, is an effect and representative of the infinite changes going on in the spiritual universe.

Yours truly,<br>W. H. H.

# LETTER XXII.

### *ADVICE TO A WOUNDED SPIRIT.*

MY DEAR MADAM:—We have read your letters with great interest and feel for you a profound sympathy. You are a good type of many wounded spirits, of many Christian daughters of sorrow. We have perceived your states, your powerful efforts to retrieve and maintain past conditions, your yearnings for light and guidance, your hopes, griefs, and despairs. We have a few things to say to you, both old and new—for he is not a good householder who cannot bring forth both kinds out of his treasure.

In the first place, break all your idols; and we have many idols whose existence we do not suspect, until we come to clean out the temple of our hearts for the entrance of the Lord. Begin the new life and re-begin it every day, by leaving the old ship and the nets, and the father and brethren behind you. Let the dead bury the dead henceforth and forever, so far as you are concerned. Abandon all the old stand-points of thought, feeling, and sentiment. There are many things which we cherish as pleasant memories, or even as sacred duties, which it is best to forget and to put away entirely; for the new proprium into which we are being born, will remember them no more forever.

"The Lord, in order to render any one blessed and happy, wills *a total submission*, that is, that he should not be partly his own and partly the Lord's; for there are then two Lords, whom a man cannot serve at the same time. (Matt. vi. 24.)

A total submission is also meant by the Lord's words in Matthew, 'Whosoever loveth father and mother above me is not worthy of me; and whosoever loveth son and daughter above me is not worthy of me.' (x. 37.) By father and mother are signified in general those things which are of man's proprium from what is hereditary; and by son and daughter, those things which are of man's proprium from what is actual."—A.C. 6138.

In the next place, dear madam, you rely too much upon books and friends for consolation and help. You go to your favorite authors for comfort as the drunkard goes to his cups. It is a species of spiritual dissipation, for you have already a great deal more knowledge than you can utilize. What you most need is to find *the Christ that is within yourself*, and bring Him down through your own spiritual structures, so that by his influx, He may give peace and joy to your heart and light and guidance to your understanding. You have infinite resources within your own soul, for all the heavens flow into you; and the Lord flows through the heavens into the truths of the Word which are stored in your memory, bringing that living wisdom which needs no clothing in earthly language.

*"Cease ye from man, whose breath is in his nostrils, for wherein is he to be accounted of?"*
*"Ye will not come unto me that ye might have life."*
*"Whosoever drinketh of the water that I shall give him, shall never thirst: for the water that I shall give him, shall be in him a well of water springing up into everlasting life."*

Another important thing for you to do, is to recognize the terrible fact, announced first by Swedenborg, that *we are all born in hell* (that is, with hereditary proclivities that are altogether evil) *and are now living in hell*, organically bound up and woven into its associated forms—from which there is no escape except through the Lord Jesus Christ; for no possible additions to us of wealth, power, influence, pleasure, etc., etc., outside of Jesus Christ, could do anything but confirm and fix us in our present evil conditions. Let us learn the truth and accept the situation. We are compelled in some shape or other to bear the burdens and share the miseries of others, for we are all bound up in the same bundle of the infernal life. We need no ideal and sentimental elevations into heavenly states of thought and feeling, above and away from the troubles and trials of the world. To bring forth the atmospheres of the Lord into the hells in which we live, is the business of the Christian life. The Lord alone can overcome the world and its tribulations. To live and work bravely, patiently, hopefully, *with* and *for* the Lord, in our own hereditary and actual hells, is the surest road to heaven.

It is a mistake, dear madam, to suppose that we have fallen from higher and happier spiritual places into our present low, external conditions, and have a reasonable right to grieve about it. It is more probable that we have passed through darker and deeper hells, which were mercifully concealed from our sight, and have advanced into more hopeful conditions, however wretched they may seem to be. Your interior spiritual states when you were the petted child of wealth and fashion, and all without was lovely and serene, were no doubt far worse than they now are, when you have been led by Divine Providence through thorny and painful paths of deprivation and sorrow, to see the old proprium as it is, to know "the depths of Satan," and to feel truly that without the Lord we can do nothing.

But what are we to do about the dear friends and relatives who are far astray from the path of duty, and going apparently to temporal and spiritual destruction? Cling to them with the utmost tenacity, through evil and good report, bearing all things, hoping all things, forgiving all things. Impatience, says Swedenborg, is an unspiritual state. The Lord is infinitely patient. Trust Him for the final welfare of those you love. The very evils you deplore in them are perhaps, in the Lord's hands, the best experiences for their final deliverance. How vain it is to judge according to appearances! We are all led by ways we know not. The Lord is often absent from places and states which we have sedulously prepared for his glorified presence. And on the contrary He is often intimately present where we would never suspect it.

"*If I make my bed in hell, behold! Thou art there:*
"*If I say, Surely the darkness shall cover me; even the night shall be light about me.*
"*Yea! the darkness hideth not from thee; but the night shineth as the day: the darkness and the light are both alike to thee.*"

What can we do but stand firm, faithful, and hopeful, in the discharge of every duty through all sufferings and tribulations? "*In the world, ye shall have tribulation; but be of good cheer, I have overcome the world.*" Let the sphere of the Lord flow through us in our states of self-annihilation, his loving kindness, his forbearance, his patience, his humility, his goodness; for these states are always really his and not our own. Thus will each of us contribute to break up the evil spheres which surround us, and reduce them into subjection to the laws of heavenly order. Then will He fill our hearts with his own joy, and give us the silent-falling manna of his wisdom for our daily thought and conduct.

How can the angels be near to us in our self-created atmospheres of doubt, anxiety, thought-for-the-morrow, and restless desire for earthly things? They are happy because they have given up all—are dead to all—have nothing, want nothing—and receive all things from moment to moment, directly from the divine hand. Let us do likewise. The Lord is now present in ultimates upon this earth, with his holy angels —or with angelic states of love and wisdom open to all, attainable by all; for verily all things are now possible to them that believe.

Now, my dear madam, these ideas seem to exhaust the subject you have presented, so far as the interior life is concerned. G. W. C. knows nothing and can give no advice about external affairs. It would be equivalent to spirit-control if he could do so. He says, stand alone with the Lord Jesus Christ, and act from the freedom and rationality He gives you, and all will be well. "*Seek ye first* (or supremely) *the kingdom of God and his righteousness, and all these things shall be added unto you.*"

May your heart be so opened to the Lord that your mind may be guided into light, and your feet into paths of safety.

Yours truly,<br>W. H. H.

# LETTER XXIII.

*COERCION IN RELIGIOUS MATTERS.*

MY DEAR MADAM:—One sentence in your letter struck me painfully, and set me to thinking about many things. "The cancer of coerciveness," you say, "is eating out the life-blood of the church, and all things are being paralyzed thereby."

It is a sign of your growing sensitiveness to the new life, that you have those feelings of suffocation and oppression in the atmosphere of the church to which you belong. Those members of it who are in harmony with its general spirit, would be simply astonished at your sensations and feelings. They are easy and happy in it, with no more sense of oppression than we have from the enormous weight of the atmospheric air upon us. The minister is talented and popular, preaches the heavenly doctrines with genuine zeal, and performs his pastoral duties with brotherly affection. The members of the church are cultivated, liberal, excellent people, quite distinguished, even in a great city, for their enlightened and earnest discharge of all their social, civil, and religious obligations. Examined from the outside and by the old orthodox standards, everything is admirable, lovely, and serene. What is the matter? Is the fault with them? or is it with you?

The truth of the matter is, you are outgrowing and outliving your surroundings. You have become dissatisfied with the standard of the spiritual life hitherto recognized and admired. There is too much light and too little heat in the sphere about you. You have learned something of the wiles of the old proprium—"the depths of Satan"—in yourself, and you see them in others. The veil of appearances, the illusions of society, the pretensions and self-deceptions of men and women are painful to you. You are yearning to realize the genuine life of heaven in your soul; to feel the Spirit of the Lord breathing upon the dark face of the waters within you, and creating new light for your guidance. You have seasons of contrition, humiliation, and despair. You have new sensibilities at your own shortcomings, new sympathies, new pities for others, a new willingness for burdens and self-sacrifices, and a deep feeling of shame when you shrink from them in the least. The Lord is coming to you personally by interior ways, and would manifest Himself through you.

Now when you broach these experiences and the new and broader intellectual views which flow from them, to your beloved pastor and to the leading members and friends in your Church, you meet with no sympathetic response. They do not wish or approve new experiences, innovations, expansions, unfoldings of any kind. They prefer the old way and its fixed and closed conditions. A good, moral life illuminated brilliantly with spiritual truths, is their beau ideal of the Christian state. Some of them doubt your experiences and question your opinions; some declare them to be visionary and fantastic; others solemnly warn you against hallucinations and enthusiastic spirits. Your best friends strongly dissuade you from reading certain books or subscribing to certain journals and papers. Some are even angry with you for doing so. Your pastor perhaps tells you gently that it is not well for the laity to encourage too much independence of thought, and that it would be humblest and best to defer, in all spiritual matters, to the superior knowledge and authority of the clergy.

Religious wars have been noted for cruelty; religious dissensions for bitterness; and the mildest discussion about religious matters rarely terminates without a disagreeable revelation of the old proprium on both sides. And these things are perfectly natural: for the religious element—a man's conception of God and the neighbor and his duties toward them, is the strongest, deepest element in his nature. Every man seems to himself to stand upon ground where surrender or compromise is impossible. When one's faith is assaulted, not only are his self-love and his pride of opinion wounded, but really believing that the welfare, peace, and order of society are endangered by his opponent's doctrines, he justifies his indifference, contemptuousness, and animosity in the most earnest and adroit manner, thinking he would do God service in the destruction of his enemies. Such men really in spirit call down fire from heaven to overwhelm those who differ in opinion. The new has pretty well displaced the old proprium, when a man can utter his own opinions gently and sweetly, listening to others freely, patiently, and charitably, trembling in heart lest he should do them injustice, and returning always to wrathful utterances "that soft answer that turneth away wrath."

The old proprium has an imperishable love of its own opinions; thinks they are exactly right and just; wishes every body to accept them; justifies them in the most zealous manner; and in proportion as self-love prevails, desires to impose them upon all the world. It is self-assertive, aggressive, and coercive in all but a physical sense. "The proprium of one man in a religious society," says a thoughtful writer, "often causes such irritation and antagonism, that the sphere of love and unity is destroyed." This sphere of coercion which we so often see in the individual, is intensified in the aggregate body according to the numbers, intelligence, and influence of the members. The church-sphere is, therefore, more coercive than the individual sphere, as the corporation is more heartless and soulless than the constituent directors. Its tendency is to restrain and constrain, to crystallize into fixed forms, to discourage progress, to infringe upon, paralyze, and finally destroy individual liberty. And all this it does in the name of charity and good-will, in the sweetest, softest, most graceful manner, pleading in its justification its inextinguishable loyalty to truth.

This sphere of authority in the individual or in the church is well described by Swedenborg as he saw it in the world of spirits.

"There was a certain spirit, who, during his life in the body, seemed to himself to be great and wise in comparison with others. In other respects he was well-disposed, and not particularly given to despise others in comparison with himself; but being of high birth, he had contracted a sphere of pre-eminence and authority. This spirit came to me, and for a long time said nothing; but I perceived that he was encompassed about as it were with a mist, which proceeding from him began to overspread the associate spirits; at which they began to feel distressed. Upon this they spoke with me and said that they could not on any account bear his approach, because they felt themselves deprived of their liberty, and as if they did not dare even to open their lips to speak. He also began to discourse, and entered into conversation with them, calling them his sons and at times instructing them, but in the spirit of authority which he had contracted. Hence may appear what is the nature and quality of the sphere of authority in the other life."—A. C. 1507.

Swedenborg repeatedly declares that the secret and holy processes of regeneration cannot go on except in states of absolute liberty of will, thought, and action. It would be well for ministers and church members to remember this, when they are endeavoring to coerce everybody into their special forms and limits of thought. We should always leave others in perfect freedom. Madam Guyon, whose remarkable experiences are only explicable in the light of New-Church doctrine, has the following judicious remarks on this subject:

"As to those directors who appropriate souls to themselves; who would fain conduct them in their own way, and not in God's way; who would put limits to his graces, and fix barriers to hinder them from advancing—as for those directors, I say, who know but one way, and who would fain make all the world walk in it, the mischief they do to souls is beyond remedy, because they keep them fixed all their lives to certain things which prevent God from communicating Himself to them without bounds. What an account will they not have to render for these souls!"

When men, professing to be Christians, have no spirit of loving accommodation, such as the Lord always exhibits, to real or supposed falsities, but insist with inflexible will upon imposing their opinions and rules of conduct upon others, there is always an unsubdued proprium at the bottom, hard, cold, selfish, tyrannical; and the spirit of the Inquisition is really concealed underneath the profitable suavities of modern life. When several such men dominate a church, it becomes a prison to the soul, where all are virtually slaves, and each is a spy on the others. Free and sensitive spirits suffocate in its atmosphere, where progress is impossible, and the truly spiritual life can never be developed. The souls who escape its bondage only by death, enter in the world of spirits upon painful experiences, that are necessary to break up the fixed and false conditions which had been imposed upon them by ecclesiastical authority.

The sphere of every being or association of beings always imposes some sense of restraint or limitation upon us, however small or faint it may be. The Lord alone leaves man in absolute liberty, exacts nothing of him, imposes nothing upon him, and is always precisely the same to him, no matter what use he makes of his freedom. Just in proportion as we have the Lord in us, will we act toward our neighbor in a similar manner.

It is clearly our duty as New-Church Christians, never to coerce and never to permit ourselves to be coerced in religious matters; to demand and to grant the largest liberty of thought and action; and to permit no possible deviations from our own standards to diminish our love for the neighbor or our labors for his welfare. There is no righteous compulsion save of a man's self. Recognizing the uses of just and wise authority in parents and teachers, in state and church, we know also their temporary character; and that the judgments of the spiritual world, beginning often in this, are for the purpose of *dissociating* us from our present imperfect, false, or accidental combinations and alliances, and *re-associating* us upon heavenly principles in the body of the Divine Man, in whose service only there is perfect freedom.

Yours in the truth that makes us free,

W. H. H.

# LETTER XXIV.

### CONVICTION OF SIN, INFIDEL DOUBTS, THE TWO PROPRIUMS.

MY DEAR SIR:—Your two long letters have been received and duly considered. Your case is common enough, and still it has something about it very rare. It is common, because there are thousands, perhaps millions of people at this moment in the world, who are undergoing similar experiences. It is rare, because not one in a thousand has, like you, the courage of his convictions, and openly denounces himself for what he inwardly feels himself to be—a thief, a murderer, a drunkard, an adulterer, an unmitigated and irredeemable sinner from centre to circumference.

You speak the language of the good in the world of spirits, when they are putting off their externals and entering into vastation and judgment in their course of preparation for heaven. The fact is, the sphere of judgment has struck you! —the heavens are opening in you, and their light shows you the old proprium exactly as it is. The same thing occurred to myself, and in reading your letters I am treading familiar ground. You give me permission to publish anything you have written. I make some extracts for the benefit of all who are now entering, or will before long enter, that descending sphere from heaven which brings with it *conviction of sin*, and leads to the humiliation and death of the old man with all his lusts.

Think of a man seventy years old, who began preaching

the gospel of Jesus Christ more than forty years ago, who stands well with his friends and neighbors, having answered all the social and ecclesiastical demands of the age—think of him throwing off the triple cloak in which we all conceal ourselves, and exposing himself in the following manner!

"Whilst I have had many seasons of joy and peace, which I would not exchange for the whole world, my life has been almost one continued scene of melancholy, caused by the almost constant reign in me of every sin; and my troubles have so much increased of late, as almost to run me deranged.

"I believe I have been the greatest sinner that ever lived. You say to me, 'Thou shalt not covet.' I answer, you had as well say to me that I must not be hungry. You say, 'Thou shalt not commit adultery.' I answer, that if we accept Christ's definition of adultery, you had as well tell me that I must never be thirsty.

"I have never seen myself so vile a sinner in my life before, as I do at present. I see that I have never done a good thing. I have performed the duties of life somewhat like other folks, but everything was done from selfish motives. Indeed I do not believe I ever performed a single act in my life, that was not in some way contaminated with sin. My very best prayers need forgiveness, my best sermons need praying for, my tears need washing.

"Yes, my condition is a thousand times worse than ever. Pen cannot describe it, nor tongue tell it! There surely can be no worse hell than that I now feel! The whole town of 'Mansoul' is full of devils! God has hardened my heart as He did Pharaoh's, and he has deserted me as he did Saul."

Now, my dear sir, all this is but the wail of a "wounded and contrite spirit." Swedenborg says that when heaven is opened to man, "he is liable to be tormented with remorse of conscience even unto death." (S. D. 1959.) The Lord in divine mercy regulates this influx from the heavens, so that we shall suffer no more than we can bear. When a man is brought sensationally face to face, as it were, with the hells within him, he cannot help feeling himself to be a perfect devil; and it is only his own finite perceptions which give any limit to the infernal influx which pervades him. He is ready to accuse himself of everything and to acknowledge any depth of infamy. Even St. Paul thought himself the "chief of sinners." My friend G. W. C. frequently says that, when he stands in the old proprium, he can imagine the salvation of the whole human race except himself. How the Lord can save *him*, is beyond his comprehension. When I see and feel the hells within myself, as I sometimes do, I can do nothing but fly in terror to the Lord, beseeching Him to withhold me from the commission of the most dreadful sins.

Now these spiritual experiences should give us no concern. They should indeed be regarded with a kind of rational satisfaction. They prove that we are in a salvable condition— that the work of regeneration is going on favorably under Divine guidance. The man who has never experienced these things, has never sounded "the depths of Satan" nor known the secret power of the Lord. He will have to find out hereafter what it has been our happy privilege to discover here. Nor need we be in the least surprised if, as we grow older and the work in us becomes deeper and more thorough, we are led into fiercer temptations and darker hours than ever before. This is all right and according to divine laws. The highest heavens antagonize the deepest hells, and we are opened first into one and then into the other. It was so with our Lord. The temptations of the Devil in the wilderness and of the Pharisees in the temple, were slight in comparison with the later temptations in the Garden and upon the Cross. What right have we to expect any better things for ourselves? Did He not say to all of us through Peter: "FOLLOW THOU ME"?

You have been reading Madam Guyon, and you find many things in her terrible experiences so fully accordant with your own! It is a good sign that the celestial degree of life is being opened within you, and that you will soon be one of the babes of the Lord's celestial church which is now unfolding in the world. *"Fear not, little flock: for it is your Father's good pleasure to give you the kingdom."*

But you are greatly astonished at a sentence from Swedenborg, which you find in the notes appended by Mr. Ford to his edition of the "Spiritual Torrents." It contains a truth of transcendent importance, repeated several times by Swedenborg in his writings, and one that may be almost called the doctrinal Key-stone in the arch of regeneration. It is this: "If man believed, as is the truth, that all good and truth are from the Lord, and all evil and falsity from hell, he would not appropriate good to himself and make it meritorious; nor would he appropriate evil to himself, and make himself guilty of it." (D. P. 320.) Treasure that thought, my dear sir, and all the other extracts from Swedenborg in your copy of Guyon, and you will come gradually into great, abiding, and consoling spiritual light.

You present me some pages of infidel doubts which arise in your mind. They are such as you find in the writings of Voltaire, Tom Paine, and Ingersoll. They are not worth answering. When you are in the new proprium and feel the Lord in you, they totally disappear. You smile at their absurdities. When you fall back into your old proprium, they need not trouble you if you will reflect that they are not your own doubts, but those of evil spirits who are near you, and who accuse you day and night of their own evil states. You will answer them to your entire satisfaction by simply getting rid of the evil spirits who cause them.

But how to get rid of them? By constantly and boldly affirming that the Lord Jesus Christ is our only God and Saviour, from whom all good and truth proceed, and who alone is the Giver of life, light, liberty, rationality, joy, and peace. By abstaining from all evils as sins against Him. By repudiating all evil things as suggestions from the hells, and refusing all responsibility for their appearance. Wait patiently on the Lord until He sees fit to remove the temptation. Accuse yourself of nothing; but face your accusers, speak to them as you would to persons in the flesh (they will perceive all your mental movements), and pray for them with an earnest, brotherly love. Evil spirits cannot abide the combined spheres of compassion, humiliation, and prayer.

Your experiences, however, are not all one-sided. No man's can be. You have states of peace and joy, little sabbaths of the soul, little foretastes of heaven. The new proprium is a new life from the Lord in us. You know a little of it now: you will live in it almost altogether hereafter. The old proprium adheres to us so long as we exist on the natural plane of life. Our states will therefore alternate. We will have day and night; summer and winter; heaven and hell; and happy are we when we feel that the Lord is present and governs in them all.

G. W. C. read your letter, and declares that you have subject for great rejoicing; that your states of conviction, humiliation, and despair, are hopeful signs of the new life dawning in you. Oh, that all the dead Christians in all our churches could thus hear the voice of the Son of God, and begin to live! Fear nothing, my dear brother! Turn away from the hells. Live and feed among the Psalms and the Evangelists and the book of Revelation.

Yours truly,<br>W. H. H.

# LETTER XXV.

### CONFIRMED IN FALSE DOCTRINES: BROUGHT INTO JUDGMENT.

MY DEAR SIR:—Your case is a very difficult one to deal with, very obscure and very distressing. Look at the spirit of your last letter!

"I have been waiting for the relief you so fondly hoped I would soon obtain. But my trouble is greater than ever. Sometimes I hope that day is breaking: but alas! alas! those moments of hope are soon dashed. My sins are strong and lively: my graces, if I have any, are weakly and soon trampled in the mire by the foe! The devil is triumphant!

"I deserve all that I feel. I do not believe that mine is a case of 'temptation,' as you suppose. I fear that God has given me up to vile affections—has given me over to a reprobate mind. I fear that the wrath of God is revealed from heaven against me. (Romans i.) Knowing God, I have not glorified Him as God, nor am I thankful. I have thought myself wise, and have become a fool. God has given me up in the lusts of my heart to uncleanness. I fear that my case is that spoken of by Jude—'Who were before of old *ordained* to this condemnation.'

"Oh! is there any worse hell than this! Me miserum! Pray for me, 'oh, wretched man that I am'! Yours in the jaws of black despair!"

Who can believe that these extracts are the words of a good and intelligent man, who has preached what he thought was the gospel of Jesus Christ for forty years? The scientist would say, this is a case of religious melancholy, dependent on physical causes. We who believe that all physical phenomena are the effects of spiritual causes, refuse to accept any but a spiritual solution of the difficulty. The solution we offer is this: Here is a man who is confirmed in false doctrines, and has been brought into judgment by changes of spiritual states going on in the interior (of which he is unconscious), but which have let in the light of heaven upon the old proprium, and revealed the inadequacy of the orthodox scheme of salvation.

Now, excuse me, my dear friend, if I tell you that you have been engaged for a great while in preaching to the people a vast system of false doctrine as divine truth; and in proportion to your own faith and religious zeal, apparently so commendable, has been your fatal confirmation in the false doctrines you preached. Among these falsities of faith, are the assertions that God is a being of infinite justice who makes certain righteous demands of his creatures, and visits them with eternal wrath if they disobey. Moreover, that He actually foreordains certain of them to everlasting condemnation, hardens his heart against them, and consigns them implacably to perdition. And now that you are nearing the spirit-world and are loosening your hold upon earthly things, these hideous perversions of truth come home to roost upon your own head, and darken your soul with secret terrors and unconcealed despair.

Now let me ask you here: Why are you not supported and comforted by the great "scheme of salvation" which you have so often and so eloquently presented to the despairing sinner? Is his arm shortened that it cannot save? How can you dare distrust the infinite atonement of Christ, or the reiterated promises of his Word? Why do you not lay hold upon his cross, claim your share in the satisfaction rendered by his blood, experience the pardon of the Father, and rise up made whole and happy with the sanctifying benediction of the Holy Ghost? Alas! my poor friend! because these are also delusions of the imagination, bound up with many others in the orthodox bundle of falsities. They are worse than useless to you; rotten staffs that break under your weight; broken cisterns that hold no water.

You will hardly believe me, but I assure you that it is true, that all the good, worthy, Christian people in all the orthodox churches, will have to undergo experiences more or less similar to your own before they are divested of their old theological delusions and enabled to receive the genuine light of heaven. You are having a slight foretaste in this world of what they all experience after death. When they find in the spiritual world no such a God, no such a Christ, no such a heaven, no such saints, no such rewards and punishments, indeed no such general or special conditions *as they expected to find*, they feel as if their Lord was taken from them and they were left in states of mental darkness and despair.

It is exceedingly difficult to eradicate these false principles from the mind after death; and many spirits linger for years out of heaven in the world of spirits near the earth, contending for the old doctrines of trinity, atonement, faith alone, foreordination, reprobation, etc., etc., resisting the gentle efforts of angels and good spirits to enlighten and instruct them. It is well for a man, as for yourself, that his judgment begins in this world, that his false idols are taken away from him, and his old states and conditions of affection and thought are being broken up, however painful may be the process. The doubts and unbelief, the secret misgivings and despairs that are now assailing thousands of souls in the Christian churches, are glorious signs of an approaching crisis which will lead us all into a new and better and higher life.

"*And ye shall know the truth, and the truth shall make you free.*"—JOHN viii. 32.

There lies your hope, my dear sir, and the hope of all men —to know the truth, and to be delivered by the truth from the bondage and slavery of error. The truth is, that no God has ever been revealed to us but the Lord Jesus Christ (John i. 18); that He is a Being of infinite mercy, who has foreordained all to heaven and none to hell; who condemns no one, punishes no one, forsakes no one; who forgives everything even without being asked; and who, instead of giving you up to your blindness and hardness of heart, pursues you even into hell with his tender mercies, and his reproachful entreaties, "Ye will not come unto me, that ye might have life." If you had possessed this true knowledge of the Lord, and built your faith upon it, you would never have fallen into the horrible pit which the enemy laid for your soul.

Other truths also, coherent parts of a vast system of truth, would enlighten your eyes as to your present condition. I said in a previous letter which was addressed to you, that the light of heaven had been let into the interiors of your soul, and discovered to you the real nature of the old proprium. But you entertain very false ideas of the changes to be effected in that old proprium or selfhood. You have persuaded yourself and taught it to others, that this old proprium—the old man of Paul is to be washed clean and made whole, to be reformed and transformed into a "new creature," so that from having been evil and false it becomes thoroughly good and true. This is a great error. The carnal mind is at eternal enmity with the spiritual mind. It is never reformed or transformed, but it must be suppressed and subdued, and finally repudiated and put off so far as can be: but it never can be totally removed, even from the angels of heaven, who are always just as ready as you to cry out of themselves "unclean! unclean!"

But the angels do not distress themselves about this old proprium, as you do. They know that the proprium is evil: they hate it and pray the Lord to withhold them from it. The devils live in it and love it, and, whenever they get a chance, accuse you of doing so too. You are really in hell; for the interior hell of your proprium has been opened, and your attendant evil spirits accuse you of every imaginable depth of sin and infamy. What shall you do about it? Acknowledge it all—confess yourself capable of every evil thing they lay to your charge. Own that you are not good, and never expect to be good, and clinch it firmly by declaring in the words of the Master, "*there is none good but God.*" Turn your back on the old proprium and all the horrible, disgusting evil spirits who obsess you through it. Turn to the Lord Jesus Christ simply by shunning all evil things because they are sins against Him; and He will give you a new life—discreted from his own flesh and blood, which never did sin and never can sin—in which life the angels stand above their old proprium in peace and glory forever.

There is no living man, however good and pure and holy, who would not think and feel just as you do, if his interior perceptions were opened as yours have been: for what is true of you is true of all men. O, poor human nature! "paint an inch thick: to this complexion must you come at last"!

You may remain long in the darkness; you may suffer a great deal; but the Lord leads you by ways we know not, and the end is certain. You will hear the voice of the Son of God, and you will arise from the grave in which you are now so deeply buried: and then you will remember his precious words—

"*Peace I leave with you, my peace I give unto you : not as the world giveth, give I unto you. Let not your heart be troubled, neither let it be afraid.*"

Yours fraternally,<br>
W. H. H.

# LETTER XXVI.

### *UNFOLDING OF INTERIOR STATES.*

MY DEAR FRIEND :—What a strange and painful revelation you have made to me of your spiritual condition ! How my heart aches over it ! I understand it, however, a great deal better than you do; for you are bewildered and unhappy, and do not seem to comprehend your experiences at all. I pray the Lord that I may be enabled to write something which will satisfy your mind and console and strengthen your heart.

When I first knew you, thirty years ago, you were a young man of fine promise, as the world says: a man with a calm, luminous, happy face ; sweet-tempered and gentle in your manners as a woman, industrious of habit and studious of the truth ; a man exceptionally good and pure, who thought with Swedenborg that it was not at all a difficult thing to live the religious life. The world was bright, heaven was near, and the future unclouded—as they all ought to be to a lovable man whom every one was obliged to love.

You were just in that transition state between the innocence and inexperience of youth and early manhood, and the time when the selfhood develops rapidly, and hereditary evil stirs itself and grapples with a man in a life or death struggle. You entered afterwards into the labors, troubles, trials, and dangers of the world. You seemed to bear yourself manfully in the fight. You had, no doubt, the usual combats with the world, the flesh, and the devil ; but you appeared to others at least to come out victorious over all. You were zealous in the performance of every duty, social and religious; an active churchman, a model citizen and neighbor, an irreproachable husband and father.

Now you assure me that your way is covered with darkness, and the light has gone out of your life. Your face is worn and furrowed with the deep lines of vexation and care. It is with great difficulty that you conceal an aching heart and a soured spirit beneath the necessary external suavities of life. You confess that your hopes have been blighted, your ambitions thwarted; that your faith is profoundly shaken, and your soul is sorrowful even unto death. Your troubles are such burdens upon you, that the heavens seem closed, the Lord entirely absent, light and peace far away, and in your despairs you have even cast your eyes longingly toward the suicide's grave.

Now you know very well from doctrine, that these states of mind are caused by evil spirits who attach themselves to you through the medium of your own hereditary evils, for which you are not responsible, and endeavor to ultimate their lives in the world. You know also that if you resist and repudiate their suggestions, you will be finally delivered from the infestations and remanded into that new proprium which has been preparing for you from your birth, which stood out so near the surface thirty years ago, and which the Lord has withdrawn from your perceptions, to save it from profanation, but which He keeps in reserve for your future use and delight.

These unfoldings of our interior states are revelations to us of the evils which lie concealed within us. Although always painful and distressing, they are exceedingly useful and even beneficent. They give us self-knowledge—that immense blessing—and they bring the truths we have stored in the memory into active combat against the hells we have discovered, and so by degrees implant those truths in our life and will. This is the office of truth. Truth is the book which the angel gave John to eat. In the mouth it was "sweet as honey," for we delight to gather and taste of knowledge. But when swallowed, it was "very bitter;" and so are truths when we begin to absorb, digest, and assimilate them to our spiritual being.

It seems singular that one so well instructed in the heavenly doctrines, and who has led such a moral and orderly life, should not be able to keep his spiritual vision clear, and his heart serene and peaceful, when the cares and anxieties of the external life crowd upon him. You know that outside of their spiritual uses, all these things are ephemeral and insignificant, not worth a sigh or a tear. Our sorrows and troubles are almost always the lamentations of the old proprium over the destruction of its hopes or the curtailments of its delights. Happy are we when we ask nothing of the old proprium but what Diogenes asked of Alexander—to stand out of our light and give us the sun. The Divine Sun cannot shine upon us until the proprium is removed.

Your unhappiness and despair are good signs that truth is living and active in behalf of your soul. When truth is defeated and the good angels leave us, we cease to struggle; the old proprium becomes quiet and happy; we sink into states of indifference or repose; the evil nature triumphs, and finding no opposition to its will, is satisfied for a while. The seven spirits worse than the first, enter the secret chambers of the heart and hold high carnival over the ruins of the spiritual life. The happiness of that hell would be immeasurably worse for you than all the miseries you now endure.

Thinking earnestly of your case, and especially of the apparent powerlessness of all your spiritual truths to aid you in trouble, even after a good life of thirty, I may say, fifty years, I seem to myself to discover the root of the evil in a single fact. You have relied too much all your life upon truth alone. You have not sufficiently looked to the Lord as our Father in heaven. You have attempted to make Jesus a King, and He has withdrawn from you as He did from the disciples, and concealed Himself in the mountain of his divine love. The consequence is, that you have gone down upon the sea of the natural life, guided only by general laws and principles, which you think sufficient because they are his laws and stand in his place, but without his personal presence in your ship. Of course the inevitable storm has arisen, the winds are contrary and boisterous, you are tossed about in the darkness, and fearful, bewildered, and wretched, you know not what to do.

Now, my dear friend, I say to you boldly, look up with hope and faith. The same Jesus who ascended to the mountain of the divine love and became one with the Father, has descended into the very ultimates of our life as the Divine Man, and He has come to bring us into personal, individual rapport with his divine-human principle; to still the raging winds and waters, to deliver us from the infestations of evil spirits, and to bring us at once ("and immediately the ship was at the land") into the peace and joy of his heavenly kingdom.

Trained as you have been in the external New Church, you will probably cry aloud at this doctrine of the personal appearance of the Divine Man in the ultimates of nature, and attribute the phenomena to spiritualism, or spiritism, or magic. But if you will exclude all other sounds and listen attentively with the ear of the heart, you will hear the voice of the Lord, proclaiming, "It is I."

The cure of your disease—for it is a state of mental and spiritual disease—is to be found in direct communication with the Divine hand or power by means of faith and prayer. It is the sphere of the Divine love which comes to help you. Evil spirits care nothing for your truths, but combat them with the utmost ferocity; but they flee from the presence of the Divine love, for it torments them like fire. An infant, says Swedenborg, can put thousands of devils to flight. Repose, as a little child again, upon the divine-human bosom of the Lord, and you will find eternal protection.

The faith to be exerted is the simple, hearty, childlike trust in the Divine Word; the prayer to be offered is an earnest desire for perfect acquiescence and coöperation with the Divine will. Prayer to be delivered from our painful conditions is mere external supplication. Spiritual prayer is, that we may be enabled to bring down the Divine life and to do the Divine will in whatever conditions his providence has prepared for the development of our spiritual nature. Seek thus, my dear friend, the "heavenly places" near the Lord, with the Lord, and in the Lord.

The practical nature of this advice will be more clearly seen, when you remember that this is the way for the internal to govern the external. "Seek ye first (that is, as the thing of supreme moment) the kingdom of God and his righteousness, and all these things shall be added unto you." Obtain peace at the centres, and it will work its way into the circumferences. The Divine will passing into our wills, moves downwards and outwards, and readjust all external relations in harmony with spiritual requirements. It gives us a new and silent power to break idols, to change habits, to pacify enemies, to attach friends, to control and transact business, and it gradually extends and deepens, through constant faith and prayer, until we know and feel the presence of the Lord in all the circumstances and transactions of life. This is the Second Coming of the Lord to the individual soul, which He is now ready to make to an extent never realized in the world before, to all who hear his voice and open the door of the heart to his entrance. So may it be with you!

Yours truly,
W. H. H.

# LETTER XXVII.

*FREEDOM OF THOUGHT, ETC. HOW IS THE LORD NEARER TO US? REMNANTS OF THE MOST ANCIENT CHURCH.*

MY DEAR SIR:—My letters and published articles interest but puzzle and almost annoy you; as well they may any one who thinks the New Church is already born into the world, and only needs a thorough education in the Science of Correspondences to enable it to absorb and supersede all ecclesiastical institutions existing. That extreme position, however, is scarcely yours; and so I persist in entertaining some hopes of you. May they be speedily realized!

"Many questions arise," you say, "and many thoughts are suggested; but it has seemed better to be silent, to wait, to ponder and think; to come out from personal spheres, much as I may enjoy them, and look at these things in the calm light of Swedenborg," etc.

All this sounds very well; but remember Swedenborg's statement, that he who continues to debate whether a thing be so or not, never crosses the threshold of genuine knowledge, but propounds questions and raises objections forever and ever, without ever arriving at any rational conclusion.

Also, my friend, do not delude yourself with the idea that your powers of thought and judgment will be improved by withdrawing from personal spheres into the calm light of Swedenborg, when perhaps you have only evaded my personal spheres to live peaceably and happily in other more congenial personal spheres—not in the calm light of Swedenborg, but in a light from Swedenborg which has been refracted by passing through other assertive but incompetent minds.

It requires thorough and unflinching self-analysis to enable one to realize the defects of mind and character which prevent him from discovering the truth, or from recognizing it after it has been discovered by others. The prime essential is freedom—*freedom of thought*—a state of mind sometimes utterly unknown to those who boast the most loudly of its possession. The most pitiable slave to his passions sometimes thinks himself perfectly free! We are all pressed upon and more or less imprisoned by atmospheres, personal, social, and institutional, of whose mastery over us, we are as little conscious as we are of the superincumbent weight of the air. In such states truth cannot be discovered or recognized, unless the general sphere in which we are immersed consents to it and acknowledges it. There is no hope for us until we detach ourselves from all surrounding spheres, and stand alone. This process is effected in the world of spirits after death, so that the spirit can choose its own fixed conditions, utterly uninfluenced by others. Such detachment is the greatest move we can make in this life toward progress. Nor do we lose anything by it; for as Emerson says, "the detached man is the universally associated man;" but just in proportion as we break the bondage of personalisms and localisms, do we rise into the atmosphere of clear vision, true liberty, and universal charity. Think on these things.

Let us study, not only for your instruction and behoof, but for my own and for the instruction and behoof of all our friends, this wonderful picture of ourselves, drawn by the inimitable Carlyle.

"An immortal nature, with faculties and destiny extending through Eternity, hampered and bandaged up by nurses, by pedagogues, posture-masters, and the tongues of innumerable old women (named 'force of public opinion'), by prejudice, custom, want of knowledge, want of money, want of strength, into, say, the meagre Pattern-Figure, that in these days meets you in all thoroughfares; a 'god-created' Man, all but abnegating the character of Man; forced to exist, automatized, mummy-wise (scarcely in rare moments audible or visible from amid his wrappages or cerements), as Gentleman or Gigman, and so selling his birthright of Eternity for the three daily meals, poor at best, which Time yields."

"Of all blinds that shut up men's vision, the worst is Self. How doubly true, if Self, assuming her cunningest yet miserablest disguise, come on us, in never-ceasing, all-obscuring reflexes from the innumerable Selves of others; not even as Pride, not even as real Hunger, but only as Vanity, and the shadow of an imaginary Hunger for Applause, under the name of what we call Respectability! Alas! now for our Historian. Instead of looking fixedly at the Thing, and first of all and beyond all endeavoring to *see* it, and fashion a living Picture of it, he has now quite other matters to look to. The Thing lies shrouded, invisible, in thousand-fold hallucinations, and foreign air-images. What did the Whigs say of it? What did the Tories? The Priests? The Free-thinkers? Above all, what will my own listening circle say of *me* for what I say of it?"

Is it not plain to you that Carlyle here unfolds almost all of the real causes why the intellectual and religious world is unable to receive the revelations and doctrines of Swedenborg? It explains also why the majority of the receivers of Swedenborg, invested still in the wrappages of ecclesiasticism, refuse to see anything between the lines of his writings, or to permit any extension of his principles, but cling with Jewish subservience and tenacity to the jots and tittles of the letter.

Enough of this strain. Let me now, from what little light has been given me, try to answer your questions.

You ask me what was really accomplished by the Lord's Glorification, and in what sense is He nearer to us now than before his incarnation. You confess that, although you have long preached the "central doctrine" of the New Church, its full meaning has somehow or other always eluded your grasp. You probably understand it quite as well as other people, for the problem itself is so vast that it can never be included in the mental field of vision of any finite creature. Yet one person, on account of organic conditions, may get a better glimpse of it than another, and thus a comparison of opinions and conceptions may lead to useful results.

The Lord is omnipresent and therefore immanent always in all men. He never ascends or descends relatively to Himself, for He never changes. But He seems to us to ascend or descend, to appear or disappear, according to our changing states of reception or exclusion of his divine influx. Nothing excludes Him but the human proprium and the hells which flow into it. Could these be *totally* eliminated, God would be manifest through all organic forms in the universe just as He was manifested in the person of Jesus Christ. But evil cannot be annihilated, and the proprium remains always with us, differentiating us from God. Therefore his manifestations, his appearings and disappearings must always be determined by our own varying organic conditions.

How shall we find the Christ within us, who is ever pressing downward for a more perfect manifestation through us? By finding the Satan within us who obstructs his descent, and casting him out by abstaining from all evils as sins against the Lord. Satan being thus removed, the Christ within stands forth manifested in us, according to our organic receptivities, without the least effort of our own. Indeed the least effort of our own proprium will cause Him to disappear again.

Now at the time of the Incarnation, or the manifestation of God in the flesh, the whole human race was sinking under the power and bondage of the hells which occupied the world of spirits and invaded even the heavens. Rationality, liberty, religion, were all about to perish. Man was about to be cut off forever from his interior connection with the heavens, the Church, and the Word. "I looked," said the prophet, "and lo! there was no man." Such was the general and individual state of man before the glorification of our Lord. How changed now!

The divine love flowing through the heavens, culminated in a new and discrete creation—a new Adam—a natural man only from the maternal side; the Lord himself being the paternal force within. Thus evading the hereditary evil proprium from the father, through which the divine life could no longer be manifested, our Lord found in the person of the Son of Mary the organic medium for contact with all the evil and diseased conditions of humanity. From this stand-point He delivered the heavens and the world of spirits from disorderly infestations, reduced the hells to order and governmental discipline, established forever the equilibrium and free agency of man; and by glorifying his humanity, even to its flesh and bones, created a new, perpetual, divine centre in ultimates, to which all forms and forces refer themselves; thus securing the incessant creation and conservation of the universe both spiritual and natural. It would take volumes, yes, libraries, to unfold even the most general of the transcendent truths involved in this little paragraph.

He is nearer to us since his glorification, because we can now approach Him directly and personally on our own low plane of thought and feeling. We have no absolute need of the heavens or the church or the Word, except so far as He is the heaven, the church, and the Word. In other words, when we have Him, we have all these things; when He enters and abides in us, He brings the heavens, the church, and the Word. If we seek these things outside of us, it is only in obedience to the law, that man delights to project around himself in objective forms the beautiful and glorious things that he possesses within. Man builds his churches on the same principle that he shapes his statues, paints his pictures, writes his books, and sings his songs; for the order of influx is from above downward and from within outward.

The Lord is always coming to us and always being manifested through us according to our states of reception; but there are special epochs of his coming, attended by judgments, revelations, and new institutions, such as occurred at the flood, in the time of Moses, in his own earth-life, and in the last century. These special epochs of his coming are not caused by any changes in Himself, but in us; and they are caused in us by rearrangements and readjustments of forms and forces in the societies of both heaven and hell, so that new and increased influxes from the spiritual into the natural plane are initiated. We are now in the midst of one of these mighty revolutions, which will go on until all things are made new. Into those who reject the new influx from heaven, the hells will enter with renewed and increasing violence. Those who receive it gladly, abjuring the proprium, will have Christ manifested within them and revealed through them as was never possible before. Paul calls this "the manifestation of the sons of God." This, my dear friend, over and beyond the coincident and necessary illumination of the spiritual mind, is the Second Coming of the Lord; and He comes to redeem our souls and our bodies from the power of *all* sin; and to fashion us according to the likeness of his own glorious body. Preach that to your people.

You seem surprised that Swedenborg should say that the Hittites and Hivites were remnants of the Most Ancient Church, and think that the Most Ancient Church must have been historically quite a recent thing, notwithstanding the geological arguments for the immense age of the earth. Now Swedenborg says that some people of our own modern times are "remnants" of the Most Ancient Church, have perceptions of truth from good, etc., and are generally misunderstood by other people and decried as enthusiasts. There have been, no doubt, multitudes of that character, from the Africans who received the new revelation, and Guyon, Fenelon, John Fletcher, Charles Wesley, etc., etc., down to Jones Very and my friend G. W. C. It seems therefore that although a New Church is always built up from the "remnants" of the Old, not all the "remnants" are used in the building. We may logically suppose that there are "remnants" of all the Churches which have ever existed in the world; and that with the opening of the interiors and the vivification of remains, all these Churches will be restored, not in discrete but simultaneous order, and we shall behold the grand solidarity of the Church wrought out in ultimates by the Divine hand.

You ask whether there were long ages of barbarism and heathenism before the establishment of the Most Ancient

Church. Certainly not. There may have been long periods of innocent and ignorant naturalism before the evolution of the celestial man: but all barbarism is the proof of decline, of decadence, of the closure of interior degrees; nor has any barbarism ever been self-developing, but has depended upon implantations of thought from sources higher than itself. I am strongly convinced that we can never get at the real facts of the earliest history of man, until by orderly spiritual unfoldings we are brought into mental contact with the spirits of our antediluvian forefathers. The process of obtaining knowledge of exterior things from interior sources, is still in its squeaking, sputtering infancy, and excites only the contempt of the natural man; but the man of spiritual insight can already imagine its enormous possibilities.

Happy if I have sent a single ray of light where it did not shine before, I remain,

Fraternally yours,

W. H. H.

# LETTER XXVIII.

*WHY SHOULD WE NOT COMMUNICATE WITH THE DE-PARTED? SWEDENBORGIANS AND SPIRITUALISTS.*

MY DEAR MADAM :—I am always pained to see people who have been recently deprived of their friends rushing excitedly and hurriedly into spiritual matters, reaching out blindly in the dark, consulting mediums or clairvoyants, and yearning after communication with the dead. It is an unhappy and unhealthy frame of mind, productive only of evil. Such persons are not disinterestedly seeking the *truth*, the only way in which it can be found. Their intellect is not calmly engaged in the pursuit of a rational philosophy or religion; but their affections are intensely aroused, and eager to find consolation in some kind of a reunion with the beloved ones who are apparently lost.

You are now passing through this sad phase of mental experience. You are dissatisfied with everything you have read, seen, heard, or tried. You would discover some trustworthy and lawful means of obtaining a personal, conscious companionship with your deceased husband. You would be assured beyond all doubt that he is still living, and that he is happy in his new life. You have been attracted to the beautiful, philosophical, and profoundly religious writings of Swedenborg; and you ask me, if there is not a pure and lofty spiritualism within the New Church, grandly different from the crude, earthy, and unchristian spiritualism of modern mediums, which can do this great work of bringing the dead and the living into open communication?

Swedenborgians are supposed by many people to be spiritualists, and even very intelligent persons are sometimes surprised to discover the antipodal relations which exist between them. The doctrines of spiritualism are thoroughly unchristian and pagan. They deny the divinity of Jesus Christ and the sacred character of the revealed Word of God; while the whole system of Swedenborg from beginning to end, is based upon the spiritual sense of the Bible, and upon the great truth that Jesus Christ in his glorified humanity is absolutely one with the eternal Father. Spiritualism, on account of the blind surrender of the mind to spirit control, is fraught with great danger to freedom of will and rationality of thought. Whatever it may mean or result in, it is now in a chaotic, certainly an embryotic condition, and offers nothing of peculiar interest to the Christian or the philosopher. It has not added the least thing of any value to the stock of human knowledge. It has proved nothing but what the Bible had already taught us; that the soul of man is immortal; that the spiritual world is close to us, and not away off in material space; that we rise at death out of the natural body in a spiritual and substantial body; and that the life after death is a real, organic life, full of activities and felicities of all kinds, as genuine and as positive as anything we here experience.

Swedenborg is the great expounder of the spiritualism of the Bible and of the Christian religion. He was duly prepared and empowered to unfold to us the organic philosophy of the universe, the laws and phenomena of the other life, the harmonies and differences between the spiritual and natural worlds, the mysteries of death, resurrection, and judgment, and all that is right or useful for us to know in the present age of the world. He has executed his mission in such a clear, thorough, and comprehensive manner, and with such a truly scientific and rational spirit, that he seems to have left nothing for others to do; so that it is exceedingly rare for a man well read in Swedenborg, to take the least interest in the phenomena or literature of spiritualism. Why should he listen to the babbling of children about subjects above their comprehension, when his eyes have been opened to a transcendent system of spiritual philosophy which has been unfolded to mankind by Divine permission? What are even the most learned metaphysical and theological discussions of the age to him, but the useless efforts of the subjects of an old *régime* to reanimate their dead king, not having yet discovered that the new king, his successor, is standing at the door?

Now what light does Swedenborg give us on this question of communication with our departed friends?

We can imagine a state of human perfection, such as is credited to the people of the golden age, when angels and men conversed together in friendly intercourse. Swedenborg says that such a state actually once existed, and was lost to mankind by the gradual development and growth of evil. The restoration of the race to that happy condition is not an impossibility, for the upward evolution of life is continually directed by a power of infinite love and wisdom, a power embodied in the divine humanity of the Lord Jesus Christ. Swedenborg teaches that these states of visible, audible, tangible consociation of men with good spirits and angels, are dependent upon the organic conditions of the human race. Only the pure in heart can see God. Nothing produces spiritual presence but thorough affinity and similarity of affection and thought. This is a law of the spiritual world from which there is no escape. When men are delivered from evil, when they abstain from all sin, when they love the neighbor better than themselves, when they manifest the operating Spirit of God in them in the minutest thoughts, affections, and actions of life, the golden age of the past, or the still more beautiful golden age of the future, will be possible—but not before.

Our practical concerns are not with the past or the future, but with our present organic conditions. The world is at this time exceedingly evil. The heavenly standard of the spiritual life, as stated above, is absolutely and utterly unrealized among men. The heavens and the best portions or elements of the world of spirits, are therefore necessarily closed against us. If the spirits most nearly consociated with us by our evil, false, sensual, and selfish states of life, were permitted to make themselves visible, audible, and tangible to us, we should find that the very hells had broken loose upon the earth. We are preserved in our present closed conditions by the providential mercy of God. Those who endeavor to pierce the veil through presumption, ambition, or idle curiosity, are most likely to come into contact with vain, selfish, cunning, sensual, dictatorial, evil spirits, and with no others. Nor could anything be expected from them but fallacy, delusion, mischief, trickery, impositions, domineering devices, and pretended revelations.

There is one grand, conclusive, and perfectly satisfactory reason why your husband cannot communicate with you, and why you should not even wish him to do so. After death the spirit undergoes various changes of state in the world of spirits, before it can be prepared for consociation with angels and entrance into heaven. These changes are made in part by putting off the forms of external thought and affection which bind it to the natural world with its limitations of time and space. Anything which would bring it back into those old earth-states of feeling and idea, would arrest its spiritual progress, draw it backward to earth, and violate the laws of spiritual evolution, which are so beneficent in their operation for the associated happiness of each and all, and for the final and perfect union of affiliated souls. The spiritualists seem to know nothing of the great organic processes by which the spirit thus puts off the natural sphere and becomes adapted to spiritual spheres—a fact which alone should make us regard their communications with suspicion and distrust, as coming from very immature, earthly, and external spirits.

The spiritualists also ignore one of the fundamental truths of Swedenborg's system, viz., that the spiritual and natural worlds are discretely separated from each other—that each has its specific forms and forces and its special life resulting from them. The other life is far more perfect than this in all its forms of public, social, and private uses. But these things cannot be communicated by the mere guidance and instruction of spirits. They grow out of ourselves after death, according to what our life has been in this world, by a process of evolution. That life is the fruit, of which our earth-states are the leaves and flowers. The two lives cannot and ought not to be mingled upon the same plane. The birds of the spiritual atmospheres cannot swim in the seas of natural thought. Our natural life must be governed by science, reason, and the wisdom of the Word of God, and not by advice and control from invisible sources, either good or bad. Nothing could be more disastrous to his spiritual welfare, and to your own welfare both spiritual and natural, than for your husband to appear regularly to you and give advice and direction in all your worldly affairs.

Although your husband has gone from you and seems to be receding still farther from you all the time, there is one sense in which you may be drawing still nearer to him, and becoming more and more closely associated with him. Swedenborg says that a man's life consists in his love and his affections; and that those who are in similar loves and similar affections are always present with each other, whether they are conscious of it or not. United at the central points of life, two souls will finally overcome all temporary separations of time, space, and accident, and become united also in their circumferences or outward surroundings, so as to be always consciously together.

Now, two souls do not attain this spiritual union which insures their eternal spiritual presence and consociation in the other life, by simply loving each other as we do upon earth. They must become spiritually similar; they must love the same things and in the same way—God, the Word, the church, the neighbor, society, and the business and uses of life. In other words, they must think and feel in perfect harmony and sympathy in the most thorough and organic manner.

The things which tended to keep you and your husband separate here, the cares and labors of the world, family, friends, men, women, and all the habits, customs, tastes, and peculiarities of the earth-life, have been all taken away from him. He is elevated into a sphere entirely above them. They separate you from him no longer. But the things which unite you and will continue to unite you more closely are common to you both. They are not taken away from you, and they are more vivid and powerful than ever with him. They are the true knowledge and love of God and of the Word of God, delight in keeping the commandments of God, in faith, charity, good works, and all the graces and virtues of the Christian soul. These are the sacred interior bonds which unite the angels of heaven, with infinite varieties and specialties, into the most perfect societary, tribal, and family organizations, blending the male and female spirit into that sublime oneness which the Word indicates when it says, "and they twain shall be one flesh."

How are you to attain this spiritual oneness with your lost husband? Not by thinking continually of his dead form, and brooding over the solitudes of the grave. He is not there; he is risen in a spiritual body; and you will never find him, or come within the sphere of his ascended soul, among the habitations of the dead. Not by clinging to him as he was in the past, and preserving his thoughts, opinions, prejudices, affections, etc., as sacred things which you must cherish for his sake. He is undergoing spiritual revolutions about all these things, casting them gradually off like old garments, and entering upon entirely new conditions. You will probably not find him in his past life any more than you will find him in the grave.

Endeavor to keep pace with him in the spiritual revolutions he is undergoing. Die with him to all earthly things, except for the spiritual uses contained in them. Abstain with him absolutely from all sins of thought, deed, and temper, so that the spirit of God can enter and abide in your heart, thoroughly vacated of self. Make yourself acquainted with that vast system of spiritual truth, revealed through Swedenborg, into which he is even now being initiated by good spirits, his instructors in the better world. Strive to enter into the ways of that new life which he is now living; and the Lord who arranges the societies and the individuals of the spirit world, and who from the beginning ordained counterpart for counterpart, will surely bring you together.

Such is the spiritualism of the New Church based upon the doctrines of Swedenborg. You see how immensely it differs from the spiritualism of the day. It has no sensations, no mediums, no seances, no advice or control of spirits, no communications from the dead to offer you. It has none but intellectual and moral attractions. It teaches that all genuine openings of the spirit and revelations from the interior, come from the Lord and the Lord alone. It repudiates as untrue and untrustworthy everything that does not bear the sign and seal of the Lord Jesus Christ.

That such openings of the spirit and revelations from the interior will occur, and even become abundant in the future of the New Church, is probable; but they will proceed unsought from within, and be subservient to spiritual uses only, connected with the regeneration of the individual or the development of the church. They will bear the unmistakable impress of the descending sphere of the Divine Humanity.

*"When He putteth forth his own sheep, He goeth before them and the sheep follow Him; for they know his voice.*

*"And a stranger will they not follow, but will flee from him; for they know not the voice of strangers."*—JOHN x. 45.

In this true Christian spiritualism, of which the revelation through Swedenborg is the beginning, you will find light and peace.

Yours truly,     W. H. H.

# LETTER XXIX.

*MEDIUMS IN THE NEW CHURCH: THE PHENOMENA AND THE LAW OF THE PHENOMENA.*

MY DEAR SIR:—I am glad you have given me so full an account of the interesting and remarkable experiences of Mr. M. They are phenomena which deserve to be studied and recorded, as all phenomena do, whether great or small. The true philosopher wants *the facts* of a case, because the facts are the ultimates, the basis, the containants of all the causes and principles involved in their production. You ask my opinion of the phenomena; and I give it with great pleasure and with great candor, for the subject is of vital interest to the church and the world.

The facts you relate are substantially these: A good man, far advanced in life (aged 65), becomes an earnest student of Swedenborg and the Bible, spending much of his time in contemplation and prayer. He enters into a state of open vision, sees the Lord and angels, passes through terrible struggles with the hells, and finally attains to a state of celestial peace and joy, free from all combat and full of heavenly light. He is now a medium of great power. Spirits or angels read the Word with him or through him, and his voice changes when they take possession of his vocal apparatus. He is frequently entranced so that he remembers nothing of what he has said. His illustrations of spiritual truth are beautiful and powerful, sometimes consciously derived from spirits, and his utterances in entranced prayer are touching and wonderful beyond description. He claims frequently that the apostles or prophets or the Lord Himself, are present and speak and illustrate through him and the sphere of his ministration is productive of great enlightenment, peace, and joy to those who hear him.

Now what is the true nature, and what is the real value of these phenomena? Is this medium "a chosen instrument of the Lord to declare the truth to man," as you say and believe? Or is this case, like all others, only one special manifestation of a universal Law infinitely transcending it, and including it and all similar correlated phenomena as the ocean includes every one of its waves?

So far as Mr. M. is an entranced medium, controlled and dictated to by spirits outside of his own consciousness, he does not rise above the level of Andrew Jackson Davis or any of the controlled mediums of modern spiritualism. To the appreciative student of Swedenborg, the utterances of a man *under such conditions* are worth very little. The sources of error, fallacy, and fantasy from such ambushed guides, are too numerous to give their dicta the least authority. What they say must be submitted to rational analysis. If they agree with Swedenborg and the Word, we will accept them at their real value. If they differ from Swedenborg and the Word, we should reject them without the least hesitation. And I am free to confess that I do not at present see the use in the spirits or angels connected with the new heavens endeavoring to preach, teach, or instruct men upon earth, when the Lord has so plainly intrusted that mission to Swedenborg in opening his Word, and when Swedenborg has executed it in such a perfect manner, that very few of his readers have ever mastered or utilized the tenth part of the stupendous system which he has unfolded to our spiritual vision.

What possible benefit can we derive from angelic instruction? Swedenborg says that when an angel descends from his own to a lower discrete degree of thought, he loses his wisdom and his insight, and becomes stupid and commonplace. An angel entering into the natural plane of our minds has his own natural degree reopened, and is simply the man he was before his departure from this world, and knows very little more than we do about heavenly matters. On the other hand, if a man be elevated into the interior degrees by open respiration, he enters into states of knowledge which he cannot retain when he returns to his natural life.

Our true bond of connection with the angels and with heaven is the Divine Word. If we wish to know more of the Word than has been revealed to Swedenborg, or to have our lives directed by a higher power than our own rational faculties, the way is very plain. It is by a far more organic and lasting process than conversations with angels. The first step is to store our minds with the knowledges of truths which lead to good. The next step is, by a genuine and thorough life according to the commandments, to conjoin our will-principle with the will-principle of the angels, and thence from good as a centre, see all *the truths flowing from good* which they see, and which are necessary to the uses of our life to all eternity.

"During man's initiation into truth, and thence into good, all that he learns is obscure to him; but when good is conjoined to him, and he thence regards truth, it then becomes clear to him, and this successively more and more; for now he is no longer in doubt whether a thing be, or whether it be so, but he knows that it is, and that it is so. When man is in this state, *he then begins to know innumerable things*, for he now proceeds from the good and truth which he perceives and believes, as from a centre to circumference. Thence the light of truth from good increases immensely, and becomes a continuous lucidity: for he is then in the light of heaven which is from the Lord."—A. C. 3833.

We must remember that the world of spirits has an increasing multitude of New-Church people in it, both from resurrection out of this world and from instruction in that one. We must, therefore, not hasten to conclude that every medium who teaches the genuine doctrines of the church, is the organ of a new revelation from heaven. He may only be brought into rapport with spirits on the interior-natural plane, who think and feel in harmony with himself, and echo his own sentiments and opinions. This is probably the case with your friend M. and with Mrs. T. of the Riverside Circle. I would not hesitate to put James Johnston in the same class, but for certain remarkable peculiarities in his history and conduct not necessary now to mention.

You say in the last meeting you held, the prophet Samuel, Michael, and John the Baptist, and others were present. Now Michael was not a personage but a name expressive of an angelic function, and so of a certain divine principle in the Lord Himself. (A. C. 1705, 8192.) In this fact you have the key to the appearance of all the Biblical worthies in the visions and trances of Christian people. It is exceedingly improbable that any of these persons are ever present with the medium. They are, no doubt, far away from us in the old heavens which were separated from the new heavens from which our present influx is received. But when spirits belonging to a certain order or type of spiritual function or use represented by Samuel, Michael, or John, approach a medium, they flow into the knowledges of his mind and produce the impression that such are their *names*. This explains many of the phenomena of Spiritism, and accounts for the very stupid things we get from Swedenborg, Benj. Franklin, Robert Hall, and other celebrities.

I am quite sure that you are mistaken in supposing that Mr. M. is opened into the celestial degree of life, or is guided by celestial angels. The celestial never teach or preach as the spiritual do. They never discuss truths, and even dislike very much to speak of faith or doctrine. They never pray with the Methodistic spiritual-natural fervor that Mr. M. exhibits (see A. C. 10,295). Nor, if he were in a celestial state, would he need any aid or suggestions from spirits, for he would *perceive truth from good* without assistance or discussion.

The states of freedom from combats and the consequent influx of peace and joy from the Lord, are common to the angels of all the heavens, celestial, spiritual, and natural. Indeed there could be no heaven without these sabbath states of the soul. Their existence does not prove that a man has been introduced into the third or celestial heaven. They only indicate that he has entered upon the second state of regeneration: that he has contended against his evils by the divine power of truth, until he has attained to states of good, or the new próprium, from which and through which our Lord descends into his whole spiritual being, and transforms him into his own image and likeness. These states of repose, peace, and joy are attainable and have often been attained in this world. Alas! for the man who calls himself a Christian, and knows nothing of these states from personal experience.

Your medium tells you that the New Church is dead, and warns you against making an idol of Swedenborg. Now all churches and indeed all men are spiritually dead, except so far as they are in the life of charity. The living presence of the Lord is evinced, not by doctrines or organizations, but by these three infallible signs—the state of humiliation, the renunciation of evils as sins against God, and the keeping of the commandments. Wherever these states are found, the Lord and the angels and the church are present, and so far as the New Church is in those states it is living and not dead; and precisely how far it may be in those states we are not permitted to judge.

When people either in this world or in the world of spirits tell us not to make an idol of Swedenborg, I do not think it is always uncharitable to suspect that they have some idol of their own to bring forward and take the place of Swedenborg. The revealer of the spiritual sense of the Word is also the great enunciator of liberty and rationality in spiritual things; and if any man makes an idol or an infallible authority of him, he does so in the face of his own incomparable teachings. He has been the medium of revealing to us inexhaustible fountains of the true wisdom from within; and whilst I retain my right to ignore or reject anything in his writings which my rational faculty cannot accept, I am indebted to him beyond all measure or power of expression.

After due consideration, my dear sir, I do not see that the phenomena presented by Mr. M. rise above the world of spirits, or have any direct connection with any of the heavens. I do not believe that all the spirits who communicate with men are evil, or come to us with evil intent. I think good phases of spiritualism may be developed to counteract the bad;

for you may be sure the Lord will guide and govern through all good or evil appearances. I have no sympathy with the fear our people have, of grappling with spirit-phenomena. The New Church alone has the light and the power to do so with benefit to all concerned. I do not believe that class of evil spirits who feign goodness, and favor a man's opinions in order to lead him into sin and falsity, can stand the sphere of one who acknowledges the Divine Humanity, and with genuine humility, self-renunciation, and prayer, looks to the Lord alone. The Peter of the New Church is sinking from lack of faith. Let him grasp the hand of the Lord and walk boldly upon the water in the midst of the storm.

Whilst, indeed, evil spirits are inconceivably false, corrupt, cunning, and subtle, and are working, and will yet work tremendous harm in the world, and are to be greatly dreaded and avoided, I think what we may call New-Church spiritualism, of which the phenomena you present for consideration are a good type, is going to increase, and may prove a power in the church and the world. It will flow from *good* spirits in the world of spirits, still probably in their external states, but anxious to comfort and enlighten the friends they have left behind. Their movements will be permissions from the Lord, who will guide them through all imperfections and appearances of truth, to genuine good. Such phenomena may be the means of breaking up existing organizations; for I believe the Lord will never permit our New-Church people to build up a great hierarchy or church-establishment on the old models. The church-building or religious proprium in both clergy and laity will resist or scout such an idea, but it will be in vain. The Lord Himself in his own personal atmospheres is moving from centres to circumferences, to establish his church and to reorganize society, not according to old methods, but in the very form and order of heaven; and all things that oppose his movements from the interior, will be swept away.

When these things come to pass, there will be cries of "Lo! here" and "Lo! there" echoed throughout the Church; and each new development will have its friends who accept it as the central point of divine influx into the world. Men will commit the serious error of mistaking the phenomena for the law by which they are manifested, and will misconstrue their character and over-estimate their importance. We may be sure that very few of these "openings" will have any real value to unfold or expound the truth. Their use and the test of their orderly or disorderly character will be found in their moral effect. If they exhale a steady, permanent sphere of chastity and conjugial purity, of personal humiliation and self-sacrifice, of independence, rationality, and all the activities of the life of charity, we may accept them as of the Lord. But the development of a thousand such centres into active operation, would not diminish one iota the necessity of the study of Swedenborg and the Word, nor the propriety of external instruction and worship, varied according to the conditions and exigencies of human life.

The law which transcends, includes, and explains all the phenomena, is this:

The Divine Humanity of our Lord is descending from primates to ultimates, moving from centres to circumferences, entering the general Body of Humanity, and manifesting *Itself* in a thousand different ways according to the organic states of affection and thought in the recipients. This is the key to all the historical, social, and religious phenomena of the century. This law explains Mr. M. and Mrs. T., James

Johnston, T. L. Harris, and my friend G. W. C.; the advanced rationality of Brooks, Beecher, Swing, Collyer, and others, the revivalism of Moody, Harrison, and Barnes, the sensational ecstasies of our friend P., the Woman Movement, the Faith Cures, the Socialism, the Scientism, the Salvation army, and all the agitations of the day. The phenomena are many, the source is One. It is the proprium which seizes upon the phenomena, and construes and appropriates them to its own benefit or gratification. They are common property and consociated parts of a stupendous whole. Foreseeing the chaos of conflicting opinions and conduct these innumerable phenomena would engender, our Lord has mercifully given us beforehand a key to them all, a guide through all perplexities, a protection against all dangers, a test of all spirits, a perfect mirror of Law, Truth, and Order in the writings of Emanuel Swedenborg.

In the study of all spiritual phenomena, the great question for us who believe the doctrine of the Divine Humanity to ask ourselves, is this: Is the Lord Jesus Christ in them, and how does He manifest Himself? The fact that spirits teach the doctrines of the New Church is of no significance by itself; for the most subtle and evil spirits will cast themselves into the molds of our own affections and thoughts. The fact that great personages profess to be present, is reasonable ground for believing that the inflated proprium of the medium is being played upon by the invisible control. Our Lord's manifestations are of a different order. They are movements upon the heart, a breath from the celestial sphere. They are shown by increased humility, by more thorough abstinence from sin, by a growing spirit of self-sacrifice and charity, and a constant, interior looking toward the Divine Man. In these states of the life, no spiritual communications can harm us. In these states perhaps none are necessary. Do not seek them; but if they come spontaneously, test them severely and thoroughly.

Yours truly,
W. H. H.

# LETTER XXX.

*THE BIBLE OF THE SPIRITUALISTS.—THE TRUE TESTS OF REVELATION.—RELIGIOUS CRANKS.*

MY DEAR SIR:—You tell me that you are deeply interested in that new, strange, enormous book called Oahspe—the Bible of the Spiritualists, a book written by inspiration or dictation from the spiritual world through a gentleman of New York city. Another friend thinks it is a perfect epitome of all the best things in all religions, and a common platform upon which Jews, Heathen, Christians, Spiritualists, and all can stand in brotherhood and peace.

You have a great deal to say in commendation of its character, its purity, benevolence, good influence, and spiritual wisdom. You are almost ready to believe that it has emanated from some portion of the new heaven which is descending to organize the new earth. I am a little surprised that so good a student of Swedenborg as yourself, should have apparently lost sight of the two fundamental points of doctrine, which constitute the final and perfect tests to be applied to everything claiming to be a revelation from heaven, viz.: the Divine Humanity of Jesus Christ, and the co-existence and correspondence of celestial, spiritual, and natural senses in every genuine Word of God.

Oahspe, you say, deals largely in the various incarnations of Jehovah, and admits the Lord Jesus Christ to be one of those incarnations, but denies his miraculous birth from the virgin. Now this idea of divine incarnations, which runs all through the oriental mythologies and religions, has something in it radically false. There never was and never can be but one incarnation of the Divine Being; and that of necessity took place through a virgin mother without the mediation of a human father. Jehovah cannot be incarnated in a man with two earthly parents. Such a man can only be filled to his little finite measure with the Spirit of God. To say that Jesus Christ had an earthly father, is to nullify the whole work of redemption; for a soul derived from a human father would interpose an insuperable barrier between the descending Divine and the ultimate forms derived from the mother.

"It is altogether impossible for any man to be born of a human parent without deriving evil thence. Nevertheless there is a difference between hereditary evil derived from the father, and that which is derived from the mother. Hereditary evil from the father is of a more interior nature, and *remains to eternity, for it can never be eradicated.* The Lord, however, had no such evil, since He was born of Jehovah as his Father, and thus *as to his internals,* was Himself Divine or Jehovah." —A. C. 1573.

This settles the question; and the author of any book who denies the birth of Christ from the virgin Mary in what we call a miraculous manner, is in spiritual darkness, has no true knowledge of the Lord, or of the uses of his incarnation, or of the glorification of the human nature, or the wonderful processes of individual regeneration.

We know nothing whatever of the Supreme Being except as He has been revealed to us in the Divine Humanity of Jesus Christ. "*No man hath seen God at any time: the only begotten Son which is in the bosom of the Father, He hath declared Him.*" (John i. 18.) The revelation of God in Christ, especially after the unfolding of the spiritual sense of the Word, is perfect and complete. With this transcendent revelation before us, how can we listen to the little cries of "Lo! here, lo! there" which echo around us? There are no true Gods and false Gods, as Oahspe has it. There is only one God—the Divine Man, Jesus Christ; and the use of the term God in relation to other persons, is disagreeable if not actually obnoxious. The word Lord seems to me greatly preferable to Jehovah.

The Divine Humanity is the only Mediator between the Divine and the human; and there can be only one Divine Humanity. So the Divine Humanity has only one Word or Logos by which He has revealed Himself to men. There can be no Bibles or revelations from heaven except through Him; and as his wisdom moves from centres to circumferences, accommodating itself to successive spheres, his genuine Word must always have celestial, spiritual, and natural meanings, one existing from the other, and the internal meanings concealed within the external. If Oahspe cannot stand this test —and I presume it cannot—you may be sure that it emanates from the world of spirits only, from the interior-sensual degree of the natural plane of the human mind, and must rank with the writings of Buddha, Confucius, Seneca, Marcus Antoninus, Mahomet, and others, according to its own merits.

The letter from your young friend W. L. C. shows that he is what I call a religious crank. He is a "Christ-child" with a great and important mission to all the "Christ-children." He will have exhibitions, public demonstrations, and deliver messages, etc., etc. Most people would advise him strongly to suppress himself, and would reason with him to convince him of the folly and vanity of his expectations. G. W. C.'s advice is different. Let him go ahead and utter himself to the utmost. Let him exhibit his mission and do his best to fill it. All men must finally be brought to that point of proclaiming in the streets those things which they have hitherto only whispered in the secret chambers. A general turning inside out is exactly what the world needs, a revelation to ourselves of the bedlams and hells which are concealed within us all.

In special relation to this "Christ-child," G. W. C. adds, that no degree of guilelessness, of good intention, pious zeal, and honest religious endeavor can save any man from the penalties of violated law,—violated from ignorance or otherwise. The animal kingdom rests upon the previously developed mineral and vegetable kingdoms. Celestial and spiritual things flow into corresponding natural things in which their power and uses are manifested. Therefore the man who utters his interior life without a fixed organic basis of genuine natural truth and common-sense, will inevitably end in disappointment, failure, exposure, and rejection. Yet these experiments and failures must needs be made, for much of the wisdom of the future will be evolved from the miserable blunders and follies of the present.

You say you are a kind of "universal believer." In a certain broad sense it is well to be a "universally associated man," an accepter of all theologies, a rejecter of none, who sees what good and truth are to be found in all things, and excuses the evil and the false. Yet theologies differ like races and men. All may possess only apparent truths; but some are far in advance of others, and all are vastly below the wisdom of the angels. It is best for us to adhere with growing affections to the highest known standard, such as that of Swedenborg, and from its stand-points to survey all others charitably, truthfully, and helpfully. Nearest to the truth must always be best for the life.

It is probably true, as you suggest, that there is great improvement going on in the Spiritualistic movement. Its advocates have discovered that there are great dangers and evils in submitting to indiscriminate spirit control; and a strong endeavor is also being made to eject the false and hypocritical elements from their midst. These advances are no doubt similar to corresponding but more concealed improvements going on in the hells, which are being ultimated in the phenomena of Spiritism. They may be matters of great interest to the philosophical student, but from a religious or vital stand-point, what are they to us? The man who has realized the stupendous light and liberty of New-Church truth, ought to have two fixed rules of conduct in relation to these things; first, never to submit himself to be the medium or victim of spiritual obsessions; and second, never to pay the least attention to anything written or spoken by any man under the control of spirits.

Hold fast the liberty wherewith Christ has made us free.

     Yours fraternally,

         W. H. H.

## LETTER XXXI.

### *THE DIVINE MOTHERHOOD CRITICISED.*

MY DEAR FRIEND:—When G. W. C. read your article on the Divine Motherhood, he exclaimed, "This doctrine of a Divine Father and a Divine Mother—a divine Two-in-One, taught by Harris and here seen and felt by P——, is more abhorrent to me than the three persons in one God of the Old Church. It is utterly false, fantastic and degrading—except when the idea is designed to be purely figurative."

We have no knowledge whatever of the Divine Being except as He has been revealed to us in the Word and in the person of Jesus Christ. Throughout the entire Word there is no hint of a female element in the Lord. He is, indeed, called Husband and Bridegroom; but the bride, the wife, is no substance or quality in Himself, but it is the church outside of his infinity—a discreted, finite, created form, which He impregnates with his Divine Love which is masculine, and from which He creates infinite series of goods and truths as children. The Church is our Mother. In the natural degree, Nature is our mother—a vast organic Form, which is impregnated by the Divine Life as a Father, and brings forth the innumerable wonders of creation.

The Lord Jesus Christ among all his beautiful sayings and teachings, makes not the faintest allusion to any feminine counterpart, or to any state of motherhood in the Divine nature. Swedenborg, moreover, in all his vast experiences in the spiritual world, and all his wonderful unfoldings of the Word itself, has no line which would warrant or countenance such a grossly anthropomorphic idea of the Divine Being. I am sure that the fatherhood of God, the brotherhood of Man, the interior motherhood of the Church, and the exterior motherhood of nature, express all the general truths on that subject which have yet been made known to us by reason or by revelation.

In the Lord the Divine Love and the Divine Wisdom are absolutely one and indivisible, and can never truthfully be conceived of as made up of two elements like male and female. It is only in finite forms that differentiations occur, and the plural number becomes possible. The "we," "us," etc., applied to God, originated in the finite mind of man, which saw Him in double or triple forms, created by the Divine Life passing through his own double or triple structures.

Your having felt the Divine-Mother-love flowing through your whole frame with inexpressible and overwhelming delights, and receiving "as from heaven" a form of prayer to the Divine Mother inside of the Divinity, can have no possible weight or value in the eye of reason. Sensational ecstasies, from the oldest Catholic saints down to the latest negro camp-meeting, have been compatible and co-existent with the wildest aberrations of the intellectual faculty. The spiritual senses like the natural, must have their fallacies corrected by a light and a power from a source above their own level.

Yours fraternally,
W. H. H.

# LETTER XXXII.

### TO A NEWCHURCHMAN INFESTED BY SPIRITS.

MY DEAR SIR:—I am very much pleased to hear from you again; and my long silence must not be attributed to any loss of interest in your welfare, but to a feeling that it was best to let you alone until you became satisfied, and perhaps wearied and disgusted, with your wanderings in the intricate mazes of modern spiritual phenomena.

I am not conscious of feeling any "displeasure" toward you. It is a brotherly sorrow that one so well acquainted intellectually with the heavenly doctrines, could be led off to take the slightest interest in any form of Spiritism. The legitimate fruit of such a state of mind is recorded in your own sad and despairing words: "I go to the Park and walk over the most lonely paths I can find, in states of anguish and expectancy, looking for light in the clouds and trees." What a melancholy picture! A man whose eyes have been opened so that he can look into the Word and see the ineffable wonders it contains, and who has learned the precious and glorious doctrine of the Divine Humanity, walking about in lonely places, seeking to assuage the anguish of his soul in the cold and dead light of natural things!

Why should there be any solitude, or any anguish, or any doubt? Why not perpetual assurance, peace, and joy? Is it not because you have turned away from the waters of the living Word—"the waters of Shiloh that go softly"—to drink of the muddy waters of that great Assyrian river that represents the self-derived, inquisitive, assertive, appropriative intelligence of the natural man? Have you forgotten the tender reproach of our Lord, "Ye will not come unto *me* that ye might have life"? or his still more tender invitation, "Come unto me, all ye that labor and are heavy laden, and I will give you rest"?

If you will earnestly and seriously study a single volume of the Arcana Cœlestia, I am sure you will find more spiritual light—genuine, soul-satisfying, prolific light—than you will ever discover "in the clouds and trees," or in the muddy streams of spiritualistic literature; or even in the highest, and best and wisest speculations of the unillumined human mind. O my friend! why should you live in the tombs and lacerate yourself with stones on the mountain of illusion? Or why should you attempt to satisfy your soul's hunger with husks in the valley of spiritual vastation? Is there not bread enough in our Father's house and to spare?

Perhaps I have said too much. Perhaps I have intruded unwarrantably upon the privacies of your spiritual life. And yet my heart would not permit me to say less. I have been in states similar to yours—but far worse. In states, not of spiritual darkness and doubt, for I knew very well where the light was, and I shunned and feared it; but in states of interior temptation of the will-principle, of the very life. I, too, have wandered alone, but in the midnight solitude of a great city, as solitary as the sparrow on the house-top, full of anguish and despair, feeling the paralyzing influx of some antediluvian hell. In and out of these dreadful states for twenty years, my religious life was truly the stormy passage of the ark upon the waters of the flood. And yet I have found peace and rest—almost perfect peace and perfect rest. And I found it where you and all others may find it—in the knowledge and belief of the stupendous fact, unknown in the Old Church, vaguely comprehended in the New, that the Lord Jesus Christ has "come again," and stands in ultimates, with "power over all flesh"! in the personal atmosphere of his Divine sensuo-corporeal degree, ready and able to heal all diseases, to remit all sins, and to cast out all devils. Individual, personal rapport with this Divine Man, by faith, by prayer, by love, will alone make us whole; and then we shall be free indeed.

Now this sublime truth which I have been called to teach and illustrate, is the key to all the wonderful phenomena which are transpiring, and the still more wonderful phenomena which are approaching their manifestation. The inquiry of my soul in relation to yourself is this: Why should he who has known and loved the genuine truth, be satisfied to dwell in the far off circumferences amid gentile and pagan elements of the New Church now universally forming, when so much clearer light and sweeter life await him nearer to the centre?

I cannot part from you, my friend: I cannot leave you as you are. Arise and follow me, for the Lord hath called us.

Yours truly,<br>W. H. H.

# LETTER XXXIII.

*IF THE HELLS WERE SUBJUGATED BY THE LORD, WHAT NEED OF A SECOND COMING?—WHY IS SPIRITISM SO GENERALLY EVIL AND FALSE?*

MY DEAR SIR:—You ask, "If the Lord subdued the hells at his First Advent and kept them in subjection, why was there no visible, historical result from it in the world? And how did the hells rise up again, and render a Second Advent necessary?"

You say truly, "These are great and deep questions;" but I think you are mistaken when you want "a clear answer put in few words, because truth is elastic and compressible." Great truths can only be seen by the combined light of many associated truths. You cannot *understand* a universal truth until you have mastered many of its contained particulars. Try to explain Swedenborg's assertion that God is not only a Man, but the only Man, "in a few words," and you will realize the difficulty of what you require.

Our Lord at his first advent entered the human form and took on all its infirmities, including the limitations of time and space. He was then like each of us, a microcosm, a miniature of the universe. From this stand-point He ascended and descended by continuous extensions of affection and thought into all the societies of heaven and hell, just as we do in a small finite way to certain societies; but his progressions of state went on until He assumed in his own person all the states of angels and devils, and reduced both heaven and hell into perfect order, so far, and so far only (mark the words) as they were ultimated upon his own glorified human nature. The relation of all other human forms to heaven and hell remained exactly what it was before. The hells are subjugated only in the Divine Natural Humanity; and no one can be delivered from hell, except as he puts on Jesus Christ, and enters into Him so as to become a member of his body— of his flesh and of his bones. There is the ark of safety.

The apostles, especially Paul, understood and taught this stupendous truth, that we are delivered from hell by the Divine Personality of Jesus Christ entering to abide with us, and to transform us to his own glorious image. If the church had continued to live and move in the personal divine-natural sphere of Jesus Christ, the history of the world would have been entirely different, and no Second Advent might have been necessary. But that such would not be the case, was foreseen and predicted. "Ye will not come unto me that ye might have life," saith the Lord.

They turned away from the Divine Man. They ceased to look to the Lord alone. They divided his divine nature and broke his unity in their souls, by the absurd figure of three persons. They perverted the truths of the Word by innumerable false interpretations, and invented monstrous schemes of salvation. The proprium even captured the ecclesiastical spirit, and ran the machinery of the church for its own benefit and in its own manner. Thus the minds of men, the world of spirits, and even the external sphere of the ultimate heaven, became blocked up with dense clouds of evil and falsity, which entirely prevented the entrance of the personal sphere of Jesus Christ through the heavens into the human race. Therefore a Second Advent became imperative.

The object of the First Advent was to lift up our Lord's human nature into oneness with the Divine. "If I be lifted up," etc. Such was the first at-one-ment—the union of the Son with the Father. The movement was ascending. The movement of the Second Advent is altogether descending. It is a movement from centres to circumferences, from primates to ultimates. It is a second at-one-ment; but it will be the at-one-ment of the Lord with his church. He will enter the body of Humanity from within, and change the likeness of our vile corporate body into the likeness of his glorious body, so that we shall be one with Him, even as He is one with the Father.

The Second Advent being a descending movement from within, can only be effected by a successive opening of the interior degrees down into the natural. When He enters our celestial degree, He vivifies remains, awakens the affection for truth, and fires us with the heavenly spirit of charity. When He enters the spiritual degree He illumines the understanding, unfolds the spiritual sense of the Word, restoring the genuine doctrines of heaven and making spiritual conjunction with Him again possible. When He enters the natural degree, He will cast out devils, He will heal the sick, He will raise the dead, He will redeem our bodies, He will reorganize society, He will establish his church in ultimates. The hopes and dreams of Christian perfection entertained by Catholic mystics, Quakers, and Methodists, will pale into insignificance before the transcendent reality, now rapidly maturing, of Christ manifested *in* the souls and the bodies of his children.

I would gladly linger long on this glorious theme; but I must proceed to the consideration of your second question. You say that some spiritist has recently published a very plausible but subtle little book, purporting to come from Swedenborg, in which he denies some of the fundamental doctrines of the church; and you ask, "Why are all the voices of Spiritism so uniform in their declarations of no evil, no Saviour, continuity, and a materialistic presence of spirits?"

Chiefly because the world of spirits is not separated from the world of nature by a discrete degree. It is in the same natural degree as ourselves, but an interior-natural, generally invisible and inaudible to us. It is a sphere of judgment and progression, and both good and evil spirits are perfectly satisfied with their progress. The good are being divested of discordant evils and falsities; they are submissive and teachable, and entirely out of the sphere of governing or teaching. That is the reason we so seldom hear from them. The evil are being divested of disagreeable goods and truths, and getting more and more into their interior loves and delights. They call evil good, and the false true; are thoroughly materialistic, conscious of no evil, feel no need of a Saviour, love to rule and to teach, and are generally unreliable and not to be trusted.

The utter uselessness, if not absolute falsity, of all the teachings of spiritism, will become more and more apparent. There is no genuine truth outside of the personal sphere of the Lord Jesus Christ and his Divine Word. The abundant spiritual communications which await us in the future from both spirits and angels, will flow down to us only from the personal sphere of the Lord and his Word, and it will be the genuine communion of the saints in heaven with the saints on earth. It will unfold itself in the future; we have nothing now but its faint beginnings. It will be *from* the Lord and *in* the Lord; and we will only feel and know it as we stand in the new proprium which is made from the flesh and blood of Jesus Christ.      Yours truly,      W. H. H.

# LETTER XXXIV.

*THE OPENING OF DEGREES.—THE NEW ERA.—RETICENCE OR REVELATION?*

MY DEAR FRIEND:—Professional work, some sickness, and much correspondence have prevented me from sooner answering your very interesting communication. It is well also not to answer such letters too soon, but to let the subject-matter lie in the mind for repeated and successively more mature consideration. I have looked earnestly to the Lord for what I should say in response; and if what I say should prove incomplete and unsatisfactory, it will be because I have not waited patiently and long enough for that perception of truth which comes only from within.

The Lord Jesus Christ is descending from primates to ultimates, moving from centres to circumferences, manifesting Himself as the Alpha and Omega, opening the celestial, spiritual, and natural degrees of the human mind, and thus entering the general Body of Humanity with his personal atmospheres, to dramatize his living Word upon the hearts and minds of men, to establish a New Church (the New Jerusalem) according to the form and order of heaven, and from thence as a centre to reorganize human society, and reconstitute the very elements of nature. It may take centuries to finish this work, but it has begun.

If you had given your strongest intellectual assent to this great universal truth which involves innumerable and wonderful particular truths; if you had brought additional and powerful arguments from the Word and from Swedenborg, throwing an increasing light upon a subject already "dark with excessive light," as Milton says of the skirts of the Almighty; it would have afforded us pleasure and satisfaction. But you have done something which is far more acceptable to "those who know the Lord from within, and not alone from without," as you have happily phrased it. You increase the light of intellectual truth, by adding to it the glowing warmth of your spiritual experiences. It is the voice of the heart we hear in the words of your letter; the sound of the Lord moving among the celestial things of life. "Out of the abundance of the heart, the mouth speaketh." "I will give them a *heart* to *know* me, that I am the Lord," etc.

I will quote a few sentences from your letter to serve as a text or basis of some suggestions, which press earnestly upon my mind for utterance.

"My experiences so far confirm every word that you and G. W. C. have said. I *know* that these new phenomena are the descent of our Lord into the ultimates of humanity."

"Little by little during the last two years I have been called to give up one thing after another, until now I feel that I have given up *all*, and all that I am is of the Lord. You well know what it costs. The old man dies hard, and with me it has been a lingering death; for I have been influenced more or less by the sphere of doubt and skepticism which pervades the external New Church."

"Are there any Newchurchmen this way to whom I may speak of my experiences freely? The day may come, and I know not how soon, when it will be necessary for me to speak more openly to my brother ministers. The Lord will open the way and give the word."

A quotation also from your friend's letter to you which you

have kindly permitted me to see, will have a direct bearing upon what I am going to say.

"Where the consciousness of interior things is dim and partial, a person will depend in some measure upon others as 'authority.' To cease to do so, requires the opening of the most interior or celestial degree of life in man. Those who have been introduced through self-denial and soul-discipline to that *sphere of conscious life*, are not under the necessity of learning from without: they perceive divine truth from within. It shines in their hearts. They are 'taught of God.'"

It is an unquestionable fact that for many years there has been going on within the limits of our New-Church organization, a deep and quiet movement—a secret but strong revival or awakening, a struggle for a more interior life, and a more thorough realization of the presence of Christ in the soul. These spiritual states were frequently suppressed from fear of "enthusiastic spirits" in the interior, or from the fear of being classed with "spiritists" in the exterior. Imperfect and partial, they were misunderstood even by those who felt them, and utterly uncomprehended and misrepresented by those who did not feel them.

This class of phenomena is on the increase. The forms and manifestations are various, but the chief fact is the development of a higher spiritual life, not through the influence of church associations or even the study of Swedenborg, but by coming into personal rapport with the descending atmospheres of the Divine Humanity of the Lord Jesus Christ. The Spirit of the Lord is brooding over the abysses of the celestial degree of human life, and is creating that light within —that truth which flows from good—and which will be found to correspond with that light from without which leads to good, and be the clearest confirmation attainable of the genuineness of Swedenborg's mission and teaching.

This vivification of Remains is truly the work of the Lord alone, and not the work of spirits or men. Its first element is conviction of sin, the realization of the perpetual and ineradicable hell within us, and a divine dissatisfaction with the righteousness of the scribes and pharisees in which we had hitherto lived in peace. Its stages are marked by self-revelations, temptations, vastations, despairs, self-loathings, self-renunciations. It breaks up the influence of father and mother, of brother and sister, and of the whole world upon us, and leaves us alone with Christ. How cold, calm, and dead is the spiritual arctic region of the mind with its perpetual snow, sunshine, and desolation, in comparison with the earthquakes, tornadoes, thunder-storms, and tempests of rain, which agitate and yet fructify the celestial tropics of the soul!

The Lord is always the same, unchangeable, immovable. He goes or comes to us according to the closure or opening of the various degrees of the mind. If the natural degree only is opened, we know Him only naturally, that is, scientifically and historically. If the rational degree is opened, we know Him rationally and philosophically; He begins to be to us the key which unlocks the mysteries of the universe. If the spiritual degree is opened, He becomes through the Word the genuine light of our understanding. If the celestial degree is opened, He becomes the central fire of life to us, and we feel and know Him in all things. One or more of the lower degrees may be opened and the celestial degree may remain closed; but if the celestial degree be opened, the Lord flows through it into all the lower degrees, and reconstructs and rearranges the whole man from centre to circumference by the laws of influx and correspondence.

The opening of the celestial degree will be attended with innumerable phenomena according to the organic conditions and spiritual receptivities of the subject. Celestial perceptions, spiritual insights, rational illuminations, opening of the spiritual senses, must and will occur in various degrees and to different extents. The phenomena will be exceedingly interesting and exceedingly puzzling, leading no doubt to innumerable false assumptions and premature utterances. We may be sure of two things: 1st, That these phenomena can never have any *universal* value like the writings of Swedenborg, because they must always be individual expressions and experiences, varying infinitely with the development or evolution of each separate spiritual life. 2d, That they cannot furnish the basis of any *organization* in the earth-life. For an orderly ultimation the celestial must be inserted or implanted in the spiritual, the spiritual in the rational, and the rational in the natural. A new and true ultimate will no doubt be finally established, and it will probably be something never heard, thought, or dreamed of by anybody in the world. That is the Lord's work and not ours; and we can contribute nothing to it except by bringing our individual lives into perfect submission to the Lord's will.

It is plainly our duty to receive these phenomena as they are unfolded from within, in the most friendly, inquiring, and rational spirit, and to judge them candidly and thoroughly by Swedenborg and the Word; and not to ignore them or attempt to conceal or suppress them by the "conspiracy of silence," shutting our eyes and stopping our ears against them, as the majority of our New-Church ministers and people seem inclined to do. Our motto should always be: "Liberty for each and charity for all." But alas! the slightest apparent deviation from the rules of faith and order laid down by the early leaders of the Church, seems to excite in the breast of some Newchurchmen that uncharitable spirit manifested by the disciples, when they said to our Lord, "and we forbade him, because he followeth not us." We are therefore justified in inquiring how far a man, having the utmost courage of his convictions, but uniting the wisdom of the serpent with the harmlessness of the dove, may still be silent or reticent about these phenomena in harmony with the law of the divine concealments.

Our Lord once asked his disciples what was the public opinion regarding Himself. (Matt. xvi. 13-20.) They answered that the people thought He was John the Baptist, or Elias, or Jeremiah, or one of the old prophets risen from the dead. The Divine influx into the old unbroken mold of Jewish thought, created the impression that He was sent to revive and reanimate the old forms and forces of the Jewish religion. "But whom say ye that I am?" Peter answered, "Thou art the Christ, the Son of the living God." Upon the rock of this truth, *God manifest in the flesh*, our Lord then declares that He will build his church—something entirely different from and superior to the Jewish religion. And now comes an astounding occurrence. Although knowing that the people were in a general state of ignorance or delusion regarding Him, and that Peter had just expressed the genuine truth of the matter, He deliberately perpetuates the public misapprehension of divine things, and charges his disciples to "tell no man that He was Jesus the Christ."

We cannot doubt that the laws of divine withholding and divine concealment are dictated by infinite wisdom and mercy. When men would deny, pervert, or destroy the true Christ within themselves, He is withdrawn or concealed from them, and they are permitted to imagine that they see and feel God in the galvanizations and perpetuations of old forms of thought and conduct. But how did Peter arrive at such a different conception of Jesus? It was not revealed to him by flesh and blood, for celestial truths, the fountain-heads of all other truths, are not discoverable by the will and the understanding of man. They are not the truths of revelation that lead to good through the understanding; but they are truths which flow from good through the heart. (See A. C. 5804-6.) It is the Father which is in heaven who reveals them to us. They come to us by way of the new will when the old will is dead or quiescent. Those who are combating evils from truths which lead to good, cannot always comprehend or receive these more interior truths that flow from good.

Now, my dear friend, God manifested in the spiritual sense of the Word, is not the rock upon which the church of Jesus Christ is to be built. Many of our New-Church people seem to think so, but it is a terrible delusion. No resurrected or unfolded Elias or Jeremiah will satisfy the divine heart-instincts of the celestial age dawning upon us. The Father will reveal to the Peter of the New Church, that Jesus Christ is not only the spiritual truth made known to us through Swedenborg, but that He is the Divine Man, having all power in heaven and earth, entering (to abide) into all the degrees of men and nature; and this is the divine truth upon which the church of the New Jerusalem will be established. And this truth will be concealed from the men of the age and the men of the church, so far as may be necessary or salutary, until the divine preparations for its general reception are perfected.

Now what shall we do about it?—we who have felt the Divine Father moving upon our hearts, until He has revealed Himself to us, not only as a spiritual Sun shining in the Word, but as God manifest in the flesh—a living Presence in us, having all power over our affections, thoughts, appetites, and desires; what must we do about it? Let us look again to the Word for light.

Our Lord took his three disciples—representing the love, faith, and obedience of the church—into a high mountain apart, introducing them into a celestial sphere of affection, and opening their spiritual eyes, so that they saw Him in a glorified form, "his face shining like the sun and his garment white as the light," conversing with Moses and Elias who represented the Word as revealed to man. When the vision passed away, these disciples knew by the evidence of their own senses, that the man Jesus Christ standing before them, apparently only a man like themselves, was interiorly the Living Word and the very God of the universe. And yet this transcendent truth was concealed from the church and the world for a time. They were solemnly charged to tell the vision to no man until the Son of Man was risen from the dead. It was plainly because preparation had not been made in the minds of men, or planes established in them for the reception of such a sublime and universal truth.

This narrative is pregnant with meaning for you and all of us. In vain will we tell the heavenly visions we have seen, the wonderful truths we have discovered, the high states apart into which we have entered, and the tabernacling of the Living Word in our souls, except to those in whom the Son of Man has risen from the dead. And instead of telling these interior things to people who are not ready to receive them, and who would perhaps reject and deride them, had we not better preach to them the resurrection from the dead, as the only process by which they can be led to feel what we have felt, and to believe what we believe?

Ah! it is well for us to question one with another what this rising from the dead may mean. It is the death of the carnal nature, the subjugation of the selfhood, the casting out of the old proprium: it is the resurrection of the Christ in ourselves, of the new proprium discreted from his flesh and blood, of a new life of which in the old proprium we had not the slightest conception. Correspondences and spiritual truths from the Word are only beautiful sports of the imagination, unless they lead to conviction of sin, contrition, confession, humiliation, repentance, self-loathing, self-renunciation, despair, and death. This is the only path that leads up into the mountain apart, where Christ is transfigured and seen in his glory. Preach their own resurrection from the dead to your people, preach the birth and growth and life of Christ in their own souls; and in proportion as the old man dies in them and the new man is created "in righteousness and true holiness," will they comprehend the Second Coming of the Lord, not only in the intellectual sphere of the mind as a spiritual light, but as a personal entrance into the Body of Humanity, and into the heart and blood and muscles and flesh and bones of our daily life.

The nature and extent of the reticence and circumspection to be employed in the enunciation of truth, must vary immensely with the individual, the uses, and the conditions. What one person may declare with propriety, another cannot. The church is not a debating society for the discussion of truths, nor a philosophical association for their discovery. It is based upon revelation, and its mission is to assert and to confirm. The atmosphere of doubt, debate, and collision would be uncongenial, perhaps inimical, to the atmosphere of acknowledgment, worship, and love of God. The things of God and the things of Cæsar must be kept separate, and each must have its due. The man who is truly dead to self and consecrated to God, may safely trust the Divine Providence to lead him through all the difficult and delicate questions which may here arise.

How can genuine liberty and rationality be enjoyed in any association, religious or otherwise, which is governed by the principles that actuate society in the present condition of the world? Suppressions of opinion, surrender of will, compromises expressed or not, accommodations, adaptations, reticences, are inevitably more or less necessary to the maintenance of any organization at all. And yet in such states men can neither clearly see the truth nor honestly live it. We are compelled to pass through death and the judgment, whereby our external life is entirely broken up and put away, in order that the internal may come forth, utter itself in perfect freedom, and choose its own fixed conditions.

Now what Swedenborg describes as happening to every one in the world of spirits, is about to happen to every institutional form of human life. "It is the sunset hour of the world." The night of death and judgment approaches. Society is about to die; governments are about to perish; churches are about to dissolve. Men do not believe it because they do not see any adequate causes to produce such stupendous results. They will be gradually, very gradually, effected by the conscious opening of the interior degrees of life. Unless the Lord was to graduate and moderate the spiritual forces now inflowing into the world, all our social and ecclesiastical systems would explode with a rapidity and violence which would produce a perfect chaos. No flesh could be saved. Were the conscious interior life of the sexes, for instance, suddenly opened in all people, as it already is in a few, the institution of marriage, the palladium of human life, would undergo such revolutions as to endanger the very existence of the race.

When the celestial degree is opened in those who have experienced the death of the old proprium, they will enter into states of perception of truth, incomprehensible to spiritual or natural men; but will have no desire to speak of them, and a genuine aversion to teaching or preaching them. "What is the use of it?" they say. "Nothing can be done from external stand-points. The Lord is moving from within, and will bring everything to pass in his own way and his own time. When the interiors are opened, men will see things intuitively and without instruction."

The unfolding of our interior states or even our interior convictions to others, must be governed with circumspection and regulated by common sense. The reticence which might be praiseworthy in you, might be blamable in me. You minister to the spiritual wants of a mixed, heterogeneous congregation, coming into contact with their personal spheres. To perform your uses toward them, you must accommodate yourself to their states and conditions, being careful not to repel, or unsettle, or mystify them by things which they are not ready to receive and perhaps not able to comprehend. You can do them most good by working in the sphere of the affections; and you can do that to the best advantage from the stand-point of cherished truths, even apparent truths, with which they are already acquainted. Teach them to do the will of the Lord, and they will come spontaneously after awhile to know of his doctrines.

Yours truly,

W. H. H.

# LETTER XXXV.

### ON SOME OBSCURE PASSAGES OF SCRIPTURE.

MY DEAR FRIEND:—I have had several inquiries made of me lately, as to the true meaning of certain passages in the Bible. I propose to answer four of these inquiries, one of them made by yourself, in the present letter. Two of them relate to passages from the Word, the other two to passages from the Acts and from Romans respectively. The Scriptures include all the sacred writings bound up in our Bible. The Word, in the New-Church sense, consists of those books only which contain a spiritual meaning within the letter. The Word contains spiritual truths clothed in natural forms. The sacred writings outside of the Word contain only the natural conceptions of spiritual truth formed by those who lived at the time of its enunciation. This idea is important to a clear comprehension of the difference between the Old Church and the New. The New Church is being built upon the words of the Master only; the Old Church was built upon the interpretation which the disciples put upon the words of the Master. This interpretation, often crude, imperfect, immature, and contradictory, has a supreme authority in the Old Church, which is repudiated in the New.

You refer me to the tenth chapter of Daniel—and a very wonderful one it is—and to verse thirteen, and ask we why the prince of Persia withstood the Divine influx for one and twenty days, until Michael came to the Lord's assistance; when yet

Swedenborg gives the prince of Persia a very high signification of spiritual and intellectual truth.

Two thoughts occur to me in this connection. One is the relation to opposites which exists in all the Divine writings. Everything which relates to good, relates also to evil; everything which relates to truth, relates also to falsity. Fire may mean the divine love which comes down from heaven and melts our hearts into corresponding love and tenderness; or it may mean the fire of evil passion, which is at once the life and the torment of hell. Mountain is the mountain of holiness where the Lord reigns supreme in us; but it is also the mountain of self-love, in the groves of which we worship our own idols. The lion is the lion of the tribe of Judah; but he is also the roaring lion seeking whom he may devour. So the prince of Persia has a good and evil signification to be determined by the context—remembering the fundamental truth, that persons and places in the Word have no individual or local significance, but are strictly representative of spiritual states and principles.

But there is another way of looking at your difficulty, and it is one of great importance. Let the prince of Persia represent the very highest forms of angelic intelligence, and yet under certain conditions he would be ready to withstand the Lord and resist his influence. See A. C. 4287, where we are taught that the Lord assumed all evil states, from those in the hells even up to those of the angels: and again, see A. C. 4295–4307, where it is affirmed that the Lord fought in temptations with the whole angelic heaven, and that these temptations were the inmost of all, because the angels act only into ends and that with surpassing subtlety. Our Lord's bitterest tears are at the graves of his friends, and his keenest cry of anguish is over the state of his own Jerusalem.

Yes, my friend, it is our religious proprium which most strenuously resists the coming of the Lord at the present day. It is our very faith and zeal and goodness, our loyalty to the church and the Word, our reverence for saints and martyrs and teachers, all so good in themselves, that make us turn away from the personal advent of the Divine Man, and reject the doctrines of the celestial life as something new and strange, or far off and impracticable.

Please notice that the prince of Persia withstood the heavenly influence "one and twenty days," and that Daniel mourned and fasted exactly the same length of time. (vs. 2, 3.) These represent the same states on the interior and the exterior planes. Men mourn and fast, or are in states of temptation, darkness, and vastation, when the Bridegroom is not with them; and it is in these same states in an interior degree, that they resist or withstand the coming of the Lord —alas! not knowing who He is or how He comes.

Some one wants more light upon the statement, that, if a man hate not his father and mother and wife and brethren and sisters, he cannot be the Lord's disciple. (Luke xiv. 26.) The common instincts of mankind revolt against the literal interpretation of this passage. No one believes it to be literally true. Even when heresy was treated as a sin and a crime, the persecuting church could never bring its wildest devotees to the point of abjuring all natural human affections even to the extremity of hate. Christians have conjectured that in some way or other it means that the evil things within ourselves are to be put away and rejected; but the philosophy of Swedenborg alone gives us clear and satisfactory information on the subject.

The relationships above mentioned are the spiritual states

of the old proprium or selfhood. These states are exceedingly numerous and varied, and they bear relations to each other corresponding to the relationships of human kindred. Our father and mother are the interior states of the evil and false which have molded our characters, begotten us as it were, and brought us to our present stand-point. The wife of the old proprium is the state of evil affections which corresponds, and is married as it were, to the falsities of the individual understanding. Our children are the other succeeding states which will surely follow in us, as the legitimate fruits and offspring of our present unregenerate conditions. Our sisters and brethren are all the collateral evils and falsities born of the same parents, and of one blood and spirit with us in our evil state. Our "own life" which we are to lay down, is the love of self and the world, which is the root of all evils, and of which all these related evils and falsities are only so many manifestations. This is a picture of the proprium or selfhood of the unregenerate man, of that carnal mind which is "enmity against God." Observe that Paul does not say the carnal mind is at enmity with God, for that might terminate; but its very essence, its definition, is "enmity against God."

Now these states of our carnal life are not only to be denounced as evil and false, and to be repudiated and put away, but they are to be *hated*. A man may resist and renounce an evil thing, and yet love it and sigh for it. Our Lord contemplates a radical, total revolution in the life and character of his disciples. Our old states, our self-importance, our ambitions and vanities, our lusts and follies, our covetousness, our falsehoods, our pretensions, our sins of omission and commission, are not only to be cast off, but to be loathed and hated to the bitter end. It is only a radical change in the will, in the vital principle, which can do that. Love is attraction; hatred is repulsion. The evil repel the Lord and the angels from themselves. Just in proportion as we repel the old selfhood from us, will we be brought into rapport with the Lord and the heavens. Thus can we become his disciples, and learn of Him, who is "meek and lowly in heart."

A dear little New-Church woman who has been emancipated from the bondage of the dreadful doctrine of predestination, desires to help her friends out of the same; and she wants to know how I interpret the ninth chapter of Romans, which is considered the impregnable stronghold of that dogma. I do not interpret it at all, for it is no portion of the Word of God, although it stands among the sacred writings. I criticise and judge it by my reason and common sense, just as I would criticise and judge a chapter of Augustine, or Luther, or Wesley. Paul's ideas are only more interesting than theirs, because he lived in the very time of the Incarnation, and was personally acquainted with those who walked and wrought with Jesus.

It is commonly supposed that the apostles were imbued with wisdom and power from on high to see the genuine truths of theology, and preach them to the world; and that therefore their words are words of unquestionable spiritual authority. This is a mistake. Their spiritual illumination was graduated according to their own states of regeneration. They understood only what they were organically capable of understanding, and they understood exceedingly little in comparison with the accumulated knowledge and cultivated thought of the present day. They were essentially Jewish, external, sensuous, legal. Paul, the most learned and pretentious of them all, darkened with his crude metaphysics the beautiful simplicity of Christ's theology. The evolution of the church and the development of doctrine took place according to the laws of the human mind; and the evolution and development from the very beginning receded from the genuine truth instead of approaching it. The Lamb "slain from the foundation of the world," means that the doctrine of the divine love in the Divine Humanity was misunderstood and rejected from the initiament of the church.

Paul judaized the Christian doctrine. He had some vague idea that the Old Testament had a spiritual meaning, but he had no key to it; and his view of the relation between the mission of Christ and the Jewish sacrifices, was exceedingly crude and incorrect. He understood the new life—the experiences of the soul in its struggle against evil—far better than he did the new doctrine. The good element of the church, John, remained until Christ came again. The truth element, represented by Peter, was soon perverted and crucified, head downward. If Paul's conception of God had risen above the Jehovah of the Jews, he would have known that God hardens no man's heart, and that Pharaoh hardened his own heart by his persistent disobedience of the divine commands. How utterly alien to the doctrine and spirit of Christ are Paul's words in this chapter!

*"What if God, willing to shew his wrath, and to make his power known, endured with much long-suffering the vessels of wrath fitted to destruction:*

*"And that He might make known the riches of his glory on the vessels of mercy, which He had afore prepared unto glory:*

*"Even us, whom He hath called,"* etc.

What but the most pitiable and trembling subserviency to a supposed infallible authority, could have made rational beings accept this miserable conception of the true God as gospel truth?

But in their predestinarian interpretation of this chapter, theologians have out-Pauled Paul, or gone a long way ahead of him. It is clear to me that Paul, here at least, had no intention of teaching that men are foreordained to be good or evil, and cannot possibly evade their final destiny. I give him credit for presenting a far more rational and beautiful idea. He is anticipating objections that might be raised against the facts, that God selected Abraham for a great mission, that He preferred Jacob to Esau for reasons of his own, that He made of the Jews a peculiar and chosen people, and that He is now ready of his own good will to extend his blessings to the Gentiles also; and that it is folly for any man to dispute or resist his will. He says virtually, that the organization of this universe containing such infinite harmony in infinite variety, is such a stupendous affair, that one great intelligence must preside, like the potter making his vessels, who foresees, provides, arranges, and consummates his work according to his own divine idea. In other words, men and nations are created for specific uses, of necessity without their knowledge or consent; but these are foreseen and ordained by infinite wisdom and mercy, and all will find the true harmony and happiness of life in their just performance. This approaches Swedenborg's doctrine of the Grand Man: that in heaven there are degrees of goodness and wisdom requiring an infinite variety of forms for their manifestation; that those represented by hair and bones and teeth and nails, are incorporated into the great body of spiritual uses, along with the greater and nobler vessels and organs; so that high and low, rich and poor, wise and simple, etc., are forever wrought into a happy and resplendent unit, as of a single being.

Paul gives us the true reason why every man should be perfectly and eternally contented with his lot; why he should accept his own specific mission (for every man has one, and was predestinated to a definite niche in heaven), and fulfill his calling, high or low, small or great, without repining at Providence. In foreseeing, providing for, and evolving the universe, which is a complex organism of concurrent and harmonious uses, it was necessary that God should appoint each individual his form, station, and function; and the evils of the universe have sprung from the selfishness, dissatisfaction, and disobedience of the human proprium, complaining of its condition, envying or assailing the functions of others, and refusing to consider itself as a mere atom whose real life and happiness are only to be found in its perfect adjustment to the service and happiness of all the rest.

I venture to say, that if Paul had evolved and elaborated his own idea more fully, he would have given us something nearer to the sublime conceptions of the New-Church philosophy, than to that dogma of predestination which has cast such a painful and hideous shadow over a considerable portion of the Christian world.

Another lady seems to think that Stephen seeing the heavens opened and "the Son of Man standing at the right hand of God," is some sort of proof of the existence of at least two persons in the Trinity. Now, what did Stephen really see? It must have been either an objective reality independent of himself, or a spiritual vision projected from his own mind and expressive of his own conceptions of truth. Can the Infinite Being ever stand before any finite creature as an *objective reality* subject to his inspection? It is, of course, utterly impossible. No man hath at any time either heard his voice or seen his shape. Only the Son hath revealed Him, and *in* the Son alone do we see Him. Therefore Stephen's vision was the projection of his own thought, which, like that of all the apostles and disciples at that time, was very immature and imperfect. Our Lord had accommodated Himself to the states of men and the limitations of time and space, and they were permitted, as a temporary or provisional necessity, to conceive of Him as a threefold Being under the names of Father, Son, and Holy Ghost, until the fullness of time when He would return again, open his Divine Word, and reveal Himself to his children as the Divine Man, one in person and in spirit.

Swedenborg's interpretation of the Word, given to him from heaven, will disperse all illusions, reconcile all discrepancies, solve all difficulties, and give us the genuine truth.

Yours truly,<br>W. H. H.

# LETTER XXXVI.

*SHALL WE STAY IN THE OLD CHURCH?—MARRYING OUTSIDE OF THE NEW CHURCH.—HOW SHALL WE BE SAVED?*

MY DEAR MADAM:—A great many people are asking the questions you have propounded; and I give you answers which seem rational to me, but I beg you to let them have no authoritative weight with you, except as you find them to harmonize with the teachings of Swedenborg and the Word.

You are an isolated receiver of the heavenly doctrines, with very uncongenial surroundings. You have been and still are a member of the Episcopal Church; but you complain that you experience no growth of spiritual life in its communion, that it has become a burden to you; and what must you do about it?

That perfect, beautiful, and harmonious adjustment of internal and external relations which will make all things congenial to us, is only to be found in heaven. It is the ideal after which we are all consciously or unconsciously striving; but as the issue depends upon others as well as upon ourselves, our aspirations are not likely to be gratified until the redemption of society from its present wild beast state into the truly human form, has been considerably advanced. In the meantime, however, is not the deep sigh for congeniality very frequently the mere cry of the old proprium for something which will make it comfortable and happy, without any genuine regard to the elevation and purification of our own states or those of others? Would it not be well to ignore that question of congeniality altogether, and to substitute the question of duty, and thus accommodate ourselves in all true and loving ways to the states of those around us, and seek our happiness, not in the consociation of congenial spirits (see Luke vi. 31–34), but in the society of those to whom we can render even the least domestic, social, or religious use?

Whether a Newchurchman should attend the services of the Old Church or not, depends upon his own spiritual condition. The more thoroughly he is in externals, the more readily will he believe that the Sabbath cannot be duly kept without a willing and reverential attendance on some divine service; and if there is no church of his own faith accessible, he will congratulate himself that he is cultivating a liberal spirit of charity toward his neighbor, by joining him in the public worship of God. He will urge, and with great reason, that external forms and ordinances are necessary to the maintenance and orderly ultimation of the spiritual life. The church, any church—Methodist chapel, Jewish synagogue, Turkish mosque, Hindu temple, Chinese pagoda, Catholic cathedral—is necessary to the instruction, peace, order, and happiness of society. We pass through a whole series of apparent truths before we reach genuine truths; and it is right and proper to recognize the uses of imperfect systems of truth and forms of worship, until better and higher things can be attained.

The Newchurchman who thinks from external stand-points, can easily persuade himself that it is a good thing to keep the Sabbath by going to church, that he thus sets a good example to others, and contributes his mite to upholding one of the safeguards of respectable society. But he has very little interior perception if he supposes these things will contribute to the development of his own spiritual nature, or if, indeed, he is not aware that there is great danger that the atmosphere of an external and dead church, will drag him down to its own level of formalism and literalism.

This question, like all others, must be determined on the principle of use. It is impossible for my friend G. W. C. to attend any church whatever. The interior states of all the people, minister included, are open to his perceptions, and are represented to him in correspondential forms. The consequence is, a bedlam, a pandemonium, a terrible confusion of sounds, colors, and odors, weeping and gnashing of teeth, contentions, mockeries, etc., etc., until he becomes so nauseated, giddy, and stupefied that he is compelled to retire. The same effect is produced upon him by the mingled spheres of public assemblies for any purpose. His strange and long-continued and oft-repeated experiences prove how little interior harmony or spiritual union there is in any of our religious meetings, and how far we all are from the perfect order and peace of heavenly associations. It is no wonder that years of instruction, temptation, and vastation are generally necessary in the world of spirits, to reduce our old proprium into sufficient subjection for us to be initiated into those stupendous gyres or harmonic movements of associated affection and thought, which make the life of heaven.

It was humiliating and incredible to me many years ago, when I was in the New-Church ecclesiastical sphere, laboring to build up an external church, enjoying the Liturgy and even submitting to re-baptism in amiable deference to the opinions of respected friends—it was humiliating and incredible, I say, to learn that G. W. C. found no particular difference between a New-Church assembly and an Old-Church one. It was interiorly equally discordant, equally actuated by the old proprium, equally remote from the perfect order, peace, and beauty of heavenly worship. How could I do otherwise at that time, than think my friend G. W. C. was the victim of hallucinations and fantasies? How long has it taken me to comprehend him, even in the partial degree that I do at present!

And now I will make a confession of my own experiences. After thorough trial of many years in both Old- and New-Church organizations, I can look back and see from far higher rational ground than I have hitherto occupied, that they were of no benefit whatever to the development of my spiritual nature; that they rather deadened my conscience by satisfying me that I was engaged in obeying and worshiping God in a most acceptable manner; that they kept me in closed conditions, in the very mold and spirit of the old dragonistic affection and thought, and hindered me from knowing or feeling that higher life which at present no external organization can either hold or expound.

It seems that people who are satisfied with the existing order of things, and who think that submission to all the social and ecclesiastical demands of the age is the life of religion, can seldom be let into those temptations and vastations which are absolutely necessary to break up the incrusted evils and falsities of old systems, and to let the light and life of heaven into their souls. They do not want to be brought into judgment, but to be left at ease in Zion. They shrink, not only from the putting away of the old proprium, but even from a knowledge of it. They love those external things which suppress or conceal their interior natures, not only from others but from themselves. (They have not realized the fact, that true worship is simply the love of the Lord and the neighbor manifested in the activities of life.) They cling to the mountains of Samaria or to the temple at Jerusalem, not understanding the words of the Lord, "*The hour cometh when ye shall neither in this mountain, nor yet at Jerusalem, worship the Father.*"

When, through the leadings of Divine Providence, I let go of all church forms and church influences, I was driven into the wilderness and passed through temptations and vastations, being with the wild beasts, until I was reduced to states of utter humiliation and despair. Nor did I get out of those hells by going back to church forms or church influences of any kind. That course I believe would have arrested the work of God in my soul. I was delivered by coming into the personal sphere of the Divine Man, who has now descended into ultimates, and has power over all flesh, and is ready to save from all sin every one who comes to Him and to Him alone for life and grace. Nor from the stand-points of this new life which has been continually growing in me for the last five years, do I feel the least necessity or the least desire to join in the external work of any ecclesiastical association, except so far as the distribution of the Word and the dissemination of the heavenly doctrines are concerned. I have learned by my own individual experiences, that the Second Coming of the Lord will not take place through an organized church, but through the individual souls of men, from which as centres He will reorganize society and establish the New Church in his own time and in his own way.

Individual experiences are instructive and suggestive, but they should never be authoritative. We are living in a transitional period, when there is no genuine church upon the earth except that which is ultimated in the good deeds of the daily life. There is nothing authoritative, because we are in the midst of the breaking up of all authorities, so that the Lord may establish his personal government among men. (Every soul must discover its own duty, and do it without reference to other people.) (The Lord leads us all differently, and by ways unknown to ourselves or others until we look back and see what He has done for us.) Consult your own conscience and reason; analyze your motives fearlessly and profoundly; act from the principle of *use*, and for the benefit of others; look constantly to the Lord and his Word; keep your heart always open to Him by faith and prayer; try all things, prove all things, put charity always in advance of faith, and He will lead you aright.

I think you experience no spiritual growth in the church because you look for it where it cannot be found. You would probably find it agreeable, instructive, and useful to attend church, if you divested it in your mind of all its old ecclesiastical prerogatives and prestige, and regarded it simply as a social institution. You would then not expect much from it, and would cease to estimate your progress according to orthodox measures and methods. You would find your true religious life in the study of Swedenborg, in frequent communion with the Word, and in that personal rapport with the Lord Jesus Christ which is attained by faith and prayer. You would feel it manifested in you and through you by a growing love of truth for its own sake, and an ever-increasing desire to do good. A genuine spiritual life works from within outward, creates its own methods and establishes itself in its own ultimates.

You next ask if it is ever advisable for a New-Church person to marry outside of the church. As I do not perceive the right of any external organization to call itself the Lord's New Church, your question practically amounts to this: Is it advisable for a receiver of the heavenly doctrines, who is endeavoring to live the life they inculcate, to marry an unbeliever of those doctrines? In the present transitional state of society, when the Old Church is dead and its successor not yet established, or at least is concealed from sight; when so few true marriages are possible; when so little is fixed or even fixable, I do not think it a matter of much importance. I do say, however, that it is better to marry a liberal unbeliever, than any strong religionist of any branch of the Old Church; for the former has already outgrown or outlived or unlearned many falsities which stand in the way of the latter, and is therefore really more receptive of the truths on which the new order will be based.*

---

* A passage in Swedenborg (A. C. n. 8998) is often referred to by New-Church writers, as teaching that it is altogether wrong—yea, *heinous* as the angels view it—for a member of the nominal New Church to marry outside of its communion. The prohibitory clause (or rather, that which is so regarded) reads: " Marriages on earth between those of different religions, are accounted in heaven as heinous." The mistake so often made here, lies in assuming that members of the organized New Church, because they understand and interpret the Word differently from other Christians, are therefore of a "different religion." This is not so. All who accept Christianity, however differently they understand the Scriptures, are reckoned by Swedenborg as of one and the same religion. But Jews, Mahometans, Buddhists, Pagans—all who do not accept Christianity—have a different religion from Christians. Christians, therefore, should not enter into marriage with persons holding some different religion from the Christian. That this is Swedenborg's meaning, is plain from his own

You say you have read with the utmost avidity and delight all I have written in the INDEPENDENT. You acknowledge with your whole heart and mind the great truths enunciated by G. W. C. and myself concerning the Second Coming of the Lord. They have vivified and exhilarated your spiritual nature, and renovated your whole life; and you want to know how and how far you can labor to impress them upon others. You can do very little in the matter, nor can we, nor can any man. The movement is from the heart or centre of the New Church, and is governed by the Lord alone. The circumferences may be in agitated and rapid motion, but the centres are in comparative rest and obscurity. Our views are quite incomprehensible to those who are unacquainted with the doctrines of Swedenborg. Even the majority of those who believe these doctrines will be very slow to receive our interpretations of them. They will be very much ignored or rejected by the present generation of Newchurchmen. It does not matter. The Lord directs the minutest things in the universe. The best way for us to coöperate with Him in instituting his church upon earth, is to open the doors of our hearts to Him, so that He can enter and abide with us. Our known influences fall incalculably short of those which are unknown, for every soul is a centre to which all other souls are circumferences.

"What shall I do to be saved?" you ask, indicating a profound dissatisfaction with the present state of the Christian life (of which your own is a fair example), and a heart-cry for

---

references in this very number to A. C. 2049, 2115, wherein he shows that, by those of a "different religion," or those "out of the church," he means "the Gentiles who have not the Word."

something higher and better, and more in correspondence with the heavenly doctrines which we have been led to believe. Oh, that this heart-cry would burst from the lips of every Newchurchman in the world! An Oldchurchman would surely answer you in the words of Paul, *"Believe on the Lord Jesus Christ, and thou shalt be saved"* (Acts xvi. 31): or in the words of Peter, *"Repent and be baptized."* (Acts ii. 38.) A Newchurchman of the external type, would answer you very truly and beautifully in the words of our Lord Himself, *"If thou wilt enter into life, keep the commandments."* But there is a more interior and exhaustive definition of the plan of salvation, also in the words of our Lord, which I commend to your studious consideration. It is this:

*"Whosoever will come after me, let him deny himself, and take up his cross and follow me.*

*"For whosoever will save his life, shall lose it: but whosoever shall lose his life for my sake and the gospel's, the same shall save it."*—MARK viii. 34-5.

To lose one's life for Christ's sake and the gospel's, is to give up our own will entirely, and to abstain from evils because they are sins against the Lord and violations of his divine law. This goes away back of the keeping of the commandments, and strikes at the root of the matter, enabling us thereafter to keep the commandments in the right way, not from the interested motives of the old proprium or our own self-derived intelligence, but because we have abandoned the life of evil in will and in deed; and the Lord's own life, the new proprium, is given to us, and flows in and enables the Lord Himself to live in us and work through us according to his own good pleasure. This is the life of the New Church.

This is exceedingly distasteful to the natural man. The

unregenerate Peter, clinging to the old proprium and savoring of the things of the world, does not understand that it is necessary to "suffer many things," to be rejected of men and crucified and buried, before he can rise again. But that was the Lord's pathway to the new life, or his glorification; and it must be ours if we truly desire to follow Him and to be where He is.

Yours truly,      W. H. H.

# LETTER XXXVII.

*THE NEW MOVEMENT, OLD AS WELL AS NEW—THAT SKELETON IN THE NEW-CHURCH CLOSET.*

MY DEAR FRIEND:—When you ask me, What is this New Movement? you ask me a question almost as formidable as an Oldchurchman would propound to you, if he said: "Now sit down a few minutes, my friend, and tell me what Swedenborg teaches." You would not know where or how to begin, on account of the immensity of the subject. And besides, the man would have so much to unlearn and to forget before your ideas could be accepted or even comprehended by him, that the task would appear futile, and indeed almost always proves so, when some enthusiastic Newchurchman endeavors to illumine the unprepared minds of his Old-Church friends. No man ever finds the truth until he seeks earnestly for it: and no man ever searches for that which he believes he holds already in his hand. No one is properly prepared to study Swedenborg, until he has discovered that his own past and present opinions are unfounded or untenable.

Still more remote from the perceptions and comprehension of the natural man—of the Oldchurchman, the scientist, the spiritualist, and even the average Newchurchman—are the series of life-truths which are being revealed and the series of events which are being unfolded or evolved, the complex of which we have provisionally called the New Movement. Apparently, and on the surface, the very least of all religious movements of the age, it is interiorly the largest and grandest in the world, for it is the centre and key to all others. If you were only curious after truth, I would refer you to a thorough study of Swedenborg as the best preparation for your final understanding of these things; for it is only in the light of Swedenborg's entire system that they can be clearly comprehended by the understanding. But I know from my conversations and correspondence with you, that you are earnestly looking for the life of Christ in the soul, for the descent of the Lord and his angels into the daily lives and business of men; and from that stand-point of affection, having been already initiated into the general principles of the New Church, you will be enabled to see and believe with the heart the wonderful things which are now rejected and ignored by the chief men of the church, mainly because they are "slow of heart to believe all that the prophets have spoken."

The New Movement is only a part and continuation of the movement already recognized in the New Church as the Second Coming of the Lord. It is the sequel and logical issue to Swedenborg's mission, and yet it began before it. It is the Lord's work entirely. The Lord comes to the understanding when it is filled with the light of truth from the opened Word. But this is only a preparatory or John the Baptist state; and yet before John appeared the Lord was. The Lord comes into the heart as the Divine Love, when we yearn to live *the life of the heavenly doctrines*—which is not a good Christian life as hitherto understood—but is *the life of Christ Himself* in the redeemed Body of Humanity.

As the understanding has been opened into a spiritual degree of light, so the will principle may now be opened into the celestial degree of love; and the Lord descending through us from centres to circumferences, from primaries to ultimates, will govern and direct our individual lives to the minutest circumstances, and will finally be the all-in-all upon earth, as He is now the all-in-all in the heavens.

There are now occurring in different centres, openings of the interior degrees of life; and from those centres the spiritual life presses powerfully downward to plant itself firmly in externals, and mold the external to its own laws and order. This is *the new life* of the New Church perfectly corresponding in ultimates to the life of the heavens.

The Lord did not establish a church through Swedenborg. Our so-called New Church is nothing but a school of instruction, very necessary, very useful, but still nothing but a school. But He sent his twelve disciples in 1770 to *preach* his new gospel throughout the spiritual world. The New Church was first established in the heavens, then in *a new earth* created in the world of spirits into which the hells can now be elevated; and from these interior centres it is going to descend into the hearts and minds of men, with infinite variety of manifestation according to the mental and moral states of the recipients. Those who are in the light of the opened Word, will be in the centre—the heart and lungs—the celestial within the spiritual, like a wheel within a wheel. From these the living New Church will evolve outward and downward to all spheres, through all degrees, the Lord alone controlling and directing, gradually knocking away all existing institutions from under our feet, and creating from within and by processes still to be unfolded, a new church, a new state, a new social life, with the conjugial love as its central fountain—all constituting a genuine and orderly basis for a heavenly life.

These stupendous events, of which these new unfoldings are only among the feeble and faint beginnings or early manifestations, imply the presence of the Lord in ultimates in a manner never before realized among men. He created a divine-natural and even a sensuo-corporeal sphere for Himself during his sojourn in the flesh, in which He manifested Himself to his disciples after his resurrection. But they could not enter into it, and He could not flow into them from that sphere, at that era of the world's history. Therefore He vanished from their sight, or passed into heavenly states of which they were organically incapable. He is now opening the interior degrees of the natural plane of the human mind, for the influx into it of his own divine-natural and even sensuo-corporeal sphere. He is coming to abide with us, to subdue *all evil*, to cure *all diseases*, to manifest his power "over *all* flesh," to reconstruct our perverted humanity, and even to change the forms and forces of nature into perfect harmony with the divine will. This will be Zion— his celestial kingdom, which He will establish in the natural degree upon this earth, because He is the Alpha and Omega ; and the people of this world correspond to the ultimate principles of the body of the Divine Man.

The tremendous consequences which are destined to flow from this genuine personal entrance of the Divine-natural Humanity with its heavenly sphere (for it flows through the heavens to earth) into the race, will not be due in any sense to the evolution of the scientific or rational man, or to the preaching and extension of the New-Church faith ; although all these will go on just as usual. It will be the work of the Lord alone ; for the angels in their co-operation, work in the Lord and He in them. It will be nothing like spirit-control.

On the contrary it will dissipate all those perverted, illusive, and disorderly spheres generated by the old proprium, and cast them out forever. It will deliver man from the infestations of all spirits, and endow him with the perfect free-agency, peace, and love of heaven.

The preparations for the New Church began on the opening of the celestial degree years before the Last Judgment, in direct revelation of the doctrine of life to certain Africans; in the spiritual experiences of the Quietists, the Quakers, the Moravians, the Methodists, etc., etc.; and in a general awakening of the emotional side of the religious nature, not due to the promulgation of religious truth, and more or less disorderly, illusory, and inefficient for want of the sound doctrines of spiritual truth.

The new awakening now occurring in the bosom of the New Church, is made upon the orderly basis of sound doctrine. It cannot fail, it cannot miscarry, for the Lord in his Divine-natural Humanity is with it and in it, and the supreme cause and motor power of it all.

Nothing can prevent or retard this downward movement from the heavens, except the impatient desire of the human proprium to direct or interfere with it for its own purposes. We are commanded to do nothing at present—but to abstain from evils as sins against God, and to "stand still, and see the salvation of the Lord."

Your other question is about the skeleton in the closet of the New-Church ecclesiasticism. Swedenborg, in Conjugial Love, n. 252-3, gives certain vitiated states of mind and body as "legitimate causes" why a Christian man may put his wife away from his bed and his house without obtaining divorce. And he also states, when treating of the unregenerate or carnal marriage, that the same vitiated states of mind and body (C. L. 470) are legitimate causes why a natural or unchristian man should be permitted to put his wife away and keep a concubine.

This is the skeleton in the New-Church closet, which all of us are afraid or ashamed of, and which all of us wish had never been created. The Old-Church people and other people have found it out, and parade it against the general truth and purity of Swedenborg's teachings. The objections are really infinitesimal; for how can a few questionable paragraphs outweigh the spiritual wisdom of twenty octavo volumes? I have a scientific friend of great intelligence, who says that he could never permit such an indecent and obscene book as the Bible to come into his family, so long as he had young children to be contaminated by it. The stories of Judah and Tamar, and of Ammon and his sister, shut his eyes and his heart against the Psalms, and the Prophets, and the Evangelists, and the Revelation. So it is with those who fasten upon Swedenborg's humiliating concession to the spirit of his age (for it is nothing else), as a general argument against all he has written.

Independent thinkers who take the good and throw the bad away, in Swedenborg and everywhere else, have no special difficulty about this matter. This man, they say, is here false to himself and to the supernal loveliness of his teachings everywhere else. Explain away as you please, there is a residuum of *wrong* in these "legitimate causes of separation from the wife." They are spots on the sun, indeed; but they are spots. Eliminate them and leave the sun to shine spotless. Swedenborg was clearly not infallible, not perfect, not entirely above or beyond his own social surroundings, or the customs and conventionalities of his age. This view settles the matter with many, myself included. The ecclesiastical special pleaders who take E. S. as "infallible authority," or his writings as "divine works," must go on trying to put spiritual garments on that skeleton; and they will probably strain at gnats and swallow camels for a long time.

Although I repudiate the paragraphs referred to in this decided manner, do not suppose that I undervalue Swedenborg's Conjugial Love. It is the most wonderful, beautiful, and interior of all his works, except, of course, those which unfold the spiritual sense of the Word of God. It teaches to those who comprehend, a morality and chastity hitherto unknown to the world. A distinguished gentleman, desirous of examining Swedenborg's claims, asked his minister to loan him one of Swedenborg's works. The clergyman gave him the Conjugial Love, as the hardest and the most puzzling. The gentleman returned it in a week and asked for more. "More?" said the minister; "what do you think of that book?" "That the writer got his information direct from the heavens," was the reply. And I concur with his opinion.

I have sometimes thought that these things, and some other mistakes and inconsistencies which may be picked out here and there in Swedenborg's voluminous writings, were permitted by Divine Providence, to preserve the future church from that insane hero-worship and idolatry of the man, which has already begun, and which tends to abolish all free thought and rationality in those who entertain the absurd idea that he was infallible and his writings divine. We may be sure that in this and all other matters the Lord will take care of the things of his church, and bring light out of darkness and good out of evil.     Yours truly,     W. H. H.

# LETTER XXXVIII.

### *SHALL WE JOIN AN EXTERNAL NEW CHURCH?*

MY DEAR MADAM:—I have answered at considerable length the question of an isolated New-Church woman, who found no spiritual strength or comfort in the Episcopal Church to which she belonged, and who desired to know whether attendance upon its services was obligatory or advisable. You ask me a different question. You are a New-Church woman, and one, permit me to say, of very great spiritual insight as well as remarkable religious experiences. You have always been isolated, or very nearly alone, and now for the first time you are going into a great city, where there is a large, highly respectable New-Church society, and a very excellent and talented minister; and you ask me whether it is your religious duty, for your own sake and the sake of your children, to join the church and participate earnestly and cordially in its exercises.

"What a strange question!" the external man says, "as if it was not the plain duty of every Christian man and woman to attend the church and labor for the church in every possible way." But you have entirely outgrown that whole sphere of thought and argument, and it has no vital hold upon your faith or your life. You see around you vast bodies of professed Christians, whose churches are saturated with false doctrines, false motives, false principles, so that you believe with Swedenborg, that as ecclesiastical institutions they are spiritually dead, and have henceforth no organic connection with the heavens or authoritative relation to men. You have not the least sense of impropriety in neglecting their ministrations.

But you search in vain for the New Church—the New Jerusalem—the promised organization which is to supersede the effete institution established by the Apostles. The Lord intromitted Swedenborg into the spiritual world, revealed to him the spiritual sense of the Divine Word; and Swedenborg announces the coming of a New Church from heaven, and publishes the heavenly doctrines which are to constitute the faith of this Church. But the Church itself does not come! The Lord prepares the man for his work, and sends us the doctrines; but He calls no apostles, commissions no preachers, organizes no Church. He simply says: Commit these things to the press, and give them to mankind—and no more.

The early receivers of the doctrines of the New Church, dissatisfied with their old associations and drawn together by affinities of faith, very naturally organized themselves into societies, which have multiplied and assumed the name of the Church of the New Jerusalem. These societies have no divine authority for their movements, and have probably no more organic connection with the heavens than the Baptists or the Presbyterians. They justify themselves on the apparently rational ground, that church organization is a necessity of the religious life, and that Swedenborg speaks of governments and churches as being equally necessary on earth and in heaven. Churches being requisite, why should we wait for any special Pentecost to indue us with power from heaven to initiate a new era? And so they went to work with the forms and spirit of the old Dispensation. The result, with such boundless wealth of spiritual truth in their hands, has not been hitherto satisfactory. The ecclesiastical proprium manifests the same old character, and the people as a body of Christians, seem to have risen but little if any above the amiable respectabilities and moralities of the older churches.

All this you know very well; and you will not suffer the bitter disappointment of many an isolated receiver who goes where he can enjoy the inestimable privileges of church association. How often have I heard the isolated receiver, particularly if he was a new convert, exclaim, "O that I could enjoy the benefit and blessing of fellowship with the people who believe these heavenly doctrines! They surely must lead angelic lives, and a whole society of them must make a little heaven." Well, he joins the church, and is politely and kindly received; and there it ends. He finds the supposed church to be a heterogeneous association of people, who are in entirely closed conditions, and who judge of him and treat him exactly as the outside world does, according to his family connections, his wealth, class, education, and manners. There are few heart-associations among them, and spiritual affinities go for little.

The organization is built upon external and natural principles, and the fruit of it is an external and natural people. They will converse freely about the truths of the church, and enthusiastically about their immense superiority over everything hitherto presented to the human mind. But if you open your hungry heart to them, and talk about the new and perfect life which must follow the new light, about the death of the old proprium, the blessings of prayer, the coming of the Lord into the individual soul, the development of the church within, the entire redemption of body and soul from the power of sin, etc., the most of them will turn you a deaf ear, and finally vote you a bore, or a crank, or a victim of enthusiastic spirits.

And yet not all; for by quiet waiting and careful observation, you will discover a few souls in sympathy with yourself, souls that are hungering and thirsting, not only after truth but after righteousness, and who are watching and praying for the kingdom of God. There are even now Simeons, "devout and just, waiting for the consolation of Israel;" and Annas who depart not from the temple, but serve God with fastings and prayers night and day. These people are not satisfied with ecclesiastical religion, nor with its most admired and beautiful products. They know there is a better, a truer and more vital kind; and they desire to walk with the Lord Jesus, "even as He walked."

There is a "remnant" of this kind in every church, and probably among the people of every religion in the world. It is the new seed for the new era—the leaven which will spread and leaven the whole. It seems to me that the Lord will revolutionize every church from its own centres: that is, by influx from within, and infinite accommodations to the states of all. Those who are most contrite and humble and therefore most open, will receive Him in the celestial degree. Those who are sincere lovers and seekers of truth, and intensely loyal to its behests, will find Him in the glorious light of the spiritual degree. And those who are religious from natural and mixed motives, and who esteem external things above their real value, will remain in the natural degree, but be brought more and more into an orderly life of use and obedience.

Thus the churches will come into the new life by interior processes, readjustments of creed, vivification of "remains" called revivals, disintegrations, and reconstructions. Unworthy elements will recede and withdraw under many pretences, but really because they will be repelled by the sphere of the Divine Love. Those who remain will draw others to them by the force of spiritual attraction; until after a while, however the churches may differ in opinion, they will be one in the heavenly spirit of brotherhood and charity.

Now, my dear madam, you and I and every one of us must play our part in the disintegrations and reconstructions which the new era necessitates. Dissociated from old things, we must become consociated with the new. Our life is bound up in the bundle of all other lives, and the religious life of the whole is the consociated religious life of the units. Asia and Africa can never be christianized, until the Asia and Africa in our own souls are reformed and sanctified. We must regard it as our most practical duty to unite with our fellows in every good work. And as men who think alike as to doctrine are most likely to harmonize as to conduct, a Newchurchman can surely find his best field of usefulness among Newchurchmen.

But, in strongly advising you, as I do, to join the church, to fulfill all the duties and obligations thereby imposed upon you, and to train your children under its influences, I beg you to keep your mind clear of Old-Church conceptions of the subject. Do not join the church because it is an institution authoritatively organized by the apostles, for that has expired; but because it is your spontaneous desire to unite with the neighbor in forms of spiritual use. It is a field of great uses, many even yet undeveloped; and you will find much spiritual benefit, not from anything the church gives you, but from the outflowing and outworking of the Lord's life through yourself for the promotion of a general good. He who gives most receives most, for influx and efflux are equal. Never be satisfied with the existing order of things either in yourself or others, but always reach out for something higher and better.

In order to look at the church from this interior standpoint, it would be well for you to keep in mind Swedenborg's distinction between a congregation and a church. He says: "A congregation in general is what is commonly called a church; but to constitute it a church, it is necessary that every individual in the congregation should be a church; for every general [thing or principle] implies parts similar to itself."—A. C. 4292.

Judged by this high standard (and it is the heavenly standard), we have no churches upon earth at present, but only congregations and societies. Our congregations have no more divine authority or essential relationship to the Divine, than any political or social organization. They are schools for spiritual instruction, and means for the cultivation of the spirit of brotherhood and fellowship.

"That which makes heaven with man, also makes the church," says Swedenborg. So that the true way to build up a church, is to plant the kingdom of heaven in the souls of its members. The true way for every man to keep the church in his neighbor, is to build it in himself. The old churches of the apostolic dispensation were constructed from without, by authority. The New Church, co-extensive with the human race, descends from within. It is the marriage between goodness and truth, the marriage between faith in the understanding and charity in the will. Its supreme centre is in the conjugial love and the love of children. From these it flows outward and becomes the love of the neighbor and of all imaginable uses to the neighbor. Such is the life of heaven, and such will be the life of the New Church which is the

Lord's heaven upon earth.  This heaven upon earth is, however, only possible in proportion as "the former heaven and the former earth" pass away from our own organic being.

Bring, my dear madam, the whole strength of your affections into the service of the society.  Study and disseminate the doctrines, visit the sick, train the children, assist the poor, cultivate friendships, lift high your ideal standard of charity and self-consecration, preach and practice the new and perfect life of peace and love: and if, on account of your advanced and liberal ideas, you are misconstrued and rebuffed and neglected, forgive the mistaken ones and labor for them with renewed zeal.

Yours truly,

W. H. H.

## LETTER XXXIX.

*THE DESCENT OF THE CELESTIAL THROUGH THE SPIRITUAL INTO THE NATURAL.*

MY DEAR FRIEND:—You ask me two questions, the answers to which involve some exceedingly interesting considerations. First, you wish to know why I call the New Church a celestial church, when we have nothing of it yet but a revelation of spiritual truth. And secondly, you ask, if the influx of the celestial into the natural without a suitable intermediate plane of spiritual thought is so dangerous, how was it with those Africans to whom Swedenborg says a revelation of the celestial life and doctrine had been made in his own time.

Let us revert to the fundamental truth, that the influx of life from the Lord is always from the celestial into the spiritual and thence into the natural. The results or phenomena produced, depend upon the organic states of the natural and the spiritual degrees into which the celestial flows. If these lower degrees are obstructed by evils and falsities, the influent life is perverted and corrupted. The inner or higher life cannot descend, until the external life and all its forms are reduced to correspondent order and obedience. Nor can it mold the external life into forms truly correspondent with itself, except through the associated and corresponding spiritual truths of the middle degree.

Every reader of Swedenborg knows that the organic function of John the Baptist was to prepare the way of the Lord, by preaching a renunciation of the life of the old Adam, and the entrance into a spiritual state which could be receptive of the divine celestial life, "the Lamb of God" then imminent in the world. In precisely the same way the vast system of spiritual truth revealed through Swedenborg, is an organic intermediate for the descent of the celestial life through its corresponding forms into the ultimates of the natural degree. The opening of the divine wisdom of the Word, must of necessity be followed by the evolution of the celestial life, which means the Lord's vital presence in the soul.

The Church began in the celestial centres. In the course of time, it fell into a lower degree and became a spiritual church. By further declension it became natural, and finally external and literal. The Lord was then made incarnate, re-opened the closed degrees of life, and inaugurated the ascending movement from circumferences back again to centres. The church which his disciples instituted was a spiritual church, corresponding, as Swedenborg says, to the ancient or spiritual church after the flood. The last and final church, the New Jerusalem, which follows the opening of the Word, is not a spiritual church on the same plane with the first Christian or Apostolic church, but a celestial church with a discretely different life. To suppose otherwise, is to violate the fundamental order and logic of the New-Church philosophy.

Swedenborg, moreover, declares that the marriage of good and truth which is regeneration, does not take place between goods and truths of the same degree, but between the goods of a lower and the truths of a higher degree. And the same relation must hold between the truths of the lower and the goods of the higher degree. No possible union of natural good and truth in the natural man, can make him a spiritual man; and no possible union of spiritual good and truth in the spiritual man, can elevate him to the celestial degree. The impregnation comes always from above. The spiritual truths revealed for the New Church are to be conjoined with celestial goods, and the resulting life will not be the spiritual states of the Apostolic church, but a discretely higher and diviner life brought down into ultimates. The Church is determined, not by doctrines but by the life of the doctrine. Swedenborg gave no hint for the institution of a Church, because he knew that his mission was only to promulgate the doctrines from the Word, which would be for the use of a Church to come, which the Lord would establish in his own time and in his own way.

The crowning reason why the New Church should be called a celestial church, is drawn from the Word itself and from Swedenborg's interpretation of it. When John "saw the holy city, New Jerusalem, coming down from God out of heaven" (Rev. xxi. 2), he also "heard a great voice out of heaven, saying, 'Behold the tabernacle of God is with men.'" The holy city with its temple corresponds to the Lord as the divine truth in the spiritual degree: the tabernacle in the inmost of the temple, corresponds to the Lord as the divine love in the celestial degree. Swedenborg, therefore, says:

"A great voice out of heaven, saying, 'Behold the tabernacle of God is with men,' signifies the Lord from love speaking and declaring the glad tidings, that He himself will now be present among men in his Divine Humanity. . . . By the tabernacle of God is meant *the celestial church*, and in a universal sense the Lord's celestial kingdom, and in a supreme sense his Divine Humanity."—A. R. 882.

Do you not now see, my dear friend, that the New Jerusalem is a celestial church or life, based upon spiritual truth,— "a woman clothed with the sun, and with the moon under her feet"? And if you will ask yourself the question, How is the Lord to be now present among men in his Divine Humanity differently from the manner in which He has been present heretofore in the Apostolic church, you will begin to see the privileges and tremendous responsibilities of those whose acceptance of spiritual truth obligates them to lead a celestial life.

Now for your second question: How was the celestial life unfolded in the Africans—which Swedenborg calls "the coming of the Lord" and "the initiament of the New Church" —without the intermediation of spiritual truth. It is a mistake to suppose that there was no such intermediation. Remember that this spiritual opening among the Africans was superintended by good spirits and angels, who no doubt taught their almost infantile minds the little modicum of spiritual truth which exactly corresponded to the awakening of their celestial affections. It was a matter of dictation, Swedenborg says; and of course we may infer that the necessary spiritual truths were supplied in the most appropriate manner.

That singular relation was for a special purpose, the opening of an avenue of influx from the heavens into the rational faculty of the human race. (T. C. R. 840.) It was of very limited extent, as the Jewish economy was, which, nevertheless, for many centuries connected the heavens and the earth together by correspondences. It was probably of short duration. The opening of the celestial degree in the most simple and childlike people, unperverted by falsified doctrines, was the gateway through which the Divine life passed into the spiritual degree of our life; but after the promulgation of a vast system of spiritual truth—the great medium between the celestial and the natural having been established—the necessity for direct dictation ceased. I suspect, therefore, that future discoveries in Africa, from which some Newchurchmen hope so much, will reveal nothing but some tribes or nations in good natural states, holding traditions of wonderful communications from angels and spirits to their not very remote ancestors.

Yes, my dear friend, the celestial influx must pass through the spiritual on its way to the natural degree, and its manifestation will be determined by the forms and molds of thought which it finds in the spiritual degree through which it passes. This is the reason why the celestial life which was evidently awakened in the Quietists, the Quakers, the Moravians, the early Methodists, and others, finding no prepared basis of spiritual truth, was choked, perverted, and almost perished in the chaos of false ideas which those people derived from the nearly consummated church in which they were born.

That the true celestial life was struggling for utterance in these enthusiasts, is an unquestionable fact. Passages selected from Guyon, George Fox, Wesley, Law, and others, and compared with passages from Swedenborg, would show clearly that "the annihilated soul" of the Quietist, "the inner light" of the Quaker, and the "witnessing spirit" of the Methodist, belong really to the sphere of celestial perceptions, and find their explanation nowhere but in the philosophy of the New Church. The same philosophy explains also the causes of their delusions, fantasies, and failures, and points us with unerring certainty to a witnessing spirit which never deceives, to an inner light which cannot mislead, and to a state of annihilation which is a resurrection into eternal life.

Finally, my dear friend, rest assured that if we prepare the way of the Lord in our own souls according to the eternal principles of truth; if in the natural degree we order our external lives strictly according to his commandments; if in the spiritual degree we illumine our understandings with the heavenly light of his revealed wisdom; if in the celestial degree we surrender our hearts and souls absolutely to the power of his love, He will manifest the presence of his Divine Humanity in us and through us, in a manner never before possible in the world. For such a universal coming of the Lord, let us all pray.

Yours truly,
W. H. H.

# LETTER XL.

### RESTATEMENT OF FUNDAMENTAL PRINCIPLES.

EDITORS NEW-CHURCH INDEPENDENT:—I have now been holding for three years, under Divine Providence, a series of epistolary communications with your readers. Those who have been immersed in the cares of business and the anxieties of the natural life, have probably paid them little attention. On some they have made favorable impressions, and these have thanked me for showing them that Swedenborg was deeper and broader than they knew. Others have expressed the profoundest gratitude for unfolding to them the true nature of the proprium, and giving a new awakening and a new impulse to their affections and thoughts. Many have been secretly troubled in soul at what seemed to them new doctrines and new explanations of doctrine, and have employed the conspiracy of silence to prevent the spread of what they considered revolutionary ideas. Many liberal Christians in other organizations, have discovered from these letters with delight and surprise, that Swedenborg teaches a more beautiful, practical, and absolute life of holiness, than has ever been inculcated by the highest evangelical authorities.

It will be well, before commencing a new series of Letters, to give a brief *resumé* or restatement of some fundamental principles which have been accepted with delight in some quarters, and received with distrust in others. These interpretations of Swedenborg bring us more closely into spiritual rapport with the whole Christian world, and invite special attention to our heavenly doctrines. For our own people I have fortified every point by copious quotations from Swedenborg, and by logical reasoning from his premises.

The coming of the Lord, or the Second Advent, is something more than his coming into the clouds of heaven, which was only the infilling of the letter of the Word with the light of the spiritual sense revealed to Swedenborg. His coming involves of necessity the unfolding of a new life in the world, the building up of a new heaven and a new church in the individual soul; for says Swedenborg, "the new heaven and the new church constitute the coming of the Lord."—A. R. 151.

This new life is a celestial life elevated a discrete degree above any religious life hitherto possible in the world except in its golden age. It is more than a life of obedience to divine authority. It is more than a life of intelligent coöperation with the movements of divine law. It is all these and more. It is a state of organic harmony with the Divine will, a life of love so thorough and positive, that the whole life of the man is the Divine will brought down into ultimates. It is the secret path by which the Lord, the heavens, the New Jerusalem, the life of the Word, are all about to descend upon the earth.

This new celestial life has been struggling for expression and ultimation for about two hundred years. It can only find its genuine expression and ultimation in the heavenly marriage of its affections to the spiritual truths from the Word revealed by Swedenborg. All efforts at the perfect Christian life will be of necessity incomplete and abortive, until spiritual truth is implanted in the understanding as the vessel recipient of celestial good. The vital elements of the Christian world are groping blindly after the very things they would find in Swedenborg whom they reject, truly not knowing what they do.

This new and heavenly life is striving to develop in the world without the apparent aid of the new doctrines or the New Church, although in a deep-rooted, hidden harmony with them. Before and coincidently with Swedenborg, but independently of him, there was a new influx of the divine love into the hearts of men, which has gone on increasing unto the present day. Guyon, Fenelon, John and Charles Wesley, Fletcher, William Law, Wilberforce, Edward Irving, and a thousand others, were the fruits of this divine seed planted we know not how. What is the meaning of these things? They are not the results of Swedenborg's teachings, nor of any direct knowledge of the spiritual sense of the Word of God. Nor does this great revival of the religious life, outside of Swedenborg and the external New Church, belong to the sunset of the Old Dispensation, but to the golden dawn of the New Era. These movements are bound up with our own in the bundle of the life of the New Jerusalem.

There are two baptisms; one of water, which means initiation into the visible Christian church, or an acknowledgment of the Christian religion and its Founder, accompanied by the desire and purpose to obey their teachings; the other of fire, which means the kindling of the divine love in the soul. Both are necessary to the perfect church. The one great need of the religious life of the age, is a knowledge of the spiritual truths to be found only in the writings of Swedenborg. The one great need of the conservators of these truths revealed from heaven, is the baptism of fire. These spiritual factors have for each other the deepest organic attraction. When they meet and unite, the angelic life can be truly unfolded among men. This will be the apostle's "manifestation of the sons of God," and we shall experience the new Pentecost.

Love is the central and supreme element in the Christian life. Truth, notwithstanding its great offices, is secondary and subordinate. All the truths of heaven in the memory of a man, could not of themselves advance him a step in the religious life. They are merely dead material until vivified into living forms by the awakening of affection, emotion, and sentiment. Our people generally are living in the mere appearances of truth, in the mere semblances of the Christian religion, in a mere routine of respectable moralism, and can scarcely be aroused to believe that there is a better way. It is because we have preached truth and doctrine too much, and the love or *doing* of truth and the *life* of doctrine too little. Let me fortify this view of the central and supreme place of good or love, by a single quotation from Swedenborg.

"That some idea may be had of the appearances of truth, and what they are, let the following cases serve for illustration: 1. Man believes that he is reformed and regenerated by the truth of faith, but this is an appearance; he is reformed and regenerated by the good of faith, that is, by charity towards his neighbor and by love to the Lord. 2. Man believes that truth enables him to perceive what good is, because it teaches, but this is an appearance; it is good which enables truth to perceive, for good is the soul or the life of truth. 3. Man believes that truth introduces to good, when he lives according to the truths he has learned; but it is good which flows into truth, and introduces it to itself. 4. It appears to man that truth brings good to perfection; whereas it is good which brings truth to perfection. 5. Goods [that is, the good deeds of life] appear to man as the fruits of faith, but they are the fruits of charity. From these few cases, it may in some measure be known, what the appearances of truth are; and such appearances are innumerable."—A. C. 3207.

Another fundamental truth repeatedly insisted on and never to be forgotten, is this: that there can be no coming or descent of the Lord into the natural proprium of man. He cannot even enter into the proprium of the angels. He can only enter into and abide with what is his own. It was for this reason He gave us his blood to drink and his flesh to eat. The new proprium thence derived, is not the old proprium regenerated, but it is the Lord's life discreted from his Divine Humanity, and given to us to feel and enjoy as if it were our own, as the angels do. Just so far as we are in the new proprium, we are in the Lord and in heaven or in angelic states; and we are in the new proprium only so far as we are out of ourselves—out of our old, selfish, and natural external life.

These ideas constitute the Key to a true knowledge of the coming of the Lord, and of the new heaven, the new earth, and the new life He will bring with Him. He comes with the holy angels when He can enter into our lives as He enters into the lives of the angels. This can be done only by our subduing and putting away the old proprium entirely. We can never do this until we know what the proprium is, until we sound "the depths of Satan" in our souls. Self-knowledge, the most difficult and painful of all knowledge, is acquired only by the constant, thorough, and unflinching exploration of our motives, purposes, dispositions, and conduct by the light of revealed truth. We will find self, in some form or other, stamped upon every iota of our social, civil, and religious life. Could we realize the hideous, sensual, selfish, and devilish nature of the proprium, we would sink into utter humiliation and despair if not sustained by the Divine Humanity or the truths of the Divine Word.

The whole modern theory of deliverance from evil, elevation of character and purification of life, by education and culture, is radically false. It can produce nothing but a suppressed proprium, refined, beautiful, charming in exteriors, but containing the unfathomable hell of self-righteousness underneath, and doomed with its correspondent civilization to radical destruction. Even Newchurchmen, deviating from the teaching of Swedenborg, have contributed to this delusion, and suffer from its evil influences—believing and teaching that the Lord gives us a new proprium to have and hold as absolutely our own, thus making one man really and organically better or worse than another; whereas all men and all angels are equally evil and false, and the Lord alone is good and true. No man or angel ever experiences a genuinely good affection, or speaks the real truth, when he feels or speaks from the proprium or selfhood, however modified this selfhood may have been by educational or religious influences.

This point ought to be definitely settled—for those, at least, who attach supreme authority to the writings of Swedenborg—by the following paragraph from D. P. 316:

"Self-derived prudence persuades man and confirms him in the belief that everything good and true is from himself and in himself; because self-derived prudence is man's intellectual selfhood, influent from self-love which is his voluntary selfhood: and the selfhood cannot do otherwise than make all things its own, for the man so infatuated cannot be elevated above it. All who are led by the Lord's divine providence are elevated above the selfhood, and then they see that everything good and true is from the Lord: nay, more, they see that what is in man from the Lord is always the Lord's, and never man's. He who believes otherwise, is like a man who has his master's goods under his care, and lays claim to them or appropriates them as his own: he is not a steward but a thief."

Yes: the apostle was clearly right when he said:—"The carnal mind is enmity against God: for it is not subject to the law of God, neither indeed can be. So then they that are in the flesh cannot please God. But ye are not in the flesh, but in the Spirit, if so be that the Spirit of God dwell in you."

From the stand-point of these truths, the Second Advent may be comprehended as a descent of the Lord into the lives and business of men; and its final effect, through innumerable intermediate causes, will be to reconstitute the church, to reorganize the state, and to reconstruct the elements of nature in perfect harmony with the influent forms and order of the heavenly world. These things can only be understood as they are unfolded; and however sublime and beautiful the subjects, it is useless to speculate about them outside of general principles. The great obstructionists to the descent of the Lord into the Body of Humanity, will be of two classes: those who scorn and reject Him altogether, and those who think they receive Him most ardently and intelligently, but who appropriate his goodness and truth to themselves, and thereby become wise in their own eyes and good in their own conceit. Overcoming all these obstacles, however, our Lord will descend into ultimates by organic processes, through the heart and mind of the church, through the conjugial love, the love of children, the love of the neighbor, and the love of uses;

and will take upon Himself the government of the world, more perfectly, universally, and efficiently, than if He had descended as the literalists expect, into the clouds of heaven with millions of angels, and instituted by external means an eternal kingdom upon earth.

A powerful mesmerist once had upon the stage a number of individuals who were brought fully under his influence. He stood in the midst of them and said in his positive manner: "I am now going away from you, and you will not see me. In a few moments I will come again, and then you will see me." He did not move from the spot. Several persons then asked the mesmerized subjects, "Where is the Professor?" They all answered, "We do not know; he has gone away." "Do you not see the Professor right before your eyes?" "No: he is not here." The Professor exclaimed, "I have come back. Do you not see me?" "Certainly," they all answered, "we see you now because you have come back." It is thus that the power of the selfhood and the evil world mesmerize us with blindness, deafness, and deadness as to the presence of the Lord who stands always in our midst.

We cannot now know, see, and feel the Lord on account of spiritual and natural obstacles and obstructions in ·the lower and lowest degrees of life. Vast processes for their removal are accordingly going on in every direction. It will be apparently true that all these things, the revolutions of social and religious opinion, the disintegrations and reconstructions in church and state, etc., are produced by natural causes and the spontaneous evolution of the race. The genuine truth will be, that in proportion as vessels are prepared for his descent into ultimates, the Lord will make his presence and his power felt in the human spirit, with infinite accommodations to individual states, and bring about a continuous re-adjustment between internal and external relations, until the New Jerusalem "comes down from God out of heaven, prepared as a bride adorned for her husband."

Looking and praying for this coming from within, and the re-adjustment of all environments by interior forces in perfect harmony for the consummation of the Divine will, I remain,

Yours truly,
W. H. H.

# APPENDIX

## THE LORD'S DESCENT
### INTO
## ULTIMATES.

# The Lord's Descent

### into

# Ultimates.

## ESSAY I.

### *OPENING OF THE INTERIORS.*

I PRAYED earnestly to the Lord to illumine my mind in relation to the method of his Second Coming and the inauguration of a new life in the world. That night I dreamed much about those subjects. Rousing once out of my sleep, I thought to myself how clear everything would be, if I could remember the glorious train of thought which had been presented to me in my dreams; but in the morning all had escaped me except a few ideas and some fragments of ideas, and a clear perception of the fact, that the solution and secret of the whole matter lay in the Opening of the Interiors.

How could it be otherwise?—when the whole story of the fall of man, from the heights of celestial perception down to the sensuo-corporeal depths of barbarism, is a story of the successive closure of the degrees of life : and the whole story of his redemption and restoration is a story of the successive re-openings of the natural, rational, spiritual, and celestial planes of thought and affection. For a knowledge of these degrees of life we are entirely indebted to Emanuel Swedenborg.

There is no opening of the sensuo-corporeal degree of life, and none can be made in it, for it is the bottom floor and there is nothing below it. It is the plane of animal life, with the instincts, ideas, and appetites associated with the senses. All the others rest upon it like a house upon its foundation. Above it rise the organic compartments of the human spirit—the natural, rational, spiritual, and celestial—like the successive stories of a house. Each has its floors, planes, or terminations which separate it from the other compartments. The discrete degrees of life are held together as one by influx and correspondence—influx of the one Divine life passing from degree to degree, producing corresponding forms of affection and thought at each successive descent.

If there were no intervening floorings or terminations the influx would flow from top to bottom without any ultimation until it reached the latter. Life as it flows from the Divine Proceeding of the Lord, is the celestial life. Therefore the first created men of the world were celestial men, with a sensuo-corporeal basis. As they passed from the earthly to the spiritual life, they formed the celestial heavens. There was then no spiritual heaven in existence. The Lord governed by influx through the celestial heaven. The good men after the flood were of the celestial-spiritual type, and were saved by the incarnation of Jehovah, and raised into a spiritual heaven. When men ceased to be spiritual, they sank to a lower degree or type, the natural. The interior men of this type, called by Swedenborg the rational man, passing upward formed the ultimate heaven. The influx of the Divine life passing now through the three heavens above us into the sensuo-corporeal basis, forms the natural man of our present world.

Although men are all now born natural, with every superior degree closed in them, still they contain those degrees embodied in their structures, so that they may be successively opened from above, and from natural they may become rational, spiritual, and celestial. Between the hells and the three heavens there is an impassable gulf; but the hells flow into and rest upon the natural plane of human life—the sensuous and scientific sphere of affection and thought; and man can only be delivered from them by the opening of the rational, spiritual, and celestial degrees which bring him into communication with the heavens and the Lord.

The order of influx is always from centre to circumference, from within outward, and from above downward, and never the contrary, however overwhelming the appearance and evidence that it is so. "It appears," says Swedenborg, "as if sensation came from influx by the externals; but it is the internal which flows into the external, and the contrary is a fallacy." Again, he declares that physical influx is against order and impossible; for all influx is from the spiritual world into the natural, and not from the natural into the spiritual. Let us fix this fundamental axiom of the Swedenborgian philosophy firmly in the mind, for it will give us a glorious deliverance from the bondage of sensuous appearances.

Another axiom of similar importance is this: "The order of all influx, thus of all existence from the Lord, is through the celestial state to the spiritual, and through the spiritual to the natural, thus according to successive order." A man therefore in the course of his regeneration, does not first become rational and then spiritual and then celestial, as seems to be the case from appearances, according to which even Swedenborg himself appears sometimes to speak. He follows of necessity the order of creation and the laws of influx and correspondence. He seems, indeed, to be regenerated by truth which is acquired or taught from without; but truth is entirely dead, until it is made alive or vivified from within by an affection for truth, or desire to know it and a will to obey it. The first step is always, therefore, an influx from the celestial degree into the affections of the natural degree.

The celestial degree is first opened in him by the vivification of "remains," and according to the measure and character of the opening, a new and corresponding spiritual life is created in his middle degree; and the same influx passing into the rational and natural degree, produces there effects corresponding to the ends and causes which had been previously operative in the interior degrees. This order seems to be reversed, because man himself is born and lives in a state of inverted order, and is overwhelmed by the sensuous appearance of a progress from without inward, and from natural to spiritual. (See A. C. 1495.)

The degrees are not opened from below upward, but the reverse. The natural cannot flow into the spiritual, nor the spiritual into the celestial. Man can become either celestial or spiritual or rational even whilst living in the natural form; but it is because the three degrees of life which exist in successive order in the heavens, exist in simultaneous order in the man, who is builded after the image of the heavens and after the likeness of God. The celestial heavens flow into our inmost degree of life, the spiritual heavens into our middle degree of life, the ultimate heavens into our natural degree of life. The whole man is determined by what is in his celestial degree—for that is his life, his love, his affections, his motives, the sum total of the ends he has in view. This celestial reproduces itself in different but corresponding forms in the spiritual degree; and these again reproduce themselves in still lower but corresponding forms in the natural degree; and what we see in ultimates on the surface is not the beginning of things, as it appears, but the ending, the basis and containant of all prior, interior, and superior things in the universe.

These great organic truths lead us to comprehend the primary principles of a true psychology—that all things exist *within* us and not only *outside* of us as they seem to do; that the three heavens are infinitesimally structured and mirrored in each individual organism; that we are microcosms of the macrocosm; that matter is plastic to the operations of spirit as the body is to the operations of the soul; that nature has no independent externeity or objectivity, but is an external picture, like an image in a mirror, representing to our sensational consciousness the wonders which are being from moment to moment enacted within our own spirits in their celestial, spiritual, and natural spheres of being.

The above statement must be slightly qualified; for the metaphor of the picture, or the image in a mirror, does not convey the exact truth to the mind. Nature has no *independent* externeity in relation to the spiritual world, but it has an externeity genuine and solid, which it is difficult for us to believe is so entirely dependent for its existence upon a continuous influx from the spiritual world. It is not, however, the shadowy image in a mirror: it is more like a projected statue. The Divine Mind is thus really mirrored in all the forms of the universe; but it is in objective, living, moving forms, which have no life but that which flows into them from interior sources.

We can now understand some of Swedenborg's stupendous generalizations: that man is a miniature image of the Lord, a miniature heaven, a miniature hell, a miniature Word, a miniature church, a miniature universe. To find the Lord, heaven, hell, the Word, the church, the world, the planets, the universe, a man never need go out of himself. All these things are inside of him, and rest upon his natural plane of life like a house upon its foundations. To find them all he must look within; and he will find them, see them, know them in proportion as the organic windows and doors of his own spiritual organization and the corresponding degrees of sensation and consciousness, are opened toward them.

This is the key to many wonderful phenomena, to many mysteries in the Word of God, and to Swedenborg's own extraordinary career. Revelation is always made by intromission—a sending within.

Swedenborg has achieved more in this way than any human being that ever lived; not by any miracle or any special work of the Lord, but by the orderly unfoldings of his own spirit in the due course of the evolution of the race. And the possibilities in that direction are absolutely limitless.

No man ever had an original thought—a thought which sprang solely from himself. We think by influx of thought from the spiritual world. The Divine wisdom—the infinity of thought—flows into the organic forms of the celestial spheres, and produces the wisdom of their inhabitants. This wisdom flowing into the corresponding forms of the spiritual heaven beneath, becomes the intelligence of that middle sphere. Thence it passes to the ultimate heaven, thence into the world of spirits, and finally into the minds of men, losing at every successive descending step immeasurable portions of its beauty, glory, and power. It is only ours when it descends into us from above and becomes ours by appropriation. There is, therefore, no such thing as natural thought excited by natural phenomena. (A. C. 6322, 3679.) Spiritual thought becomes what we call natural thought, when we are brought to a consciousness of it by the natural phenomena which correspond to it and represent it. (A. C. 4526.) These successive changes of the same thought may be vaguely compared to the different appearances of the same substance, in steam, water, and ice.

It is absolutely true that "a man can receive nothing except it be given him from heaven." Swedenborg affirms that even scientific truths in the external natural, are given to man by influx from the Lord, and are not acquired by any power of his own. (A. C. 4151, 5649, 5660.) He also says, if man were in the true order of life, the order in which he was created (and to which he must return), wisdom, intelligence, and science would flow down from within to his exterior consciousness. If all the knowledges and sciences of the present day were utterly obliterated from the human mind, they could be reproduced, if it pleased the Lord, increased a thousandfold, through regenerating mediums; and the mouths of spiritual "babes and sucklings" could utter them far more readily and perfectly than the most capable and learned men in the world.

The celestial, spiritual, and rational degrees which exist in simultaneous order in each individual, connect him with the three heavens,—the Divine life flowing through the celestial of the third heaven into the celestial of the second heaven, thence into the celestial of the ultimate heaven, and thence into the inmost degree of the human mind on earth. Therefore each man is organically connected with the Lord and with the entire universe; and by the opening of degrees and extensions of affections and thoughts into societies, he might be brought into visible, audible, emotional, and sensational contact with everything in the universe without ever leaving his natural body, which, with its indwelling soul, is a least form or miniature of the whole.

It is, therefore, not at all incredible that Andrew Jackson Davis when an ignorant boy of nineteen, had a great volume of immense learning and genius filtered through his mind from the spiritual world above and within him. That, however, is no reason for accepting a communication from the interior; for the evil and the false as well as the good and the true flow into us from the spiritual world. It is not at all incredible that an old negro woman in Brooklyn, as some of our friends there affirm, was taught the True Christian Religion from within, without knowing anything of the external book which it is our privilege to read. Nor is it incredible that Madam Bourignon, an old Catholic mystic, whose external acquaintance with the Bible was exceedingly slight, had the

Word of God given to her from within, with many beautiful perceptions of its more interior significations and their teachings. And it is not only possible but absolutely true, that a friend of mine, whose case I have carefully studied for many years, received a knowledge of the doctrines of the New Church and much of the spiritual sense of the Word of God, without having read a line of Swedenborg or any of his expositors.

Yes, my dear reader, it is true: you have all things within yourself—royal avenues through all the kingdoms of heaven upward and inward to the Lord—dark and devious and terrible pathways downward through all the hells into the nethermost abyss. You are susceptible to all Divine influences; you are capable of committing the whole catalogue of crimes. You are possessed of all knowledges, all power, all delight. The entire organic universe is inscribed upon your mental structures as the sun and the sky are pictured in the drop of dew. Your apparent life, as felt by yourself, is that little infinitesimal fragment of the life, affection, thought, and actions buried within you, which comes to the surface of your organic frame and is consciously realized as your own. What part and how much of the infinity within you comes to the surface, depends entirely upon what windows and doors in your soul leading out into the heavens and the hells, are opened and what are shut.

With the opening of the interiors all things are possible. Heaven was lost by their closure, it will be regained by their unfolding. By the opening of the interiors, the Holy Spirit, the Comforter, descends and leads us into all truth. Regeneration is an opening of the interiors. The judgment is an opening of the interiors. The coming of the Lord is an opening of the interiors. The final and perfect Church will be an opening of the interiors, so that the heavens and the earth shall be as one in affection, thought, and conduct.

Alas! for those who think that the heavens have been opened but one time in our modern ages, and then closed indefinitely, leaving the race in its natural darkness to be taught and governed by a new ecclesiasticism built upon the doctrines of the gifted seer. Swedenborg was but one product of the openings which preceded him, and one cause of the openings which have followed. He was but one of our "fellow-servants and brethren."

The openings of the celestial, spiritual, rational, natural spheres of the human mind in the last century, have been very numerous; imperfect, partial, indefinite, abortive it may be, but they were beginnings which are progressive. Openings are now going on everywhere, bringing the spiritual and the natural spheres into closer conscious communion. The very air is full of spirits, and the ultimate heaven hangs immediately over us, or, in more philosophical terms, is about to burst forth within us.

Hear what the Spirit saith:

"*Open thou mine eyes that I may behold wondrous things out of thy law.*"

"*O Lord open thou my lips, and my mouth shall show forth thy praise.*"

"*Knock, and it shall be opened unto you.*"

"*Behold I stand at the door and knock: if any man hear my voice and open the door, I will come in to him, and will sup with him and he with me.*"

"*Hereafter ye shall see heaven open, and the angels of God ascending and descending upon the Son of Man.*"

"*The kingdom of heaven is within you.*"

"*And I John saw the holy city, new Jerusalem, coming down from God out of heaven, prepared as a bride adorned for her husband.*"

"*And I heard a great voice out of heaven, saying, Behold the tabernacle of God is with men, and He will dwell with them, and they shall be his people, and God himself shall be with them, their God.*"

The whole question of regeneration depends on the opening of the interiors. Unless they are opened above the natural degree, and planes are formed in the celestial, spiritual, and rational spheres for the arrest and appropriation of the Divine life, that life will pass entirely through the interiors of the man into the natural plane, into which the hells flow, and it will then be turned into false and filthy forms so that men become selfish, devilish, and bestial. In proportion as interior openings occur, man is brought into contact with new societies of angels and into new heavens, with larger multiplication of truths and richer fructification of goods.

Swedenborg repeatedly declares that man at present is in a state of inverted order, utterly immersed in the sensual life, with little or no thought or love of spiritual things; but that if the order were reversed, in other words, if he laid down his own inverted life and entered into the life of Jesus Christ, he would be delivered from the terrible bondage of sensualism, would become conscious of spiritual things, have communication with spirits and angels, be gifted with heavenly perceptions of truth, recover the lost sciences and correspondences of the ancient church; and, living and thinking consciously from within outward, he would perceive that nature was nothing but the representative image in ultimates of the Lord's kingdom in the heavens, and would assign to all natural things the low and humble position and use for which they were created. Why should the receivers of the heavenly doctrines, who are under the divine protection of the Lord, shrink from the contemplation of these sublime possibilities? —these states which *must* be realized upon earth, unless the Divine Man shall fail in his work of redemption, which it is blasphemous to suppose.

The phenomena attending an opening of the interiors must be exceedingly various. The opening may be only of the interior-natural plane of the mind, which connects us with the world of spirits and thereby with heaven or hell. Or it may be an opening of the internal man who is celestial, spiritual, and rational; and the opening may take place into any one of those degrees which connect him with the three heavens, into each successively, or into all at once. Any of these openings may be partial or complete—of a single sense, hearing, sight or touch, or of the whole man; and his rapports or communications may have infinite variations of extent and character.

The degrees below may be shut or closed. The phenomena of trance and somnambulism occur when the sensuo-corporeal degree is quiescent or unconscious, and the interior-natural is open. I think the phenomena of being carried unconsciously from one place to another physically, whilst engaged with spiritual scenes, as in the experience of the apostle Philip and of Swedenborg, is of a similar character. The natural plane may be thoroughly closed whilst one or more of the interior planes are opened, when the man would be as it were taken out of his body, and elevated into one of the heavens within him.

The interior degree of life, the heaven in which we are hereafter to live, and the very society of that heaven, are all opened unconsciously in us and to us according to the life we have lived upon earth; for we really live simultaneously in both worlds. If the natural plane of the human mind was opened to a consciousness of the influxes descending into it, the man regenerating in the celestial kingdom of either degree, would find himself in more or less developed states of celestial perception, unitized sex, and heavenly wisdom: the man regenerating in the spiritual kingdom of either degree, would find himself in states of spiritual intelligence and a knowledge of the spiritual sense of the Word; while a man not regenerating at all, but opened into the interior-natural, the degree of the world of spirits, would come into more or less audible, visible, and sensational contact with mixed spirits of all sorts, and even with the demons from the hells. Thence flow the direful persuasions and falsities of modern spiritism, and the danger of having anything to do with it outside of faith in the Divine Man and the protection of his presence.

There are two misapprehensions about the opening of the interiors—universal in the Old Church, too common in the New—which need correction. One is, that a man cannot be opened into celestial and spiritual spheres, unless he is an exceedingly holy man, far advanced in the work of regeneration. This idea is radically false. No man can *live permanently* in those spheres, and be associated and consociated with the angels there, unless he has become organically celestial or spiritual. But any man, good or bad—any spirit, good or bad—having celestial remains within him, may be *introduced* into those atmospheres, may see and comprehend things before invisible and incomprehensible; and if the natural plane of the mind were simultaneously opened, as in the case of my friend, he might reveal the spiritual mysteries of the inner world, so far as realized by himself, just as well as Swedenborg or any other seer. This is the reason why the person communicating is nothing, and the only authority for truth is the truth itself.

Another misapprehension is, that the Lord must have an exceedingly pure and holy medium through whom to manifest Himself to men. This is contrary to the teachings of biblical history, and to the philosophy of Swedenborg. The men who represented the Lord among the Jews, and through whom the Lord spake and acted, as Abraham, Moses, David, etc., were wholly unregenerate men. The difference between "the celestial remains," or "the human internals" (H. & H. 39) of the lowest man and the highest angel, must be to the Lord entirely inappreciable. By the opening of the interiors to the descent of his life, and by the quiescence of the proprium which is equally evil in angels and devils, He can infill the organic human form (whosoever it may be) with his presence, and speak in the first person. Were the natural plane of the human mind thoroughly open to spiritual influxes, as it was with the Most Ancient Church, the Lord might appear and speak to us now as He did to them. Nor would the Lord select the man on account of his personal excellencies, as men suppose—all men and angels being in themselves equally evil—but on account of his organic receptivities, and the infinitely varied and consociated uses of the divine economy.

The human race began in the celestial degree of life. It lapsed into the spiritual, and thence into the natural, and thence into the sensuo-corporeal. Each individual follows the same course, the angels from the celestial heavens guarding his infancy, and new and lower societies being opened to him as he sinks downward and outward, closing the planes behind him.

If a man were successively opened from the celestial degree downward, with interior perceptions of the course and phenomena of his regeneration, it would appear to him that he had been receding from the Lord all the time, and that the Lord had followed him downward step by step; nor would he realize the true power of the spiritual forces within him, until they obtained their ultimate forms in the lowest degree of life.

The Lord is the Divine-Celestial, Divine-Spiritual, and Divine-Natural Man; and when the men of ancient times sank downward from one degree to another, and the heavens were closed behind them, they passed by degrees out of the Lord, out of his Word, out of his Church, and would have perished in sensualism and animalism, had not the Lord descended and assumed a human form for their redemption.

He bowed the heavens and came down. He clothed Himself successively with the atmospheres of the three heavens; and by his perfect union with the Father—the Father descending with Him and abiding with Him—He re-opened those closed degrees of life in his own glorified Humanity, making it possible for men to be opened again into the heavens by a work in their souls similar to that which our Lord effected in Himself.

The Lord has thus opened all the heavens in his own glorified Personality, and is ready to open them all in us according to our states of love, faith, and receptivity. He has thus been standing, as it were, for eighteen centuries, inviting us to Himself—Divine even as to his flesh and bones, and able to spiritualize us, our whole being from centre to circumference. What more is necessary?—what more is possible?

Alas! the whole history of Christianity—the present dead state of the church and the evil state of the world, the presence of the rider on the pale horse among us—all things, show that much more is necessary, that much more is possible; that this incarnation of Jehovah, this first Advent of our Lord, was not a finality, but only a means to an end—a great step, but not the last one in the work of redemption.

In opening the interior degrees of his own life, the Lord did not open them in any one else, for He respects always the free agency of man, and He only knocks at the door of the human heart, waiting for the human will to open it. In his elevation, however, He draws all men unto Him. What hinders that his divine love does not draw all men into spiritual union with his glorified Humanity? Organic obstructions, hereditary and self-erected, in our own wills and our own understandings against his descent—organic closure of the interior degrees of life. Why has it taken eighteen hundred years of organic preparations for their re-opening? Only a perfected philosophy of history can answer that question.

It was necessary for Him to go away and to come again. Now the Lord Himself never goes away, never comes again. The apparent motion in Him is due always to a real motion in us. Why did the Lord ever disappear from his infant Church and the world? What is the meaning of his ascension? He disappeared from his disciples because they possessed no organic states of life and doctrine which could keep hold of Him and make them feel and know that He was always present. They were like spirits of a low degree, elevated by special arrangements of societies into one of the superior heavens, where they saw and understood all the wonderful things about them; but so soon as they were remanded into their own states of life and will, everything vanished from their sight. He disappeared from them because the celestial and spiritual degrees of their minds were closed, their organic conditions forbidding that they should remain open.

The Lord, however, is always present with us in the celestial degree of our life; for He flows into our goods, but not into our truths unless they correspond to our goods. He tarries always with John, but He disappears from Peter. John and Matthew give no account of his ascension, no hint that He was ever taken away from the world. John is the celestial-rational, and Matthew, who gives the full Sermon on the Mount, is the celestial-natural man : Luke being the spiritual-rational and Mark the spiritual-natural man. The Lord sups with the celestial-rational man, and he with Him; He takes him to his bosom; He gives his mother—the affection for all divine truth—into his keeping; He reveals Himself to him in apocalyptic splendors; He tarries always with him; they are never parted. And to the celestial-natural man, the celestial in ultimates as our Lord Himself was, He says, "Lo I am with you always, even to the end of the world."

The angels have a continual perception of the presence of the Lord (A. C. 5962, '3), and so would men upon earth, if the celestial, spiritual, and rational degrees of their life were consciously opened into the natural, so that the Lord with his holy angels could flow into it. This would be the Second Coming of the Lord, indeed—a descent, not into the external atmospheres as a human Personality, and not merely into the opened mind as the Divine Truth, but a descent into the entire Body of Humanity, filling all its degrees, celestial, spiritual, rational, and natural, with the conscious life of heaven.

When the disciples were gazing after the vanishing figure of their Lord, the angels said unto them:

*"This same Jesus which is taken up from you into heaven, shall so come in like manner as ye have seen Him go into heaven."*

He was taken away from them by the closure of the interior degrees of life and thought which had been temporarily opened in them. The cloud which carried Him out of sight, was not only the cloud of literalism which prevented them from seeing the divine truth, but also the cloud of their own carnalism which separated them from the divine good. How is He to re-appear? for He has really never been away. How are we to see Him, know Him, feel Him again? He will re-appear, and it will be the judgment to us all, by the re-opening, according to the laws of order, of the degrees which are closed. This great work has already begun, and will henceforth be continuously done by the Lord alone; for no one else can open the book of life but the Lion of the tribe of Judah, whose other more interior and celestial name is the Lamb of God.

The Second Coming of the Lord into the Body of Humanity is effected, according to the order of creation and the laws of influx, degrees, and correspondence, by the successive opening of the celestial, spiritual, and natural degrees of the human mind. The wonderful phenomena of this Event, now rapidly progressing, will be considered in another essay.

# ESSAY II.

*THE LORD'S DESCENT THROUGH THE HEAVENS.*

WHY did our Lord incarnate Himself in this particular earth of the universe?

Swedenborg gives two weighty reasons:

First: Because the inhabitants of our earth correspond to the external, corporeal, and ultimate principles in the Grand Man. The Lord would not have been the Alpha and the Omega, the First and the Last, nor would He have acquired to Himself in his glorified Humanity all power in heaven and earth, unless He had appeared in human form in some world bearing that specific and organic relation to the rest of his created universe.

Second: Because the Word which connects heaven and earth, the internal with the external, could be revealed in its natural and literal forms, in which E. S. declares the fullness of its power resides, only on such an earth holding such ultimate relations to all the heavens. And as there are no spaces or times in the spiritual world, the ultimation of our Lord and his Word on this globe alone, makes them manifest, as Swedenborg says, "to all in the universe, who come into heaven from any other earth whatsoever." (A. C. 9356.)

Our world, then, has been the seat of the most stupendous phenomena; the revelation through organic media, and in its lowest ultimate forms, of that Divine Truth which pervades the spiritual universe; and the incarnation of the Supreme Being, his presentation in our midst with objective forms, conditions, and circumstances, corresponding to the subjective states of human receptivity. Our world is the ultimate battle-field between heaven and hell—the basis of that ladder of descent and ascent upon which the divine powers are manifested—the theatre upon which the transcendent work of Redemption is being wrought. The reality and fullness of that Redemption—the fact that the Lord Jesus Christ has all power in heaven and earth, that He is the Alpha and the Omega, the Beginning and the Ending, the First and the Last, the All-in-all from centres to circumferences, from primaries to ultimates, will be stamped ineffaceably upon the future history of this little globe; for all power is in ultimates.

Therefore the prophecies of the Word, infinitely outreaching the vision of Swedenborg who supposed all things would go on as before, declare that the old order of things shall utterly perish, and all things be made new; that the power of evil shall be radically destroyed; that God Himself shall tabernacle with men, and his divine law be written on every heart, so that heaven and earth shall be one in spirit, faith, and action, bound together in the indissoluble perfection of the divine order.

This happy and enduring state of things will be brought about by the Second Coming of the Lord; or, to use a more philosophical expression, by the Descent of the Lord into Ultimates.

The first coming of the Lord was also a descent into ultimates, but under different conditions and with different results. He bowed the heavens and came down, clothing Himself with each successive degree of life, until He appeared in the ultimates of nature with flesh and bones like our own. Nothing but Swedenborg's doctrines of the organic coherence and successive derivation of all things, his doctrine of discrete degrees, influx, and correspondence, and his declaration that each human being is a miniature or least form of the universe, can make the incarnation and glorification of Jehovah at all comprehensible.

Our Lord apparently descended the ladder of life as the Son of God, the Divine Proceeding from the Father, and ultimated Himself in a miniature or least form of the universe. From that form He re-ascended to the Father, by extensions of affection and thought into societies and into heaven after heaven throughout the universe, until He took upon Himself all the states of men, spirits, and angels. From one point of view, He is the man Jesus Christ—a least form of the universe like ourselves, baptized and praying, and looking upward until the heavens are opened unto Him. From the other point of view, He is the Divine Man—the sole life and power in the spiritual universe. (A. C. 3637.)

The Lord disappeared from his disciples and ascended to the Father, because the interior degrees of the human mind were closed, and the divine-natural, the divine-rational, the divine-spiritual, the divine-celestial could not be seen, felt, or comprehended in the dark clouds of literalism and carnalism which shrouded the world. The work of Redemption was but half accomplished. Order was restored, but only upon the spiritual side; for the earth was the seat of increasing anarchy, misery, and crime. The Divine Man had conquered the hells, but only in his own person; for they have ever since darkened and saddened the hearts and minds of men. And so his church has gone on through centuries of suffering, temptation, and doubt. The world has lost all faith in spiritual things. His children are "eating and drinking, and buying and selling," and making all sorts of base compromises with the world, the flesh, and the devil, saying in their hearts, "My Lord delayeth his coming."

Now what is this Second Coming of the Lord which has been so clearly promised, so ardently expected, so long delayed, and so utterly misunderstood?

The Old-Church theory of the literal, personal descent of the Lord into the clouds of heaven, has no weight with those whom the spiritual sense of the Word has delivered from the gross materialism of the letter. It is needless to refute a literal dogma or series of dogmas founded on sensuous appearances, which, however weighted with authorities and respectabilities, will dissolve away on the presentation of a rational philosophy of the connection between the spiritual and the natural universe.

The theory of T. L. Harris, that by organic preparations made in the spiritual world, the Lord is about to descend into ultimates through himself as pivotal man and spiritual King, seems to be only the dark shadow of the old Babylon cast upon the sphere of the New Church, and may be safely consigned to the realm of stupendous fantasies.

The majority of the readers of Swedenborg believe that the Second Coming of the Lord is the unfolding of the spiritual sense of the Word: and that the New Jerusalem descending from God out of heaven, is an external Church which shall derive its doctrinals from that sense, and preach the life corresponding to them.

Now this is true, and a truth so vast and essential that its character can never be overestimated, nor its meaning fully comprehended. The riches of divine truth drawn from the Word by Swedenborg, whose receptive mind was directly illumined by the Lord for that purpose, are inexhaustible, and constitute the rational and intellectual basis upon which the external Church of the future will stand forever, however many different forms it may assume.

But in recognizing the revelation of the spiritual sense as a veritable coming of the Son of Man into the clouds of heaven, have we grasped or exhausted the whole meaning of the Second Coming of the Lord? Have we not a part only? Is it not a means to an end, and not the end itself? Is it not rather a middle term, a cause, an instrumental means whereby an end can be carried into effect?

Man is not saved by faith alone, or by truth alone. Truth alone, however lofty its degree, does not form the Lord's Church. The Lord cannot come to us so as to abide with us in truth alone. The understandings of men and spirits can be elevated into the divine light of the heavens above them, so as to comprehend the spiritual mysteries of truth, but it does them no good; it is barren and fruitless unless the will also has been elevated into a corresponding heat of the superior degrees. Truths are mere vessels for the reception of something greater and more living.

The Ancient Church from Noah to Abraham, was in possession of most of the spiritual truths offered us by Swedenborg; but its people perverted, falsified, and finally lost them entirely. Their mere restoration in the present age, can develop nothing but an ecclesiastical Intellectualism. And why is it that we cannot point to a general, genuine manifestation of the heavenly life in the thousands of so-called Newchurchmen who have believed and loved the spiritual sense of the Word? Is it not because they have accepted the coming of the Lord as a manifestation of divine truth to their understandings, and know nothing of Him as the Divine Man entering, and entering to abide, into all the degrees of life, celestial, spiritual, and natural—individual and general?— Swedenborg's mission and all its phenomena being only the consequence of his passage through the spiritual degree.

Let us consider this subject in the light of the spiritual philosophy of Swedenborg. Why do we speak of the descent of the Lord into ultimates, when we know that, on account of the glorification of his Humanity, He is already and always in ultimates, even as to the principles represented by flesh and bones? It is because the degrees of the human mind are closed to the reception and acknowledgment of that transcendent truth, and to the glorious consequences which follow the living consciousness of the presence of the Lord in ultimates. To *know* that He is here is one thing, a mere article of faith; to *feel* that He is here, tabernacling and abiding in our souls and bodies, is another and a different thing. This latter is a life—the life of heaven. The first was the privilege of the Old Church,—" for lo! I am with you always even to the end of the world." The last belongs only to the New Jerusalem descending from God out of heaven.

It was necessary for the Lord to go away; for the human race, even "his own," could not receive Him, or hold Him, or live Him out in ultimates. It was necessary for Him to come again to finish his work of redemption. Nearly nineteen centuries of our time have been employed in organic preparations for that descent. It is going on now with ever-increasing rapidity. It is a descent from highest to lowest, from primaries to ultimates, from centre to circumference. It is a successive opening of the celestial, spiritual, and natural degrees of human life—which will go on, both in the individual and in the race, until the Lord infills the world with his presence through the general Body of Humanity, just as He fills the heavens with his presence through the angels, and becomes the Grand Man. It is thus that the Lord will descend with his holy angels, and heaven and earth be united in one Church, with many varieties, multiplicity in unity. It is thus that the will of God will be done upon earth even as it is in heaven. Then will the Lord reign supreme, from that "inmost heaven" in the spirits of men and angels, "known only to Himself," down through all his creation, into the very sensuo-corporeal principles of the inhabitants of this ultimate earth in the universe.

The opening of the celestial degree of the human mind for the Lord's descent into ultimates, began partially in the interior of Africa, a little before the spiritual sense of the Word was revealed to Swedenborg. He first mentions the fact in a portion of the Spiritual Diary written about 1750-2, some years before the Last Judgment, and when he was publishing the first volumes of the Arcana. But as he states that these revelations to certain people in Africa had been going on *for a long time* ("*quod diu habuerunt revelationes e cœlo*" —4774), and even points out very considerable regions over which they had spread, it may be safely concluded that the opening began antecedently to his own opening into the spiritual degree.

Why do we think this opening into the African mind was an opening of the celestial degree of life in the human race? For several very cogent reasons:—

Africa in the spiritual sense, is the east, or the state of life nearest to the love and wisdom of the Lord. (A. E. n. 21.) Swedenborg repeatedly says that the Africans are of the celestial type or genius; the most beloved of all the gentiles in heaven; the most capable of interior and intuitive perceptions of truth, a state so very different from its exterior acquisition. It was therefore into those children of the race, those relics of "the days which were before the flood," that our Lord first descended or appeared, opening a degree of life which, historically speaking, had been long closed, vivifying "remains" which had been for ages quiescent, and thus rendering possible again the reproduction of the golden age and the celestial life upon earth. Thus was planted the invisible seed of that tree of life, whose leaves are the divine truths revealed through Swedenborg, and whose fruit is not yet.

Again, it was a celestial opening because it was not an elevation of those African minds into spiritual light such as Swedenborg enjoyed, but a direct dictation from the Lord, through good spirits and angels, of the simple doctrines of the Divine Humanity and the New-Church life.—Contin. L. J. n. 76.

We may yet again infer that this was an opening of the celestial degree, from the following extraordinary statement of Swedenborg: "I heard the angels rejoicing over that revelation, because through it a communication was opened to them with human rationality [the human rational] till then closed up by the universal dogma, that the understanding should be held in obedience to the faith of the ecclesiastics." (T. C. R. 840.) How many Newchurchmen have read these singular lines without any conception of their real bearing and immense importance!

The angels here state that by means of these revelations to the African mind, they have access, in a manner not possessed before, to the rational sphere of human life. It is not a relation between the few angels speaking and the few Africans instructed; but it is a general relation, an avenue opened between the heavens and the earth, a new way or path of influx from angelic spheres into the rational faculty of man. Now it is the celestial with its good, that flows first into the rational and gives man that liberty and rationality without which all revelation of truth to him is utterly vain. Swedenborg says that the celestial is the internal of the rational, as the spiritual is the internal of the natural: also, that the rational is predicated of the celestial man who has a perception of good and of truth from good, but not of the spiritual man, because he only knows truths by instruction and is properly called interior-natural.—A. C. 6240, 3747.

The first step therefore of the Lord in his Second Coming, was to open the celestial degree of life, and establish a communication with the rational sphere of human thought. Such is the organic connection of all spiritual things, and their independence of natural times, spaces, and quantities (witness the spiritual power of the Jewish economy), that this opening, however limited in extent and duration, however secret, obscure, and unknown to the race, was the means whereby the angels could flow down and vivify the celestial remains and awaken the rational faculties of mankind. The concealed influences of that opening have been felt in every human heart and mind throughout the world ever since it happened. It is the heart of the New Church, the hidden spring whence have flowed all the emotional revivals of religion, the love of liberty and truth, the renaissance of charity and brotherly love, and all the chastened and renewed affectional life of modern times.

This opening could only have occurred among an obscure, ignorant, docile, childlike people, far removed from the contaminating influences of our diseased civilization, and utterly unacquainted with the terrible falsifications and perversions of the Christian religion. Swedenborg, from the purely spiritual standpoint of his own mission, may not have seen this subject in the full light with which we are now permitted to behold it; but he saw clearly enough to call this opening among the Africans *the initiament of the New Church and the advent of the Lord.*

In number 4770 of the Spiritual Diary, under the title, *De Novæ Ecclesiæ initiamento*, he says:

"After the atheistic crowd which appeared within the Church had vanished, it was said by many that it was announced, that somewhere among the nations a revelation from heaven has begun, that spirits and angels truly speak with them, and teach the celestial doctrine, especially concerning the Lord, and that they receive it, and that so the New Church springs forth out of heaven (*et sic quod nova ecclesia e cœlo exsurgat*)."

Again, and with still more emphasis, he declares (S. D. 4777):

"Thereupon the angels were gladdened, because now the advent of the Lord presses down (or begins working), and because the Church, which now perishes in Europe, may be renewed or restored in Africa, and that this is being done by the Lord alone through revelations, and not by means of Christian missionaries."

Thus Swedenborg, at the very time when he was unfolding the spiritual sense of the Word, and was in his full state of spiritual light, affirms that the initial steps of the coming of the Lord and the institution of his New Church, had already been made by direct revelations of the doctrine of life to people who were capable of receiving it in the interior of Africa.

Now there was something else involved in these extraordinary statements of Swedenborg, over and above what he himself saw. In the spiritual sphere there is no Africa, Asia, or Europe, but the states or degrees of the human spirit to which they correspond. Africa represents the celestial degree everywhere and always, Asia the spiritual degree, and Europe the natural degree. The revelation of the doctrine of the new life to Africans, meant not only that literal fact but also the revival of celestial affections everywhere in persons of the celestial type—of whom Swedenborg says there were "remnants" in Europe in his own day. It meant the opening of the celestial degree wherever possible, and its impregnation with the fire of the divine love. This is the true key to the extraordinary revival of the religious life in the Quietists, Moravians, Quakers, Methodists, and others for half a century antecedent to Swedenborg's spiritual intromission.

In his descent into ultimates, whether into his own natural body, or into our individual souls, which is regeneration, or into the general body of the race, the order of the Lord's procedure is always the same. The law is that of influx through the celestial or sphere of affection, into the spiritual or sphere of thought, and thence into the natural or sphere of conduct and life. He has thus always three manifestations —as the Father, the Son, and the Holy Ghost; as the Divine Love, the Divine Wisdom, and the Divine Power.

Having therefore entered into the celestial degree of the race through the revelations in Africa and elsewhere, He proceeds by the laws of influx and correspondence to pass into the next discrete degree below, viz., the spiritual; and He there manifests Himself as the Divine Truth, and of necessity through the mind of the man best fitted at that time to receive, arrange, and publish to the world the spiritual truths of the Word in which the Lord Himself resides. That man was Emanuel Swedenborg.

This "servant of the Lord" declares (T. C. R. 779) that, as the Lord cannot manifest Himself in person (that is, cannot appear in a material body as the Old-Church people have expected Him to do), He has manifested Himself spiritually to him—opened his spiritual senses into the heavens and the hells, and taught him the doctrines of his New Church, not through spirits or angels but from Himself alone, whilst he (the humble medium and agent) was reading the Word of God.

By the laws and processes of spiritual consociation, radiation, and propagation from centres to circumferences, the descent of the Lord into the spiritual degree of the mind of Swedenborg, was virtually his descent into the spiritual sphere of the human race. It was the lightning which shineth from one end of the heavens unto the other. "Spiritual light," says Swedenborg, "does not pass through space like the light of the world, but through the affections and the perceptions of truth, therefore in an instant, to the last limit of the heavens." It was the same coming of the Lord which had passed through the celestial, and was now manifested in the spiritual degree under suitable forms. The revelations of life to the Africans and others, and of life and doctrine to Swedenborg, are one and the same thing, by influx from the higher and correspondence in the lower degree. They are different but harmonious movements of the descending Lord.

Therefore the writings of Swedenborg, so far as they unfold the spiritual sense of the Word and the doctrines of the New Jerusalem, are of supreme and unimpeachable authority. These writings are authoritative, not on account of the man whose relation to them was entirely mediumistic and impersonal, but on account of the Divine Truth in its spiritual degree (the Lord on his way into ultimates) which shines in and through them. By extension of affections and thoughts into heavenly societies, we may enjoy in future innumerable "multiplications of truths" and revelations of things never seen or heard by Swedenborg; but they will be in thorough and organic harmony with all he has uttered; they will be rivers of water flowing from this same fountain; they will be leaves and flowers and fruit from the seed here planted.

These openings or avenues of descent, were no doubt made from the celestial and spiritual kingdoms of the Lord in the ultimate heaven, into the corresponding celestial and spiritual degrees (in simultaneous order) of the human mind in the world of spirits, of which world we are all the time unconsciously inhabitants. Of the preparations made in the celestial and spiritual heavens for the Lord's descent into the celestial and spiritual of the ultimate heaven, we have no revelation and could probably form no conception. But we can easily understand that, when the spheres of the divine love and the divine wisdom found appropriate media and channels in the ultimate heaven connected with the world of spirits, the first effect would be a judgment upon those who were in mixed states of good and evil. Hence the phenomena of the Last Judgment in 1757.

The opening of the celestial degree in the Africans and others, the illumination of the spiritual degree in Swedenborg, and the execution of the Last Judgment, were consecutive and associated phenomena, the first being preparatory to the second, and the first and second united being preparatory to the third.

If the natural plane of the human mind throughout the race had been opened from above at that time, the Divine power manifested in the imaginary heavens by the upheaval and destruction of all their institutions and surroundings, as described by Swedenborg, would have displayed itself in corresponding forms throughout the consummated church on earth and the world of nature. In mercy to mankind the gates were kept shut; and although it is now imperative that they shall be opened, it will be done in the most gradual, gentle, and orderly manner.

The descent of the Lord into the natural degree of the human mind, where He will not only build his temple but pitch his tabernacle and abide forever with men, is a subject of such vast importance that I must devote a separate essay to its consideration. We are surveying in the present essay only the grand, spiritual, organic preparations which have been made for that culmination of prophecy, that transcendent Event,

"Toward which the whole creation moves."

According to Swedenborg, the Christian heaven with its three degrees, celestial, spiritual, and natural, was a new heaven made up of the good who passed from the earth after the Incarnation; and it was discretely separate from the ancient heavens which were peopled before the birth of Christ. It is from this new Christian heaven that the Lord's New Church, in which is the Lord Himself, descends upon earth. The spiritual sense of the 14th chapter of Revelation describes the process, and is worthy of profound study in connection with the views I have just advanced.

*"And I saw, and behold a Lamb standing upon Mount Zion, and with Him a hundred and forty-four thousand, having the name of his Father written upon their foreheads."*

This indicates "the presence of the Lord in heaven and

the church," and it is in the *celestial* degree of heaven, the church and the human mind. This is plain, because "the Lamb" is the Lord in his Divine Humanity; Mount Zion is the state of celestial love; the hundred and forty-four thousand are the angels who are in truths from the good of love; the Father is the divine love itself; and "written on the forehead" is acknowledgment from love and faith. (A. E. 612, 613.)

It is still more clear that influx into the *celestial* sphere is meant, when we consider the spiritual meaning of the things which follow, the new song they sing, their being virgins without guile, without fault, following the Lamb, "the firstfruits" of God and the Lamb, etc. All these forms correspond to celestial and not to spiritual things.

Swedenborg says there is a perpetual presence of the Lord in the heavens and the church, whereby all things in the universe are kept in order and connection; "but," he continues, "the presence which is here understood by standing upon Mount Zion is the extraordinary, active presence of the Lord, to the end that his Divine may flow in through the heavens into the lower parts, and there separate the good from the evil." This flowing in of the Divine from the heavens into the lower parts, will continue even into the ultimates of nature.

It was in connection and correspondence with this "extraordinary, active presence" of the Lord in the celestial heavens, and to bring the corresponding degree of the human mind into rapport with Him, that He vivified the "celestial remains" in Africa and elsewhere, and made the initial point of his coming and of his Church in the world. "*Adventus Domini*" was no doubt written on the books of Swedenborg in the spiritual world, indicating their use in the manifestation of the Divine Truth; but "*adventus domini et initiamentum ecclesiæ*"—the coming of the Lord and the inauguration of the Church—had already been inscribed on the hearts of his babes and sucklings, his "first-fruits," by the Divine Love.

This prophecy of the Lord's clothing Himself with the celestial heavens, so that He could enter by influx and correspondence into the celestial degree of the human race, is immediately followed by another which describes the sphere of divine truth in the spiritual heavens, preparing for the glorious manifestations of the everlasting gospel—the Lord's advent and the New Church upon earth.

*"And I saw another angel fly in the midst of heaven, having the everlasting gospel to preach unto them that dwell on the earth, and to every nation, and tribe, and tongue, and people."*

It was in connection and correspondence with this "extraordinary, active presence" of the Lord in the spiritual heavens, that the spiritual degree of the human mind was opened first in Swedenborg, and the spiritual sense of the Word was revealed to mankind. This is the coming of the Son of Man in the clouds of heaven—the middle term of the Second Advent of the Lord.

The divine influx with its "extraordinary, active presence" is then continued downward into the ultimate heaven; for the next verse of the prophecy says:

*"And there followed another angel, saying, Babylon, that great city, is fallen, is fallen,"* etc.

This angel and a third who follows, represent, according to Swedenborg, the truths from the Lord which brought into judgment the imaginary heaven of the Catholics and the Reformed Church, whose externals corresponded with those of the ultimate heaven, so that they were conjoined with "the lower parts" of that heaven, and intercepted the light of that heaven flowing into the world of spirits. The last judgment was not executed upon those in the world of spirits (L. J. 69; Contin. L. J. 30), but upon those who were organically connected with the ultimate heaven. The world of spirits received as much light as the men on earth did, from the removal of the vast spiritual cloud which shut out the light of heaven.

The ultimate heaven is sometimes called by Swedenborg the natural heaven, and its inhabitants are sometimes called the interior-natural, sometimes the rational. From and through that heaven flow the spiritual forces which make us rational, and which, by means of the rational, connect the spiritual and natural together in mutual correspondence. So that when our Lord clothed Himself with the three heavens, or descended into them with "an extraordinary, active presence," and when He opened the corresponding degrees in the celestial, spiritual, and rational planes of human life, by the revelation to the Africans and others, the illumination of Swedenborg, and the execution of the Last Judgment, He obtained a new and interior access to the human race.

What is to be the end of all this? The establishment of a single organized Church which is to evangelize the world by preaching a new system of spiritual truth according to the old methods? The ecclesiastical proprium, both lay and clerical, can find many cogent and gratifying reasons for so believing; but what does Swedenborg say about it? He says that the Advent of the Lord and the inauguration of the New Church began by dictation from the Lord through angels and good spirits—a kind of Christian spiritualism leading to a new life—in the interior of Africa. He says his own writings constitute an authorized revelation of spiritual truth from the Lord, and are the coming of the Lord as to that Truth. He says, moreover, that in the year 1770 the Lord called his twelve Apostles together, and commanded them to preach this new gospel throughout the spiritual world. The Lord, however, makes no provision through his illumined mind for the establishment of a church or the preaching of its doctrines on earth. Swedenborg's only mission was the enunciation of truth, and his only agent the press. He kept aloof from the Old-Church organizations, and made no movement toward the organization of a New one.

The New Church is a celestial life, with its corresponding body of spiritual doctrine. It is the Bride, the Lamb's wife. It is no tower of Babel built up from the ground of literalism, and aspiring to the heavens. It is built *in* the heavens and in the heavenly life of the individual, and, unlike all other churches, descends from above. It is coming, but it is not come. It is indeed the Lord Himself, descending from primates to ultimates, passing from centres to circumferences, to ultimate Himself in the Body of Humanity, and to be upon earth what He is in the heavens, the all-in-all. He will thus unite the Grand Man, from the inmost celestial to the external-sensual (to which our earth corresponds) into a perfect whole, and so be the First and the Last forever. The New Church will be simply heaven upon earth.

The descent of the Lord into the world of spirits, which is the sphere of our natural life above its animal basis, the continuous opening of the three degrees of the life of men, the prolongation of the judgment, the subjugation of the proprium, the expulsion of the hells, the redemption of our souls and bodies, the reconstruction of nature and the "restitution of all things" will be considered in the next essay.

# ESSAY III.

*THE LORD'S DESCENT INTO THE NATURAL PLANE OF THE HUMAN MIND.*

THE Son of Man who is revealed in the clouds of heaven is not the Divine Humanity, but only one phase of it. He is the Lord as to the Divine Truth only, and his coming is the revelation of the spiritual sense of the Word, which was made through the instrumentality of Swedenborg. These spiritual truths are for the use of the angels, and of the men of the coming Church who shall be in rapport with angels. They do not constitute a church, least of all the final New Church which is a life flowing from conjugial love and the genuine marriage of good and truth. Until that regenerated state of the sexual sphere descends from heaven, the spiritual truths revealed through Swedenborg are little more than dead scientifics in the mind. And every effort at church organization on the basis of spiritual truth, which does not involve the vivification of celestial remains and the regeneration of the conjugial sphere, is the work of the ecclesiastical proprium inherent in us all, to seize and appropriate divine truths for its own benefit and gratification, and is thoroughly Old-Church in spirit.

The general expectation of the Christian world, the spiritual philosophy of Swedenborg, and the reiterated prophecies of the Word, all demand that the Second Coming of the Lord in its full and final sense, shall be something more, something larger and grander, something more organic and universal than a revelation of spiritual truth, however important a part the latter may play in its accomplishment.

The Second Coming of the Lord is the transflux of the

Divine Humanity from primaries to ultimates, through the three heavens in successive order; and its corresponding transflux through the degrees of the human mind in simultaneous order from centres to circumferences. It will be a successive opening of the celestial, spiritual, and natural degrees of human life; and a corresponding simultaneous development of religious affection, thought, and conduct. It will be the reappearance of "this same Jesus" on the ultimate plane of the human mind. It will be the unfolding of the New Jerusalem "from God out of heaven." It will be the coming of the Bridegroom; and the Bride, "the Lamb's wife," will be the New Church, whose starting point is the celestial life and the conjugial love.

The Second Coming of the Lord, by the organic laws of the spiritual universe, cannot stop at the coming into the ultimate heaven, and the Last Judgment upon the imaginary heavens which had been reared between the ultimate heaven and the world of spirits. It must be final and complete; it must pass down into the world of spirits, and through the natural plane of the human mind into nature itself in all its elements and all its departments.

The rational mind can see that such must be the case by the light of illustration from the Word, whether the statement can be found in Swedenborg or not. It must be so, because the Lord is the Alpha and the Omega: because the natural sphere is the ultimate, basis, and containant of the spiritual: because all power is in ultimates: because the Lord was born upon our earth, and assumed our humanity, and glorified it even as to its flesh and bones, and has promised to reappear to us upon the lowest plane of life: and finally, because our world corresponds to the external sensual principle in the Grand Man; and the Lord cannot truly reach and save us, unless He descends to our own organic level and conjoins us with Himself.

Therefore, after clothing Himself with the three heavens and executing the Last Judgment (not in the world of spirits itself, but in the provisional world, the imaginary heavens which were attached by similar externals to the ultimate heaven), our Lord proceeds to descend into the natural plane of the human mind, from which as an ultimate centre He can destroy the old order of things and construct the new.

What and where is this natural plane of the human mind?

In general terms the universe is divided into two parts, spiritual and natural. The natural includes the material universe, and the lowest or natural plane of the mind into which man is born. The spiritual includes the spiritual universe, and the three degrees, rational, spiritual, and celestial, into which man rises after death, or which were opened in him by a good life in the world.

These are again divided into internal and external. In general terms the spiritual is internal and the natural is external; but every man, every degree, every heaven, has its internal and its external forms, and the external of the higher degree is connected with the internal of the degree below it. And again: every form—every man, angel, society, heaven, has three degrees of altitude (successive or discrete degrees), and three degrees of latitude (simultaneous or continuous degrees), all represented by the terms, celestial, spiritual, and natural.

Although the Lord has two kingdoms pervading all the heavens, called the celestial and spiritual kingdoms, still the third and second heavens are pre-eminently celestial and spiritual; and the quality of the inhabitants of the first or ultimate heaven is rational or interior-natural, or as Swedenborg says, celestial-natural and spiritual-natural.

Now all below the three degrees of the heavens and all below the internal man, is the natural plane of the human mind. This plane is common to us living men, to the inhabitants of the world of spirits, and to the hells. It contains within its outer circle, strictly natural, two inner circles constituting its celestial and spiritual degrees in simultaneous order. These inner degrees are closed to evil spirits and to unregenerate men. The hells, therefore, can only flow into the outermost degree of the natural mind.

That outermost degree of the natural plane of the mind constituting the natural man, has also its three degrees, rational, scientific, and sensual; and each of these degrees has its internal and external. The highest, the internal of the rational, connects us with the heavens; whilst the lowest, the external-sensual, immerses us entirely in nature, and we share it with the beasts.

We are in the world of nature only as to our animal life, or exteriorly; we are in the world of spirits as to our human life, or interiorly; and so far as we are evil we are in hell. We are not in heaven, or heaven is not forming in us, until the rational is opened in us, and so connects us with the spiritual and the celestial. When the "extraordinary and active presence of the Lord" is felt in the natural plane of human life, He will have passed or descended through the heavens, and have come into nearer contact with devils, spirits, and men. What tremendous issues may we expect from such a coming in the ultimate sphere of his creation!

Hell is entirely outside of the Grand Man. Its three degrees of evil are antipodal to the three degrees in the heavens, and no influx passes *directly* into the hells from the opposite heavens. The Lord flowing through the heavens only meets with the hells in the natural plane of the human mind; and then only in its outermost or strictly natural sphere, for the celestial and spiritual of simultaneous order are closed in the devils. The hells are hells because there are no planes formed in the celestial, spiritual, rational, and interior-natural degrees of its inhabitants for the arrest of the Divine influx, but it passes through into the sensual sphere, and is there turned into evils, fantasies, and abominations.

Jehovah came into contact with the hells by assuming the maternal heredity in the plane of the natural mind. He put off everything derived from the mother, because He subdued all the hells which flowed into the proprium of his infirm humanity *which then ceased to exist;* and He stood in his own proprium, which is life itself, the Divine Man from inmost to outmost. When we abstain from evils we desist from our own wills, so that the proprium is subdued, and we receive from the Lord that new proprium which is his flesh and blood. The new proprium grows in us as the natural plane of the mind becomes reduced into more and more perfect correspondence with the rational degree above it; for so the Father is united to the Son in us, the hells are cast out, the heavens inflow, and the life of the branch in the vine is established in our souls. This will be the perfect and permanent state of the men of the New Church.

The world of spirits, like the hells, is no necessary part of the organic framework of the universe. Its existence depends upon our transition from external states in which our interiors are concealed, to internal states in which they are unfolded. If we were not in mixed states of good and evil, but if the natural plane corresponded perfectly to the spiritual, we would pass at once after death into our special heaven, just as infants do at present. The interiors of the natural mind are implanted in the world of spirits; and there are two worlds to us only because our interiors and our exteriors do not correspond to each other, or to the threefold expanses of the heavens within us.

Nature is the ultimate plane in which divine, celestial, and spiritual things are terminated. All the interiors close in together and rest upon the exterior and extremes, thus upon the sensual or ultimate of man's life; and this is illustrated by the skin, which contains all the interiors of the body and holds them in connection. The natural plane of the human mind is the gateway or medium for the descent of the Lord into the ultimates of nature. It is, indeed, the centre from which the natural world is created, and the states and phenomena of the natural world exactly correspond to its operations. The fixity of the natural world is due to the fixity of the natural plane of the human mind.

These grand fundamentals of the New Church philosophy, worthy of the profoundest study, explain the facts of the Incarnation and its so-called miraculous phenomena. When the Lord Jesus Christ assumed the natural plane of the human mind in a finite body, He occupied the central point from which the external universe is constantly being created. He could, therefore, by the influent life of the Father, still the waves and the winds, turn water into wine, materialize bread and fishes apparently from nothing, and dissipate instantaneously the organic elements of disease in the human body; and all these things done according to the supreme laws of order, appeared to the uninitiated the most extraordinary violations of those laws.

When He comes again and enters the general body of Humanity, He will occupy standpoints in the natural plane of every man who receives Him, similar to those which He occupied in his own material form in Judea. When He has gathered together his elect, and arranged and structured them into the form and order of the heavens, the divine influxes passing through the unobstructed natural plane of the human mind, will reconstruct the physical universe according to the laws of spiritual regeneration. The very elemental substances and forces of nature will be modified. The causes of storms, accidents, diseases, and all disorderly phenomena will be eliminated. The ferocities of the animal kingdom will disappear: the lion will truly lie down with the lamb; the serpent will cease to be poisonous; and our own bodies, perfectly chastened and purified, will become temples of the living God. *"Greater works than these shall he do, because I go to my Father."* O, the power and glory of the actual and organic descent of the Divine Humanity!

All these things can only be effected by the subjugation of the human proprium, the birth and growth of the new proprium from the Lord, and the elimination of the hells from the natural plane of the human mind. This involves a prolongation of the Judgment begun in 1757, which is effected by the continuous descent of the Lord, with an "extraordinary and active presence," down through the world of spirits into those ultimates of the natural mind, which really constitute the world of nature.

This judgment is now going on in the world of spirits with ever-increasing rapidity. It is entering the interiors of the natural man, and they will be progressively laid open, so that the interior man will be compelled to utter himself externally, regardless of all restraints or bonds, social or legal. The processes of putting off our external states and appearing in our real characters, will take place before death just as they now do after it. The atmospheres of the Divine Humanity, penetrating the interiors of every human being, will bring into judgment, not only the individual, but through associated individuals, the churches which are the imaginary heavens of the natural plane, and all the social, civil, and institutional life of the race.

The celestial and spiritual forces evolving from within, will work their way downward and outward, creating external forms in correspondence with themselves; and during this stupendous process, all opposing things will gradually give way. Churches will disintegrate and dissolve; governments will be revolutionized and reconstructed; and the competitive elements of human life utterly broken down, and society rearranged upon permanently coöperative principles. Thus our hells of individualism will perish, and the divine socialism of the heavens be inaugurated upon the earth.

The series of stupendous phenomena of judgment, happening and about to happen, is unfolded in the book of Revelation from the 15th chapter to the end, in that "spiritual-natural sense" of the Word mentioned in A. E. 630. It may be given by "illustration" to those who are in the genuine love of truth for its own sake, and who preserve in thought the distinction between the internal and the external man. (A. C. 5822.)

Now is the time (or the required state of the external church and the world), when the seven angels having the seven last plagues are coming forth out of the temple of the tabernacle; which Swedenborg says "signifies a preparation from the Lord to operate by influx from the inmost heaven into the church, that its evils and falsities may be universally disclosed, and that thus the wicked may be separated from the good." (A. R. 670.)

The plagues that follow, which are now appearing and will indefinitely increase, are the results in ultimates of evil devastated, separated from good and left to itself, so that by the eternal laws of order, it runs into punishment and destruction. The judgment upon Babylon is the judgment upon the universal evil state of the human will; the judgment upon the beast and the false prophet is the judgment upon the universally false state of the human understanding, preceded by revelations of spiritual light from the Word, indicated by the opened heavens, and the appearance of the White Horse followed by the armies of heaven upon white horses.

All these things are necessary, organic preparations, proceeding from above downward, from centres toward circumferences; and they ultimate in the binding of Satan with chains in the bottomless pit. This is the final and perfect subjugation of the proprium of the individual soul, so that Christ reigns supreme in the life for a thousand years, or to the fullest and extreme extent. Then the spiritual triumphs permanently over the natural.

But the work of the Christian is not done. He is the medium of bringing all lower things into judgment. When "the thousand years" are finished, that is, when the celestial and spiritual states of the church are full enough for the purpose, the divine influx is directed upon "the rest of the dead." Satan released from prison and besieging the camp of the saints, is the proprium of the hells infesting and assaulting the religious life. But as this life is now centered in the divine love, spiritual fire from heaven scatters and destroys its enemies. Then follow the grand ultimate scenes of the spiritual resurrection and the final acts of spiritual judgment or separation in the extremes of the natural plane of human life. The Lord has then passed from primates to ultimates, and the new heaven and the new earth are rendered possible, and therefore appear upon the stage. Until that state has been reached, all church organizations are merely man-made and originating in proprium — externals without corresponding internals.

The hells will not be regenerated as the universalists think, nor will they be annihilated as some believe. They will be subdued and reformed; and instead of being infesting enemies, they will become tributaries, dependents, and servants of the human race, or friends and allies, according to their own external and internal states. (A. C. 1695.) The regenerate men of the new earth will constitute the exterior of the ultimate heaven, and no influx into the human mind from the hells will any more be possible.

The Lord, however, will make merciful provision for those in hell, as He does for all his creatures. The general proprium of hell will be subdued, although its inhabitants will be receptive of only a low, sensual, and scientific life. They will be wisely governed and controlled from their own selfish standpoints. They will be in rapport with the subjugated proprium of the heavens. They will render willing obedience, for they will discover the Lord to be their best friend, who saves them with a powerful hand from themselves and from each other. They will exclaim, "The empire is peace."

The effect of the descent of the Lord into the ultimate plane of the regenerating mind will be, to separate the good and truth in the man from the evil and the false in him, in such a manner that he will perceive the presence of the Lord in him with a new consciousness. He will feel and realize his two propriums—the old proprium which is conjoined to hell, and the new proprium which is the Lord in him, an absolutely new life, organized, as it were, from the flesh and blood of the Divine Humanity, and given to him to enjoy as if it were his own. He will clearly perceive that everything good and true in him is the Lord's and not his, and that everything evil and false in him flows in from hell, and is not his own, except so far as he accepts it and approves it. He will clearly understand the words of one who has long borne the Lord consciously in his bosom—"Outside of the atmospheres of the Lord, I am Satan; within the atmospheres of the Lord, I am the Lord."

In proportion as the old proprium passes off to the circumferences or to the feet, and becomes the mere basis or pedestal upon which the man stands, and not the man himself, the Lord takes possession and abides in the soul. This is the new life, which will be considered in the next essay. It will bring with it, after indescribable tribulations and combats, internal respirations, celestial perceptions, the heavenly marriage, angelic communications, and the sense of power and the perpetual peace of the life of heaven. Then and then only will the divine petition of the Lord's prayer be realized, that the Father's will may be done on earth even as it is done in heaven.

Now, my dear reader, I am only offering you in these essays a bare outline of general principles, a mere statement of universals which it would take volumes to infill and vivify with particulars, with the necessary facts, illustrations, and arguments. That work will be done by other hands than mine. At present I invite you to survey with me a few of the incidents and signs of our modern times, which show what progress the race is making toward a realization of the tremendous issues I have suggested.

It was shown in the last Essay from the spiritual sense of the 14th chapter of Revelation, that the Lord descended through the celestial and spiritual into the natural or ultimate heaven, for judgment and the creation of a new order of things. How also the revelations in Africa and elsewhere, the spiritual illumination of Swedenborg, and the judgment executed upon the church in 1757, were connected with and caused by the superior and interior events. The effect or consequence has been the continuous opening of the three degrees of man's life, which exist in simultaneous order within the natural plane of his being.

The first appearance or movement of the descending Lord into the natural plane—*adventus Domini*, and also *initiamentum Novæ Ecclesiæ*—was made in its inmost degree by a revelation of the doctrines of life, what Swedenborg calls "the celestial doctrine," to certain people in Africa who were "opened" to receive dictations from angels and good spirits, and to many persons of the celestial type of character in Europe.

This secret and concealed vivification of celestial remains, like a stone dropped into the centre of a pool of water, pulsated and radiated from its unseen sources throughout the entire affectional or emotional sphere of the human race.

It was a spark of heavenly fire, appearing everywhere, and tending to kindle into gentle affections and brotherly love every kindred germ of celestial remains, which could be found anywhere in the human heart. We may fairly presume that one of its first effects was to vivify the dormant religious nature of Swedenborg himself; for we find the cold, mathematical scientist and philosopher, over fifty years of age, suddenly entering upon strange religious experiences, and writhing under conviction of sin and contrition of heart like the mourners at a Methodist altar.

Indeed the great Methodist movement was one of the first fruits of the dawning of a celestial life upon the race; and if that remarkable people had possessed a true system of doctrine to correct, explain, systematize, and shape their experiences, the effect upon the world would have been tremendous. But it was heat without light; whereas our Swedenborgian movement has been characterized by light without heat. The religion of the future will be the married union of the two.

Emotional Methodism, however, was but an exaggerated expression of the general revival of religious affections which has been going on ever since throughout the world, from the same undiscovered cause, the influent heaven of the celestial degree. From this inmost fountain which lies in every human heart, have sprung forth all the great humanitarian, missionary, socialistic, and co-operative movements of the Age, all the generous and liberalizing outbursts of the human feeling of sympathy, and the far-reaching cry of "Liberty, Equality, and Fraternity."

The interior-celestial is concealed and conceals itself from the world. The greatest uses are performed by those whom we know least, and of whom we hear nothing. Since the opening in Africa there have, no doubt, been many openings, many communications, secret and unannounced. There are people at present throughout the world, who breathe in and from the heavens, and feel consciously the presence of God, who assume nothing and reveal nothing, but like Mary brooding over the signs of the Christ, ponder these things secretly in their hearts.

In the bosom of the external New Church, more than sixty years ago, the angels were permitted to reveal themselves to an exceedingly poor mechanic in England, James Johnston by name. They did not come in apocalyptic splendors, but descended into the interior-sensual of the natural degree, and accommodated themselves in dress, manners, names, and conversation, to the opinions, ignorance, and prejudices of the old man's mind. They lifted him, however, out of the atmosphere of the little ecclesiasticisms which surrounded him, and taught him by suitable representatives that the heavens and the earth are conjoined together, and the church established in the heart of man, by the simple duties and charities of life. It was, perhaps, more than a mere teaching. It may have had organic values not yet revealed to us.

We are indebted to the liberality of Mr. A. W. Manning, of San Francisco, for the publication of this remarkable Diary of James Johnston. The extreme simplicity of the statements and the apparent insignificance of the things revealed, might induce us to ignore it as a matter of little worth; but the opening among the Africans stands in our way as a warning, and we dare not assert that this mission of the poor, old, honest, truthful mechanic, "the celestial representative" as his angels called him, was not somehow or other a mission of concealed but real importance, in the inmost conjunction of the heavens and the earth in the simple life of charity and duty.

Every student of Swedenborg knows that spiritual phenomena vary immensely according to what degree of the mind is opened, and according to the conditions and circumstances of the opening. In James Johnston's case there was clearly no opening of any of the discrete degrees leading into the heavens, but such an opening of the interior-sensual leading only into the world of spirits, that spirits representing angels could flow in and apparently project themselves into the world of nature. Abraham's vision and entertainment of the three men (Gen. xviii.) were analogous phenomena, explicable by the same laws. Swedenborg says that Abraham's washing their feet, was in order that the Divine should approach nearer to the human "by putting on somewhat natural," and that he offered them food so that the human and the celestial should be brought nearer together. These and similar things in the Word will throw great light on Johnston's, and other cases, now discredited only because they are not comprehended.

It is highly probable that the revelations to Johnston constituted an exterior movement corresponding to the interior movement among the people in Africa. The latter was an opening of the celestial-rational, the former of the celestial-natural. The celestial Church which is the New Church, is thus ultimated or established upon earth, with the conscious concurrent influx of the angelic heavens. It was absolutely necessary, however, that this initiation of the *life* of the New Church should take place secretly, among obscure people and in obscure places, so that it might be utterly concealed from the church and the world.

The woman seen in heaven represents the celestial affections of the New Church about to be established. The man-child born of her represents the doctrine of spiritual truth—more especially the doctrine of charity or the good of life—as revealed through Swedenborg. The woman flying into the wilderness where she is secretly nourished, and the child being caught up to God, signify the Divine circumspection and protection extending to the infant New Church in its feeble beginnings, manifested by concealing it from its enemies. Even to this day, the highest, holiest, most powerful elements and forces of the New-Church life upon earth, are undiscovered and undiscoverable.

Swedenborg says that if the order of man's life had not been inverted, celestial affections flowing into the middle degree of his mind, would produce corresponding states of spiritual intelligence, and he would need no man to tell him of the Lord or the mysteries of his kingdom. If the order of man's life had not been inverted, there would have been no need of Swedenborg or any unfolding of the spiritual sense of the Word, for the celestial affections vivified in Africa, would have gradually brought the race, by the power of influx and correspondence, into the perception of spiritual truth. It is, indeed, because the original order of man's life is being gradually restored by regeneration and the continuous opening of degrees, that approximations to the doctrines of the New Church are being gradually made throughout the Christian world, without any knowledge of Swedenborg or his expositors.

One of the most extraordinary instances of this was the case of Edward Irving, the great Presbyterian orator of London. This man, from states of childlike simplicity, fervent piety, intense love of use and self-abnegation, was brought by interior ways to see in a great measure the doctrine of the Divine Humanity and the true nature of the Atonement, whilst his preaching was followed by remarkable spiritual manifestations among his people. He died of a crushed spirit and broken heart, without disease, a martyr to the new faith which had literally come down into him from heaven. He was arraigned by his church for abominable heresies, tried, convicted, and expelled. A perverted ecclesiasticism is always in the hells of the crucifixion; and he who brings it a new truth, out of correspondence with its states of affection, hears the old cry, "Away with him, away with him! Crucify him, crucify him!"

Since man is not in the true order of his life, and his evil affections can only flood his mind with falsities, the Lord has mercifully provided that his understanding may be elevated into the light of heaven by means of truths revealed from heaven. As he cannot receive through his own affectional sphere the truth that flows from good, the Lord reveals to him the truth that leads to good. The Lord therefore comes into the clouds of heaven, revealing the spiritual truths of his Word for the future establishment of a celestial church. Truths and goods of the same degree are not married, but those of one degree are married to those of the degree above it. (A. C. 3952.) The natural or literal truths of the Word attracted spiritual goods from the degree above it, and their marriage made the spiritual life of the Apostolic Church. The spiritual truths now revealed through Swedenborg, must attract and be married to celestial goods, so that the New Church which will be the last, will be a celestial church corresponding to the Most Ancient Church which was the first. Swedenborg answers the cry of the celestial for light.

But the New Church cannot be established in the world, celestial goods cannot descend through spiritual truths into ultimates, until the natural plane of the human mind is prepared for their reception. This plane has been the seat of the most wonderful organic preparation for nearly one hundred and fifty years. The divine influxes flowing through the celestial into the rational, and through the spiritual into the natural—the Last Judgment having cleared the way for their passage—have produced all the rapid and extraordinary changes, religious, civil, social, rationalistic, scientific, and material, of our modern times. It is the Lord descending as the Divine Love and the Divine Wisdom into the interior degrees of the human mind in the world of spirits, who has caused all the agitations, the doubts, the fears, the aspirations, the ecstacies, the revolutions, the progressions, personal and social, individual and general, of the whole race. He thus enters the general body of humanity at his Second Coming. He moves from centres to circumferences. He now approaches the surface.

Our life is threefold : the inmost sphere of it is the life of affection, the middle sphere is the life of thought, the ultimate or external sphere is the life of sensations and motions in which the affections and thoughts embody and express themselves in actions. This is true of every man, spirit, and angel. Every one also has interior affections and exterior affections, interior thoughts and exterior thoughts, interior sensories or sensuals as Swedenborg calls them, and exterior sensuals. Our exterior sensuals are the affections and thoughts ultimated solely in the life of the senses of the body. Our interior sensuals open into the world of spirits, and are illustrated abundantly in the phenomena of dreams, mesmerism, clairvoyance, transference of sensation, and the astonishing developments of modern spiritualism.

The Lord flows "with an extraordinary, active presence," as Swedenborg calls it, into our inmost life, the sphere of affection, when we get into states of profound conviction of sin, contrition, and humiliation, and our souls are stirred with all the passional elements of love, hope, fear, aspiration, self-contempt, self-renunciation, and despair. Ever since the opening of the celestial degree, there has been a constant influx from that sphere tending to bring all men into these emotional states. This is the secret of the Methodist conversion, one of the most extraordinary spiritual phenomena of all the ages. There have been millions of intelligent witnesses to its facts.

When a man, profoundly humbled with a sense of his ineradicable sinfulness, resolutely determines to leave the world, the flesh, and the devil, and falls in strong faith and absolute self-surrender at the feet of the Lord Jesus Christ, the "celestial remains" concealed within him are touched and vivified—a thing which, since the opening of the celestial degree in Africa, is *possible* to multitudes, and even to the whole world at once. According to interior states and organizations the penitents have the celestial degree measurably opened in them, and, when wholly abstracted from sensuals, they come into perceptive and sensational contact with the states of their attendant angels. Sooner or later, gradually or suddenly during the excitement, a great light breaks in upon them, an unutterable peace, an indescribable joy, a sense of holiness and freedom from sin, a love toward the Lord Jesus Christ which beggars all description. The soul is flooded with the light of heaven.

The Methodist explanation of this wonderful but transitory state, is altogether erroneous. There is here no justification by faith, no forgiveness of sin, no regeneration or redemption whatever. The biological and materialistic hypotheses are equally untenable. The truth is simply this: the man by certain genuine and indispensable spiritual exercises, has come into states of mind receptive of celestial influx; and as the Lord is now opening all the interior degrees of life wherever the conditions presented render it possible, the celestial degree opens in him, the angels inflow, and communicate to him their own states of blessedness and delight.

"The perception and sensation of delight and blessedness thence resulting," says Swedenborg, "surpass all description. . . . When good spirits, who are not yet in that delight because not yet taken up into heaven, *perceive it from an angel by the sphere of his love,* they are filled with such delight that they come as it were into a delicious trance."—H. H. 409.

The Methodist conversion is, therefore, the temporary transference or induction of the angelic state upon the human mind, and not its own condition. Such condition is only created and fixed, as it is in the angels, by the long and arduous work of regeneration. So the convert soon finds the heavens have closed, the vision has fled, and Satan who had departed for a season, returns to tempt and torture him again. Only those who have sufficient depth of earth and look constantly to the sun, bring forth the fruits of a good life.

Now, why cannot this beautiful gleam of heaven be permanent? Because celestial goods with their corresponding delights must have a basis of spiritual truths into which they may flow. The plane for the reception of these spiritual truths, can only be formed by the knowledges derived from the revelations made through Swedenborg. Nor even then, with the celestial and spiritual degrees opened in us, could we realize the peace and joy of the heavenly life in ultimates, until the Lord had descended into the natural plane of the human mind and opened it to the influx of the heavens. That great work is now going on; and as it progresses, regenerating men will feel the joy and peace of the angels descending through their spirits and pervading even the sensories of the material body.

As the work of judgment proceeds in the world of spirits (of which we are all inhabitants), the presence of the Lord will become more and more distinctly *perceived* in the hearts of those whose evils are being cast out and whose proprium is being thoroughly subdued. There will be such openings of the interior sensuals, that our Lord, entering into the natural plane of the mind, may be projected objectively out of the man by the laws of spiritual creation, and seen either as the Divine Man Himself, or as an angel infilled with his presence (H. H. 121), or as a whole society of angels under one human form (A. C. 10,810,'11). There are men now living who have thus seen Him, although their declarations, like those of the women respecting the appearance of Jesus after his burial, will be regarded "as idle tales"—relations not to be credited.

The spiritual history of man since the time of Swedenborg and the early Methodists and the early Newchurchmen down to the present hour, is full of extraordinary and constantly increasing phenomena, irreconcilable with the old theologies and philosophies, explicable only by the genuine truths of the New Church, and which all tend to prove that the world of spirits is being gradually opened to the interior perceptive faculties of the human race. Many of these remarkable phenomena have occurred among the receivers of the heavenly doctrines, few as they still are in number. Some are only whispered from friend to friend: some no doubt are unconfessed and unrecorded. This is only the beginning. After a while they will come in torrents—by thousands. Nor can they be concealed or repressed; but the interiors will shine down and out through the externals, and stand confessed before the world.

And here the inexorable logic of that spiritual truth which reasons from centres to circumferences, from internals to externals and not the reverse, points out the true significance and value of the wide-spread and wider-spreading events of modern Spiritualism. They are proofs, and at the same time consequences, of the opening of the interior-sensual degree of the natural mind, so that the world of spirits and the world of nature are coming together. As the natural plane is opened, the heavens and the hells both rush in; and the combats of the world of spirits will be apparently led down into the world of men.

Why are the phenomena of Spiritualism productive of so many unmistakable evils and falsities, whilst the good of it is yet so unapparent? The heavens cannot descend into the present activities of the natural life of man, because they spring from and are saturated with his evil proprium. The hells, however, flow in first, take possession at once, and vivify all the energies of man from the selfhood. They find the ground already prepared for them, and their own energies coincide with the selfish and sensual rush of human motives and appetites. But the heavens are equally immanent and active. They work more interiorly, nor can they fall into the currents of human thought and feeling except so far as the proprium is subdued. Therefore they come to destroy before they can rebuild; they come to lay waste and to bring low, for thus only can they prepare the way of the Lord.

Swedenborg, from the spiritual standpoints of the last century, asserted that communication with spirits was disorderly and dangerous. His disciples have therefore very generally avoided and ignored the developments of Spiritism, classing them with the old arts of magic and necromancy which are forbidden in the Word. The phenomena, however, are entirely different. The latter arose in the corrupt ancient Church from the abuse of correspondences, which were then in power. It was an effort to force one's way into the world of spirits, and to ally one's self with the evil powers of that world for selfish purposes. Modern Spiritism is a spontaneous, unsought, unheralded descent or opening from above. It is the world of spirits rapping at our natural doors, appealing to us for recognition and intercourse—first by hearing, then by sight and touch. It is a new development, unforeseen by Swedenborg, fraught of course with disorder and danger, for it will bring us into audible, visible, and sensational contact with evil spirits. But by the same law it will bring us after a while into audible, visible, and sensational contact with angels: and at the worst, it cannot unfold to us any hell but that which already exists in our own bosoms.

Although Swedenborg says that in his own day it was disorderly and dangerous to hold communication with angels and spirits, he often qualifies his statements by adding, unless a man be in the true faith, or in the acknowledgment of the Divine Humanity, etc. He also declares that if man was in the true order of his life, it would not be disorderly or dangerous, but perfectly natural and proper, to hold communication with the heavens.

In the great openings which are preparing for the world, the well-instructed student of Swedenborg will be the last man to be deceived by fantasies, or carried away by false Christs. He holds in his hand the true means of testing all phenomena. He will care nothing for communication with spirits and angels. He will stick closely to the ultimate duties of life, knowing that the Lord comes first and the angels afterwards. He will shun all evil things as sins against God, and look to the Lord alone for life, wisdom, and power; and he will then accept gladly such communications with the other life as the Lord may give him, for the purpose of aiding and perfecting his uses in this life. This was precisely the case with Swedenborg; for in all that he saw and heard, in all his communications with the spiritual world, he was so directed and guided by the Lord in every event, every change of state, every conversation, that he could truly say that he received nothing from angels or spirits, but every thing through angels and spirits from the Lord alone.

One sure sign of the impending judgment in ultimates, is the growing lawlessness of the world, the increasing contempt for authority, the breaking of old bonds, external and internal. It is the beginning of the end. It is the process by which exterior restraints are laid aside, and the true interior comes forth to sight. The conservatives will labor to strengthen or re-impose the old fetters both in church and state; but in vain. They are all doomed. The evil will despise them more and more. The good will require them less and less. The internal will cleave down through the external, and reveal itself and assert itself regardless of all bonds. The eyes of the future will see strange sights. Tribulations unheard of before, earthquakes in church and state, dissolutions and reconstructions; precipitations like Lucifer's, resurrections like Lazarus', the renewal of magic, the repetition of miracle, the unfolding of all secrets, the hyena in the pulpit, the dove in the brothel. "The last shall be first, and the first last."

These are not prophecies, dear reader, but legitimate deductions from the teachings of the Word, and from the general laws and principles laid down by Swedenborg.

As the interiors are opened, the results will be determined by the organic states and receptivities of the medium. There will be innumerable cases of false utterance, of premature philosophizing, of abortive efforts, movements of the proprium to maintain its status or increase its power. Amid the chaos of opinions and sentiments which will ensue, the Word of God and its spiritual interpretation as revealed through Swedenborg, will be our sure refuge and rock of defense. Whoever clings to the atmospheres of the Word in which the angels breathe, will be saved from the infestations of evil spirits and be guided to the light.

It is probable that many beautiful and wonderful sayings of the Divine Man, unrecorded by the Evangelists, floated about in traditionary forms among the early Christians for a long time. One of the most extraordinary of these is the following found in the second Epistle of Clement, chap. 10, v. 2.

"*For the Lord Himself, being asked by one when his Kingdom would come, replied: 'When two shall be one, and that which is without as that which is within, and the male with the female, neither male nor female.'*"

This abstruse answer, concealing its meaning from those

who could not see, is now intelligible. "That which is without" shall be "as that which is within," when the internal is opened and flows down into the external, compelling it and transforming it into correspondence with its own structure and order. "Two shall be one," when the male shall be with the female and the female with the male in such a manner, that neither is male or female alone, but the two souls are so united that "each feels himself or herself in the other mutually and interchangeably," as Swedenborg expresses it. (C. L. 178.) This mystery of the heavens is going to be realized on earth, for it is the outbirth of the heavenly marriage of goodness and truth. The interiors and exteriors are to be made one; and so, through the conjugial love which is the life of the New Church, and the opened heavens, the Lord will descend into ultimates and establish his everlasting kingdom upon the earth.

The transcendent meaning and use, the previded and provided end of all these phenomena, is the inauguration of the New Life, the life of the branch in the Vine in this world of ours, whose inhabitants correspond to the sensuo-corporeal principles of the Grand Man. Then will the spiritual universe be held together from primaries to ultimates, from centres to circumferences, in the loving embrace of the Divine Man. Light upon this sacred subject, drawn from Swedenborg and the Word, will be presented in the next essay.

# ESSAY IV.

*THE LORD'S KINGDOM ON EARTH.—THE NEW LIFE.*

WHAT is the New Life which the entrance of the Lord into the Body of Humanity will inaugurate?

It is the Kingdom of Heaven, which is said to be *within* us. It is the answer to the petition of the Lord's prayer:

"*Thy kingdom come. Thy will be done on earth, as it is in heaven.*"

It is the fulfillment of prophecy:

"*Now is come salvation and strength, and the kingdom of our God, and the power of his Christ.*"

It is the realization of the promise of the Master:

"*And I appoint unto you a kingdom, as my Father hath appointed unto me.*"

The Church of the Future will be a celestial church; but it will constitute the heart and lungs of the world, and not the whole man. The Christian life of the future will not be a celestial life alone, converting the world into a third heaven; nor a spiritual life alone, confounding it with the second heaven; nor a regenerate natural life alone, making it one with the first heaven. In a world which corresponds to the sensuo-corporeal principles of the Grand Man, upon which the Lord was Himself ultimated even as to flesh and bones, there can be no celestial church, without spiritual intermediates, and natural and even sensuo-corporeal foundations.

The natural plane of human life is the ultimate, basis, and

containant of all the interior discrete degrees which flow into it and spread themselves out upon it, in correspondential forms in simultaneous order. It is like the human skin, into which the nerves and blood-vessels and cellular tissues of the body descend, and arrange themselves in stupendous order, constituting a broad, vital membrane which contains, represents, and repeats the whole man. Such will be the Lord's kingdom in ultimates. It will be a miniature form of all the conjoined heavens, an image of the Grand Man.

It is because the Lord descends into the Body of Humanity from and through the heavens, that the natural plane of the human mind will be hereafter infilled and structured according to the form and order of the heavens. There will be members of the Church universal on earth composed spiritually of all the churches, who will correspond to every degree of the heavens, to the interiors and exteriors of every degree, and to all the intermediate forms which connect and bind the parts of the Lord's celestial and spiritual kingdoms into a transcendent whole.

In the spiritual world, times, spaces, distances, and phenomena are determined by the spiritual states and changes of state in the inhabitants. Therefore the celestial, spiritual, and natural degrees, and the interiors and exteriors of those degrees are separated from each other. And even in every society the spirits of the most interior nature occupy the mountains; those of a less interior nature live upon the hills; while those of the least interior nature dwell in the valleys. Or if the society occupies a plain, the most interior are grouped in the centre, the less interior are arranged around them, and the least interior are located in the circumferences. So also the relative position and arrangements of good spirits and angels as to east and west, north and south, are determined by their states of love and wisdom, and their receptivity of the Divine Sun.

In the world of nature, however, which is a fixed plane for the insemination, birth, growth, and translation of human beings to higher spheres, no such grouping or arrangements will ever be possible. Men will continue to organize themselves into families, tribes, nations, churches, societies, associations, unions, etc.—occupying external relations as heretofore; but the interior forms of these larger bodies will approach nearer and nearer to the use and perfection of the human form, as through individual regeneration they are led more and more into the life and order of the heavens.

Every church for instance, every congregation or society, will be composed of celestial, spiritual, and natural men; of interior and exterior celestial men, interior and exterior spiritual men, interior and exterior natural men, and of all the intermediates between them; so that it will be a little form or image of the heavens, its component parts differing immensely as to opinions, but held together as one whole in the bonds of charity. The Lord will flow into it as He does into the heavens, assign each his place and functions, and vivify the whole by his presence. Whatever may be the external appearances and differences, the celestial man (spiritually speaking) will occupy the mountains and the centres, the spiritual men the hills and the middle places, and the natural men the valleys and the circumferences, all resting upon a sensuo-corporeal basis reduced into order by the influx and presence of the sensuo-corporeal life of the Divine Man.

The fixity of the natural plane of the human mind, makes it the seed-field of creation and the basis of the heavens above it. It is the centre from which nature is created and brought into the field of our consciousness. The laws and phenomena of nature, therefore, will remain forever the same, after the perturbations produced by evil have been eliminated. The laws of regeneration also, its processes and phenomena, so elaborately unfolded by Swedenborg from the Word, will remain forever unchanged. While the order of influx and evolution is from primates to ultimates and from centres to circumferences, the order of progression or development is the reverse. We have first the elemental kingdom, then the mineral, then the vegetable, then the animal, and lastly the human. Man will continue to be born in mere sensuals, and to pass from them into scientifics; from natural to become rational, from rational spiritual, and from spiritual celestial. He will first be taught the Word in the letter. Advancing from appearances to realities, he will comprehend it in the spiritual sense, with Swedenborg as his guide. A discrete step further, and the celestial sense will be unfolded in his affections and dramatized in his life according to the opening of his inmost degree.

The perfection predicated of the New Jerusalem, is and always must be relative and not absolute. It will be ineffably superior to anything hitherto attained, but it will be forever inferior to the higher and grander progressions of the heavens. And it is well that it is so. The possibility of our perpetual advance toward perfection, lies in the fact that we are organically and permanently imperfect. The highest angels have their states of obscurity and twilight, of indifference and something akin to sadness. They are drawn toward their proprium again, however dead and conquered it seemed. They must then learn new truths for higher steps in regeneration. They must again ascend the ladder of prayer, of self-compulsion, and obedience, before they can descend again with new love and wisdom and power. And so will it be on the earth forever; for these are organic necessities.

The apostle John is the prophet of the states of the New Life. The burden of his song is the coming of the Lord, not merely as a revelation of spiritual truth, but as an organic, vital, universal descent of the Divine Humanity, for judgment and reconstruction, into the very ultimates of his creation. Nothing less than that can produce the form and order of heaven upon earth. Nothing less than that can fully explain the book of Revelation. Judgments in the world of spirits and new revelations of divine truth, are only organic preparations for the actual descent of the Divine Being. His First Coming was his own incarnation in a human body. His Second Coming, for which the first was only a preparation, is his descent into ultimates and his virtual (not actual) reincarnation in the Body of Humanity.

The new life or kingdom of God upon earth is fully described in the twenty-first chapter of Revelation. It is a new heaven and a new earth, or a new state of existence both spiritual and natural. It will be a new structure or new order of things; a new soul (the new proprium) and a new body to correspond with it. This new life will fill the whole man individually, and the whole church and world collectively. Therefore there will be "no more sea"—no more external, outlying regions of scientism or heathenism in the man or the race, out of harmony with the interior life.

It will be a celestial life—a celestial church—all of whose outflowings into lower degrees are from the throne of the Lamb, or from the power and glory of the Divine Love. The holy city, New Jerusalem, is therefore called the Bride, the Lamb's wife, from the mystical marriage of the Lord with the church in man. The creation of the universe flows from the marriage of the Divine Love and the Divine Wisdom. Its first proceeding is the marriage of the divine celestial and divine spiritual in the Infinite Humanity of Jesus Christ. This marriage produces the marriage of goodness and truth in the heavens, and is imaged in the marriage of spiritual heat and light in the creation of the spiritual universe, and in the marriage of natural heat and light in the creation of the natural universe. From the marriage of goodness and truth flows conjugial love—the first of all the affections coming from God, the highest and holiest, the fountain and progenitor of mutual love, and of all the infinite varieties of it, which constitute the life of the human race.

The new life of the Church of the future is therefore centered in the regenerate condition, the marriage of goodness and truth, of charity and faith, of the will and understanding, in the marriage of two souls in the bonds of conjugial love, so pure, so perfect, so absolute, that they are no longer two but one; and the man carries the woman in himself, and the woman carries the man in herself, consciously, emotionally, intellectually, sensationally, wherever either of them may be. (C. L. 178; Spl. D. 4407.) This profoundest mystery of the heavens, which must exist organically even if unconsciously in every man and woman in the world, according to his or her inmost states of regeneration, is now being faintly unfolded upon the earth; and it will grow and develop in the Church in proportion as the interiors of men are opened, and the Lord descends through them according to the laws and processes of divine order, down into the sensories of the body and the ultimates of nature.

The reconstruction and sanctification of the married relation upon earth, will begin from regenerate centres in the New Church. Only the spiritually married are admitted to the marriage supper of the Lamb. In proportion as the old Babylon of self-love, that "mother of harlots," who has made the inhabitants of the earth "drunk with the wine of her fornication," is cast out of the human heart, the heavenly marriage will take place in the souls of men; and descending into the sensories of their bodies, will chasten and modify all other loves, radiating celestial influences from centres to circumferences, until the church and the world are "permeated and perfumed with the airs of heaven."

The Lord is present in conjugial love and in the mutual love which flows from it. These constitute the new or celestial proprium, which is the new life from the Lord given to man to enjoy *as if it were* his own. It is the means of conjunction between the Lord and the soul. It is the life of the Lord *in* the disciple, not only *known* but *felt* to be such. (A. C. 8865.) It is the realization of the Lord's words, "As thou, Father, art in me, and I in thee, that they also may be one in us."

Therefore when John *saw* the New Jerusalem "as a bride adorned for her husband," or comprehended its truths with the understanding, he also *heard* "a great voice out of heaven," or perceived its inmost life from the affections; and that voice said:

"*Behold, the tabernacle of God is with men, and He will dwell with them, and they shall be his people, and God Himself shall be with them, their God.*"

Hear moreover what our Lord says:

"*And the glory which thou hast given me, I have given them : that they may be one, even as we are one.*"
"*I in them, and thou in me, that they may be made perfect in one.*"

Hear, too, what the apostle Paul says:

"*I am crucified with Christ : nevertheless I live ; yet not I, but Christ liveth in me.*"

Hear, also, what Swedenborg says:

"The things appertaining to the internal man are of the Lord, so that it may be said that the internal man *is* the Lord." —A. C. 1594.

The Lord is therefore descending, with what Swedenborg calls "an extraordinary, active presence," into the body of Humanity. He is being felt, according to the opening of the celestial interiors, as a living Guest, a pervading Presence, a divine Guide, in the souls of men. He is no longer to them an objective Being, represented by sun or moon, and to be worshiped in temples. He comes independently of all ecclesiasticisms. He is seen *within* by a spiritual light; He is felt *within* as a spiritual "glory." In his presence there can be no weeping, or sorrow, or pain, or death: in his atmospheres, no fear, or unbelief, or falsehood, or any unclean or evil thing.

This angelic state is now possible to men upon the earth. It is an altogether new state, never before possible. It is the beginning of the marriage-union of heaven and earth. The Lord is not in love alone, but in that love only which produces truth. He is not in truth alone, but in that truth only which leads to good. The celestial life described in this marvelous chapter (Rev. xxi.), is therefore rooted, grounded, and imbedded in that infinite system of spiritual truth, represented by the Holy City, with its walls of jasper, its gates of pearl, its streets of gold. Therefore whoever has the celestial degree of life opened in him, has received the good which leads to truth; and he enters, according to the degree and quality of his good, into the spontaneous and intuitive perception of the corresponding spiritual truths of the Word as revealed through Swedenborg. On the other hand, he who has stored his mind with the spiritual truths of the Word revealed through Swedenborg, has within him the sacred vessels which are receptive of the celestial life; and woe to him if it comes not to the birth!—if the Rachel of his soul does not exclaim in agony, "Give me children, or else I die!"

How can this holy state of life be realized in the individual and in the race? The processes are described in the spiritual-natural sense of the preceding chapters of Revelation. These can be clearly comprehended, if we will bring the spiritual sense as revealed through Swedenborg down into ultimate application, guided always by the infallible science of correspondences he has unfolded, and remembering the following universal principles he has laid down : 1st. That the interior senses of the Word rise above time, space, persons, names, or things, into the abstract regions of good and truth. The judgment upon Babylon and the Dragon, therefore, were not only personal judgments upon Catholics and Protestants in the world of spirits, but universal judgments upon qualities or states of life and thought wherever they may be found. 2d. That the spiritual world is the world of causes, and causes produce their effects by influx and correspondence, moving from above downward and from within outward. Therefore the judgments initiated upon the qualities and states of life and thought in the spiritual world in the last century, must of necessity be prolonged and repeated in the natural sphere, where similar qualities and states exist, and obstruct the Divine entrance into the lower realms of human life.

The woman arrayed in purple and scarlet, and "decked with gold and precious stones and pearls," sitting upon the scarlet beast, "full of names of blasphemy, having seven heads and ten horns," is the human proprium as to its evil affections, its love of self and the world, the root of all sin and folly, the source of all wicked desires and false principles, the fountain of self-righteousness and self-aggrandizement and of the lust of spiritual domination. The powers of this evil proprium "make war with the Lamb," the divine goodness, and not with Christ or the Word, the divine truth. They are overcome by the Lamb, and cast down and cast out, so that the proprium can rule no more forever. The tremendous wail of sorrow and despair which goes up from those who have loved it, and believed it, and lived in it, can only be appreciated by those who have awakened to a sense of its terrible nature, and have discovered how hard and painful it is to die thoroughly to the last one of its infernal affections. Those, also, who have laid down the life of the old proprium to take up the life of the new, can understand the gladness and triumph of the heavens at the removal of this proprium, and their saying, "for the marriage of the Lamb is come, and his wife hath made herself ready."

All this takes place in the sphere of the affections, in the inmost or celestial degree (in simultaneous order) of the natural plane of the human mind. In strict correspondence with these things, the divine prophecy goes on to state what occurs in the spiritual degree. The heaven of that degree is opened, and the White Horse and his rider, the Word of God, appear, followed by the armies of heaven. This is the revelation of the Lord to us as the Divine Truth. The Divine Truth overcomes all falsity, and enlightens the spiritual understanding into correspondence with the regenerate movements of the celestial will. Therefore the beast and the false prophet and the kings of the earth make war upon him and are overcome by him and cast out forever. Note well, however, that the King of kings achieves for us in the sphere of thought, the corresponding work which the Lamb of God had already accomplished in the sphere of the affections. They move together on their discrete planes *pari passu*, or step by step, because they are the divine heat and light whose marriage-union creates the universe and regenerates the souls of men.

The spiritual sense of the Word as revealed through Swedenborg is a middle term, something without independent use or meaning, and only existing because connected with the two other terms. It is like the beautiful light of winter, smitten with barrenness when standing alone. Its truths fall like scientifics into the memory of man, and lie fruitless and lifeless until the celestial degree is opened and they are vivified by the fire which descends from heaven. When, however, they are so vivified, they become the winged lightnings of the divine wisdom, and passing into ultimates, manifest that power which resides in the letter or the lowest plane, because it is the basis and containant of all interior forces. The successive opening of the three degrees, and the descent of the Lord through them as the Divine Love, Wisdom, and Power, will produce the final and astounding effects of the judgment described in the twentieth chapter of Revelation, which we will now examine.

There are here three great events which occur, by the laws of influx and correspondence, in the three degrees (in simultaneous order) of the natural plane of the human mind. First: The binding of the evil principle in the bottomless pit, and the reign of the good with Christ for a thousand years (vs. 1–6). Second: The last contest between the saints and Satan, who besieges the beloved city (vs. 7–10). Third: The general resurrection of the dead and the vanishing away of heaven and earth, so that the new heaven and the new earth, with the New Jerusalem of the next chapter, become possible (vs. 11–15). Swedenborg here unfolds the spiritual sense of the Word only so far as it relates to certain movements in the world of spirits in the last century, and which seem to have for us only a certain historical and philosophical interest. By the descending and increasing light of the Word, the rational mind may now perceive that these astounding events are occurring and about to occur in every individual soul, so as to prepare mankind for the evolution of the new heaven and the new earth.

The angel coming down from heaven, "having the key of the bottomless pit and a great chain in his hand," is the Lord descending for judgment and salvation from primaries to ultimates. The Lord alone opens and shuts, and our regeneration is effected by his opening our interiors to heavenly associations, and shutting off the influx of the hells into our life. The evil principle, represented in its three degrees —the evil (devil), the false (Satan), and the sensual (serpent) —is cast into the bottomless pit, which is the hell of our own hearts. This is the subjugation (laying hold of and binding) and removal of the proprium, concealing and shutting it up, to make room for the life and reign of Christ in the soul. This is the state of the angels whose proprium, bound, sealed, and shut up within them, is just as evil as that of the devils in hell. But it is utterly separated from them, and they live in the new proprium, formed out of the substance of the Divine Humanity, and given to them to occupy and to feel as if it were their own. Such must be the state of the man of the New Church, else he is of this Church only in name.

In exact proportion as the proprium is removed from man, does he turn away from the worship of the beast, which represents all the evil lusts engendered by self-love and the love of the world. In the same proportion does he obey the commandments of God, and is guided and judges himself and all others by the truths of the Word. He lives and reigns with Christ, because Christ lives and reigns in him. As this heavenly life opens and deepens in him, he will surely be "beheaded for the witness of Jesus;" that is, he will be misunderstood, misrepresented, repudiated, and scoffed at, especially by those in the church to whom his celestial state of life and love are incomprehensible. Thanks to the mercy of the Lord, these dawning states of the perfect life in us are concealed under his altar, and protected from the infestations of evil spirits and of men.

"A thousand years" has no relation to time, but means the persistency and intensity of the holy state of life involved in the context. Ten signifies the remains of good and truth implanted in the internal man by the Lord. One hundred means the same thing in greater fullness or realization. A thousand years still further intensifies the quality or state of life. "The rest of the dead lived not again until the thousand years were finished" means that the "first resurrection," or the vivification of celestial remains, always precedes the awakening of the intellect and the resurrection of the senses to the divine life. Swedenborg says that the process of regeneration by knowledges and intellectual truths, cannot take place until a plane has been first formed in infancy by the insemination of celestial affections (A. C. 1555). The thousand years ending, does not mean that the states of the celestial life cease; but that on attaining a certain fullness of state the representation changes, and the celestial passes down into the spiritual degree, producing a new and different but corresponding series of phenomena.

These phenomena of the spiritual degree relate to the contest between the true and the false for the possession of the human mind. Therefore Satan appears again, out of prison, to deceive the nations; that is, to persuade us that our apparent good is real good, that our thoughts and opinions are true and right, that our goodness and truth are our own, and that we may righteously congratulate ourselves upon being what we are. He therefore gathers together all the lies and falsities that have ever blinded the intellect and darkened the understanding, to make war upon the heavenly doctrines which resist him, and to besiege "the beloved city." These confederated false principles are overcome and cast out by fire from heaven—by the descent or influx of the conjoined good and truth (heat and light) from the celestial and spiritual heavens. These also reveal the great fact that Satan (the false principle) is really the devil or the evil principle: and he is cast out into the hell of lusts and falsities, with the beast and the false prophet. Thus regeneration proceeds through the spiritual degree.

The Lord, having thus taken possession of the sphere of affection as the divine love, and of the sphere of thought as the divine truth, descends for judgment and reconstruction into the ultimate plane of the life and conduct. The great white throne represents the power and purity of the divine truth descending into the natural plane. The heaven and earth that fled away, are the internal and external life of the proprium—for the proprium of the natural man has its heaven or its religious life, and its earth or its social and business life, and these cannot stand a moment before the face of the Lord. All the dead things of the natural life—the spiritually dead, externals without internals—are brought into judgment, and inspected from the books of the memory and of life according to the deeds done in the body. All the evil and false things of the natural man are thus separated and cast off into the subdued and conquered hell of the proprium, nothing remaining whose name or quality is not in harmony with the divine life in the soul. After these things have been accomplished—the individual soul and the church having been structured and ordered according to the forms and the laws of heaven—the apostle sees the new heaven and the new earth, and the New Jerusalem descending from above.

The spiritual truths of the Apocalypse, passing into the natural mind of the apostle, entered the sphere of times and spaces, and the representative events and visions are related as if they occurred in successive or historical order, and we are obliged to think and speak accordingly. But we can never understand this holy book, unless we also grasp the idea that these things are always happening, simultaneously, at once and all the time, with infinite varieties, to every individual soul. Thus the Babylon is not utterly cast out of the man's soul, and then the Divine Truth revealed to him on the White Horse, and after that Satan bound in chains, and still after that a judgment of externals, and still later the appearance of the new heaven and the new earth. This is indeed partially true, for one thing springs from another and effects follow causes; but it is not all the truth.

The other part of the truth necessary for our comprehension of the whole, is, that the destruction of Babylon, the binding of Satan, and the unfolding of the new heaven within us, are simultaneous and identical processes. So of the appearance of the rider on the White Horse, the descent of fire from heaven to destroy Satan, and the revelation of the spiritual truths involved in the descent of the holy city, New Jerusalem. So, also, of the great white throne in ultimates, and the evolution of the new earth in which there was no more sea. The three discrete degrees are, moreover, so made one by influx and correspondence, that the religion and business of the external life will always reveal, in the individual and the church, how far Babylon has been destroyed, Satan chained, the new heaven opened, etc., etc.

The heaven and earth of the proprium of the natural mind is now being visited by the "extraordinary, active presence" of that Divine Power which sits upon the great white throne. The internal and external of that proprium is about to be explored through the books which will be opened. The religious life and the social and business life of that proprium will be found so evil and false, that they will be disorganized and dispersed by the presence of the face or the interior manifestation of the Lord. Little or nothing will be found in them but the evil and false things from the sea and from death and from hell. There will be a remnant left, however—that very small portion of genuine love of the Lord and the neighbor called "remains"—the name or quality "written in the book of life;" and from that the new life of the individual and of the church will begin.

When the proprium even of the highest angel is altogether evil and false, how can there be any religion of the proprium? It is, of course, an evil and false religion; but the proprium of the natural man is exceedingly religious. It seizes upon the religious idea with the utmost avidity, appropriates it to itself with the greatest delight, busies itself incessantly in church-building and church-going, in organizing societies, conventions, and hierarchies, and actually enjoys all kinds of self-sacrifice, humiliation, and suffering. Swedenborg saw men of this kind in the other life, who had been models of piety and had preached the gospel with zeal and power, who, when interiorly examined, were found to be consumed with the love of self and the world. (S. D. 4325.) Nor are these men always, or even often, hypocrites, who consciously and of set purpose subordinate the truths of heaven to their own selfish interests; but they are deceived by the cunning Satan of the proprium, and have no conception of the true nature and tendency of the false sanctities in which they are immersed. (A. C. 215.)

I am indebted to Henry James, one of the profoundest thinkers of our faith, for my first clear conception of the church-proprium or ecclesiastical spirit as the root of self-righteousness—an evil far worse than lust, intemperance, or gambling; for these run by organic laws into punishment and correction, but self-righteousness ends in spiritual insanity—one of the saddest and most incurable of all states. This cunning, cruel, and malignant church-proprium, buried deep under beautiful and lovely externals, is not confined to ecclesiastical bodies, but is rampant in us all, building up our absurd personal and private pretensions, disguising and extenuating our evils, and defending our falsities with the fervor, humility, and sincerity of truth itself. "The heart is deceitful above all things, and desperately wicked; who can know it?" (Jer. xvii. 9.)

The proprium of the natural man is hell (A. C. 694, 987, 3812); and therefore the religion of the proprium is the religion of hell. Think over the majority of motives which lead men and keep them in what they call the religious life. Fear is the principal one—fear of God (not the holy fear), fear of punishment, fear of each other (a demon who loves to haunt ecclesiastical bodies), fear of the congregation, fear of the minister, fear of inconsistency, fear of the world's opinion, fear of the loss of reputation or position, etc. Then self-interest, which is the love of self and the world in one— ambition, love of approbation, the hope of reward, sense of personal worth and dignity, motives springing from policy, fashion, respectability, conformity to social demands, and all shades and varieties of self-seeking. All these elements of the religion of the selfhood, constitute that heaven which fled away from before the face of the Lord, and which is doomed henceforth to utter destruction. When these elements (which belong to the sea, death, and hell) are detected and exposed in us, and cast out of us into that "lake of fire" where they belong, we shall find out how much or how little there is in us of that saving name or quality which is "written in the book of life."

"The devil," says Henry James, "has been from the beginning our only heaven-appointed churchman and statesman, the very man of men for doing all that showy work of the world, namely, persuading, preaching, cajoling, governing, which is requisite to be done, and which is fitly paid by the honors and emoluments of the world." And again he says: "I admit, nay I insist, that the devil is fast becoming and will one day be a perfect gentleman; that he will wholly unlearn his nasty tricks of vice and crime, and become a model of sound morality, infusing an unwonted energy into the police department, and inflating public worship with an unprecedented pomp and magnificence."

The earth which corresponds to the heaven of the natural proprium, and which dissolves away with it from the face of the Lord, so that no place is found for them, is the external, social, business, and institutional life of man. This is just as false and evil as the religion of the proprium, which is the interior source from which it springs. It is a vast tissue of frauds, shams, illusions, selfishness, and injustice, with might instead of right, with cunning instead of wisdom, with policy instead of virtue, with competition instead of co-operation, with the irredeemable love of self and the world instead of the love of God and the neighbor. The general character of this life will be exposed and revealed by the light of heaven; for the sea, death, and hell will be compelled to disgorge their secrets for universal inspection. By what revolutions, catastrophies, tribulations, and chaoses all this is to be accomplished, it is useless to conjecture; but whether it takes ten years or a thousand, the prophecies of the Word will be fulfilled, old things will pass entirely away—the old wine and the old bottles—and all things will be made new. "Even so, come, Lord Jesus!"

The secret of the New Life and the kingdom of heaven in the soul, is the binding of Satan, that old serpent which is also the Devil, in the bottomless pit. This is the subjection and suppression of the proprium. Only in proportion as this is done, are the truths of the Word so vivified in us as to become genuine forces of life. (S. D. 1877.) Only in proportion as this is done, can we be delivered from the sea, death, and hell of the natural man. Only in proportion as this is done, can the new heaven and the new earth be formed in us.

The subjugation of the human will and its incorporation into the Divine will so as to be one with it, constitute the sum total of religion. Man's whole work is to acknowledge the Divine Humanity of the Lord, to rely on his mercy, to trust in his power, and to abstain from all evils as sins against Him. His natural instinct is to will to do evil. (S. D. 4241.) When he therefore wilfully desists from evil, his own will is subjugated and suppressed, and the Lord's will reigns in him. The ten commandments teach only the acknowledgment of God and the abstinence from evil. This abstaining from evil as sin against God, is an entirely different thing from self-denial, which is capable of enormous abuse, and has been in all ages a prolific source of self-righteousness and fantasy.

The proprium is organically and eternally evil, for it is never changed. No man has an independent selfhood which is better or worse than that of other men. No man is ever better at one time than he was at another. There is not a particle of individual goodness or holiness in any man, spirit, or angel. Man can never, never, of himself, do anything good or think anything true. He receives all things from the Lord—his perception of life, his affections, his thoughts, his ability, his sense of power. He may believe and even acknowledge that his goodness and wisdom are from the Lord; but if he thinks that *he* has really become good and true, and therefore is now better or wiser than he was before, or better and wiser than his neighbor who does not acknowledge the Lord, he is in spiritual darkness; he appropriates both good and evil to himself, and his real states, however pious and good he may seem to be and feel himself to be, are full of self-love and fantasy.

The false interpretation put upon Swedenborg's statement that we must do good "as of ourselves," has reduced the standard of New-Church life quite to the level of the standards of the dead church. It has led even such men as Prof. Parsons to believe that the life of the Lord is given to us to be *absolutely and actually our own*, and of course that his goodness and his wisdom also become absolutely ours. This is the basis of the Roman Catholic doctrine of merit. It is the root of all self-righteousness. It harmonizes thoroughly with the aphorism of the natural man, "God helps those who help themselves." In opposition to this gospel of materialism, Swedenborg teaches that the life, goodness, and wisdom of God apparent in us, are *always his* and not ours; that their seeming to be ours, is always an appearance and not a reality (D. P. 308); that we are organically and forever ineradicably evil and false, and that nothing but the personal presence of the Lord in us, prevents us all—men, spirits, and angels—from obeying our infernal instincts and rushing headlong into hell.

The difference between men, outside of special organic differences, lies in the fact, that some are more or less withheld from our common evil nature than others: and that some are more or less willingly receptive of the Lord than others. To acknowledge that all goodness and truth are *from the Lord* in us, is one thing—and is the Old-Church standpoint; to see and feel that all goodness and truth apparently ours, *is really the Lord in us*, is a different thing—and is the New-Church standpoint. If the Lord ever enables *us* to be good and true, we are justified in all our self-righteousness; but if only the Lord Himself is good and true in us, then are we nothing but the branch in the Vine. Then also do we first become capable of realizing his personal presence and guidance in our souls. The proprium, with its sense of individual life and personal pretensions, must be seized, bound, and sealed up in the pit of our inherent hell, before Christ can reign in us and live in us forever.

The men and women who are undergoing this secret, silent, but stupendous process, are the spiritual martyrs of the age, ignorant of the causes and misinterpreting the phenomena of their martyrdom. As a general rule, to which there may be exceptions, men whose proprium is being seized, bound, and sealed up forever, and who are being unfolded into the new heaven and the new earth, gradually lose interest in external things—in men, parties, churches, organizations, etc., etc. They become indifferent and flag in their business activities. They sometimes appear stupid, and seem to forget everything they had ever known. Swedenborg himself was reduced to this state before he conversed with angels and spirits. (S. D. 3904.) These men who are thus dying to the proprium, neglect even their duties—for the discharge of all duties has hitherto been saturated with the spirit of proprium. They are blind to their own interests and careless of the opinion of others. Most of them fall behind in the race of life, and become poor, or sick, or embarrassed, or unpopular, and so fade away from the sight and thought and care of their fellow men, misrepresented, misunderstood, and held in comparative contempt.

Their spiritual trials are very great, and the vast majority do not interpret them correctly. These "babes and sucklings" conceal their experiences, having no one to sympathize with them or to comprehend them. The evil spirits about them are troubled at the impending loss of proprium, and infuse into the sufferers all sorts of doubts, reproaches, self-accusations, despairs, and temptations. Men in this state of life have committed suicide, or sunk into temporary insanity, or rushed as by insane impulse into evils of that sensual degree, which is the last stronghold of the devil and is regenerated with so much difficulty. They are weary, struggling, reticent souls, whose deep religious nature finds no expression. And yet they belong to the class of those who are beheaded for the testimony of Jesus, and who come up out of great tribulation and are washed in the blood of the Lamb, and who live and reign with Christ a thousand years.

On the contrary, men who are well-to-do, contented and happy, satisfied with their uses, falling in with the general current of human feeling and thought, admiring and admired, doing good and seeking truth "as of themselves"; "eating and drinking, buying and selling"; who float on the tide of popular favor, and command the greatest attention and respect, and who are in the most honored and prized positions of religious activity, are immersed in the spirit of the Old Church, and are obstructionists to the true kingdom of God. Their vastations, judgments, and deliverances are of necessity deferred to the next life. The roots of their proprium, of all their affections and thoughts, are planted deep down in the soil of the present state of things; and they can only be held to their excellent and necessary uses (for the Lord never breaks but bends), by being kept in closed and fixed conditions as to spirit. Nor can they rise at present, without great interior struggles, above their ecclesiastical naturalism; but they will deny, repudiate, and resist the coming of the Lord into the Body of Humanity, instead of into the little organic forms they have prepared for his reception; and his coming will be as much "like a thief in the night" to them, as to any ecclesiastics of the Old Church.

It is an utter fallacy to suppose that the New Life, the kingdom of heaven upon earth, can be attained by any possible extensions or intensifications of the sanctities and spiritualities of former dispensations. Men who live in those sanctities and spiritualities will refuse to come to the Supper of the Divine Man. They have bought land and must see it; or they have obtained oxen and must prove them; or they have married a wife and cannot come. The guests of the Lord are found in the highways and hedges, and they are the spiritually poor, maimed, halt, blind, miserable, and naked.

The road to the New Life is not through prayers, and praises, and sacrifices, and glorifications. It is through abandonments, and privations, and sufferings, and death, and annihilation. (S. D. 2043, '4, 1708.) The true disciples must leave their nets in the ship with their father Zebedee. They must sell all they have and give to the poor, and follow Christ. They must hate father and mother, wife and children, brethren and sisters, yea, and their own lives also. They must lay down their own life, the natural proprium, freely and forever; and the life they take up will be the new proprium, made from the flesh and blood of Jesus Christ. "Whosoever he be of you," saith the Master, "that forsaketh not all that he hath, he cannot be my disciple."

My friend who enjoys spiritual vision, always wide awake, once received a striking representation of how the business of the world will be transacted when the Lord is all in all upon earth as He is in heaven. He seemed to be in a livery-stable where horse-trades were going on. While looking at the people standing about, he perceived that the atmospheres of the Lord filled the place. Examining the persons more closely, he discovered that the Lord occupied the interiors of every man—that He was transacting all the business Himself, did all the talking and all the listening, all the buying and all the selling, and all by wonderful influxes, without infringing upon the sensations of life and independence peculiar to each individual.

This statement, so extraordinary and incredible to most men, is perfectly clear to the readers of Swedenborg who has revealed to us the structure of the heavens and the phenomena of the other life. "The functions of the angels," he says, "are functions of the Lord through the angels, for the angels discharge them, not from themselves but from the Lord."—H. H. 391.

Again he says:

"An angel does not speak from himself but from the Lord. . . . The angels are indignant if anything of good and truth is attributed to themselves in what they speak; . . . for they know and perceive that they have from the Lord, that is, from the Divine, everything good and true which they think, will, and do."—A. C. 4085.

When the Lord has entered the Body of Humanity, coming to abide and to tabernacle with men, such will be the manner in which all the work and phenomena of life will take place. We can imagine what stupendous revolutions will occur in the social, commercial, political, and religious life of the race! How will He scourge out of his temple the money-changers and those who sell doves!—the manipulators of markets, those who make and sell liquors, who put false marks upon goods, who gamble in stocks and futures, who exploit their fellow-men, congratulating their souls upon the riches they have acquired! How will He extirpate the self-seeking, the avarice, the ambition, the vanity, the flatteries, the competitions, and all the other spiritual infamies of the present Christian world!

Now, dear reader, I have finished these four essays, the substance of which was foreshadowed to me from the interior about six months ago. I beg you to read and re-read and ponder well everything I have said, by the light of Swedenborg's revealings and the Divine Word. The seeds of truth here planted under the guidance of Divine Providence, may be hidden from sight and forgotten for a while; but they will return to the surface in due time, and bring forth flowers and fruit.

THE END.

www.ingramcontent.com/pod-product-compliance
Lightning Source LLC
Chambersburg PA
CBHW020104020526
44112CB00033B/807